CLYMER®

YAMAHA
XS750 & XS850 • 1977-1981

CLYMER®

P.O. Box 12901, Overland Park, Kansas 66282-2901

FIRST EDITION
First Printing March, 1979
Second Printing May, 1979
Third Printing August, 1979
Fourth Printing February, 1980

SECOND EDITION
Updated to include 1980-1981 models
First Printing April, 1982

THIRD EDITION
Revised by Ron Wright
First Printing October, 1983
Second Printing February, 1985
Third Printing January, 1987
Fourth Printing June, 1988
Fifth Printing March, 1989
Sixth Printing September, 1990
Seventh Printing January, 1992
Eighth Printing June, 1993
Ninth Printing January, 1995
Tenth Printing December, 1996
Eleventh Printing November, 1998
Twelfth Printing December, 2000
Thirteenth Printing July, 2003
Fourteen Printing February, 2006

Printed in U.S.A.

CLYMER and colophon are registered trademarks of Prism Business Media Inc.

ISBN: 0-89287-243-8

MEMBER

MOTORCYCLE INDUSTRY COUNCIL, INC.

TOOLS AND EQUIPMENT: K & L Supply Company at www.klsupply.com.

COVER: 1978 XS750(E) motorcycle and photography courtesy of Rod Ratzlaff.

CLYMER ®

Publisher Shawn Etheridge

EDITORIAL

Managing Editor
James Grooms

Associate Editor
Steven Thomas

Technical Writers
Jay Bogart
Jon Engleman
Michael Morlan
George Parise
Mark Rolling
Ed Scott
Ron Wright

Editorial Production Manager
Dylan Goodwin

Senior Production Editor
Greg Araujo

Production Editors
Holly Messinger
Darin Watson

Associate Production Editors
Susan Hartington
Julie Jantzer-Ward
Justin Marciniak

Technical Illustrators
Steve Amos
Errol McCarthy
Mitzi McCarthy
Bob Meyer

MARKETING/SALES AND ADMINISTRATION

Sales Channel & Brand Marketing Coordinator
Melissa Abbott Mudd

New Business Marketing Manager
Gabriele Udell

Art Director
Chris Paxton

Sales Managers
Justin Henton
Dutch Sadler
Matt Tusken

Business Manager
Ron Rogers

Customer Service Manager
Terri Cannon

Customer Service Representatives
Felicia Dickerson
Courtney Hollars
Jennifer Lassiter
April LeBlond

Warehouse & Inventory Manager
Leah Hicks

Prism Business Media
P.O. Box 12901, Overland Park, KS 66282-2901 • 800-262-1954 • 913-967-1719

The following books and guides are published by Prism Business Media

More information available at *clymer.com*

CONTENTS

QUICK REFERENCE DATA

TIMING MARKS

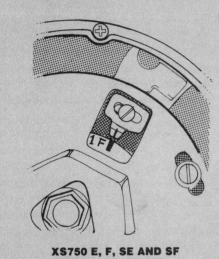

XS750 E, F, SE AND SF
XS850G, SG, LG

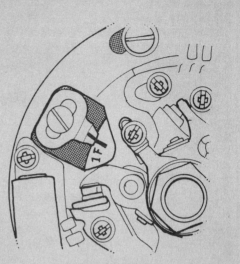

XS750 D AND 2D

TIMING MARKS
XS850H, SH, LH

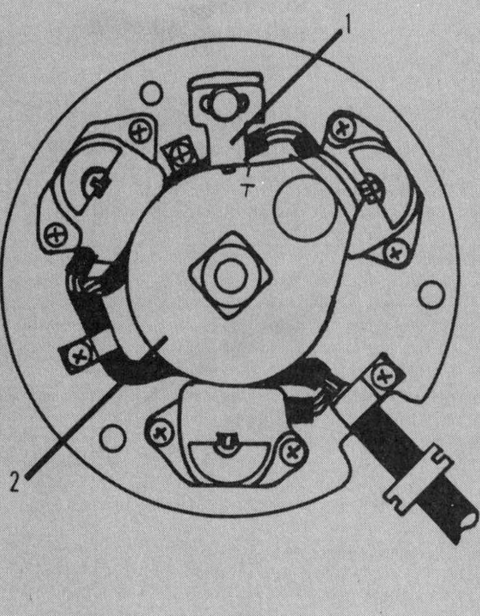

1. Stationary pointer
2. Timing plate

TUNE-UP SPECIFICATIONS

Cylinder head bolts	
8 mm	14 ft.-lb. (19 N•m)
10 mm	25 ft.-lb. (34 N•m)
Valve clearance (cold)	
XS750	
Intake	0.006-0.008 in. (0.16-0.20 mm)
Exhaust	0.008-0.010 in. (0.21-0.25 mm)
XS850	
Intake	0.0043-0.0059 in. (0.11-0.15 mm)
Exhaust	0.008-0.010 in. (0.20-0.25 mm)
Spark plug	
Type	NGK BP-7ES, Champion N-7Y
Gap	0.028-0.031 in. (0.7-0.8 mm)
Idle speed	
XS750 D and 2D	1,050 rpm
XS750 E, F, SE and SF	1,000 rpm
XS850	1,100 rpm
Compression pressure	
Cold at sea level	142 +/-14 psi (10 +/-1.0 kg/cm^2
Breaker point gap	
XS750 D and 2D	0.012-0.016 in. (0.3-0.4 mm)

Champion RN9YC (handwritten annotation)

FREE PLAY ADJUSTMENTS

Clutch lever	
At end of lever	1/2-1 in. (13-26 mm)
At pivot	0.08-0.12 in. (2-3 mm)
Front brake lever	0.2-0.3 in. (5-8 mm)
Rear brake pedal	1/2-5/8 in. (13-15 mm)

OIL Filter 1J7-13441-10

APPROXIMATE REFILL CAPACITY

Item	Quantity
Engine oil	
Oil and filter change	
XS750 (1977)	3.4 qt. (3,200 cc)
XS750 (1978-on)	3.3 qt. (3,100 cc)
XS850	3.3 qt. (3,100 cc)
Oil change only	
XS750D	3.0 qt. (2,800 cc)
XS750-2D	3.3 qt. (3,100 cc)
XS750 (1978-on)	3.0 qt. (2,800 cc)
XS850	3.0 qt. (2,800 cc)
Fork oil	
XS750D, 2-D	5.75 oz. (170 cc)
XS750E	6.8 oz. (200 cc)
XS750SE, F	6.4 oz. (190 cc)
XS750SF	7.91 oz. (234 cc)
XS850G, H	6.59 oz. (195 cc)
XS850SG, LG, SH, LH	9.30 oz. (275 cc)
Middle gear case*	12.0 oz. (375 cc)
Final drive case*	10.0 oz. (300 cc)
Fuel	4.5 gal. (17 liters)

* Verify with dipstick.

RECOMMENDED LUBRICANTS

Item	Type
Engine oil	
Above 40° F (5° C)	SAE 20W-40
Below 59° F (15° C)	SAE 10W-30
Fork oil	SAE 10 or 20
Brake fluid	DOT 3
Middle gear/drive case gear oil*	
All weather	SAE 80W-90 GL4
Above 40° F (5° C)	SAE 90 GL4
Below 40° F (5° C)	SAE 80 GL4
Fuel	Regular or unleaded

* Hypoid gear oil.

TIRES

Load	
Up to 198 lb. (90 kg)	
Front	26 psi (1.8 kg/cm^2)
Rear	28 psi (2.0 kg/cm^2)
198-410 lb. (90-186 kg)	
Front	28 psi (2.0 kg/cm^2)
Rear	32 psi (2.3 kg/cm^2)
Maximum load limit	
Front 470 lb. (214 kg)	40 psi (2.8 kg/cm^2)
Rear 615 lb. (280 kg)	40 psi (2.8 kg/cm^2)

(continued)

TIRES (continued)

Size
    Front   3.25 H19-4PR*
    Rear
        XS750   4.00 H18-4PR*
        XS850   4.50 H17-4PR*

*Tubeless on XS750F and XS850

FRAME TORQUE VALUES

Item	Ft.-lb.	N•m
Steering stem		
Top bolt	40	54
Pinch bolt	11	15
Top fork bridge	11	15
Handlebar holder		
(upper and lower)	13	18
Front axle nut	76	103
Front axle holder nuts		
(Models D, 2D and E)	16	22
Front axle pinch bolts		
(Models SE and SF)	15	20
Rear axle nut	108	147
Rear axle pinch bolt	4	5
Rear swing arm pivot		
Bolt	5	6.8
Locknut	73	99
Shock absorber nut		
Upper	21	29
Lower	28	37
Engine mounting bolts		
8 mm flange bolts		
and nuts	14.5	20
10 mm flange bolts		
and nuts	40	54
12 mm flange bolts		
and nuts		
XS750	69	94
XS850	18	25
Final drive flange nuts	29	39
Brake rotor to wheel bolts		
Front and rear	12-16	16-22
Front caliper assembly		
Models D, 2D and E		
Mounting bolt	32-36	45-50
Support bolt	11-15	15-20
Models SE and SF		
Mounting bolt	25	34
XS850	19	26
Brake hose union bolts (all)	16-20	22-27
Rear master cylinder to frame		
XS750	11-15	15-20
XS850	16	23

NOTE: If you own a 1980 or later model, first check the Supplement at the back of the book for any new service information.

1

CHAPTER ONE

GENERAL INFORMATION

This book provides maintenance and repair information for the Yamaha XS750 and XS850 models.

Read the following service hints to make the work as easy and pleasant as possible. Performing your own work can be an enjoyable and rewarding experience.

MANUAL ORGANIZATION

Chapters One through Twelve contain general information on all models and specific information on 1977-1979 models. The supplement at the end of the book contains specific information on 1980 and later models that differs from earlier years.

This chapter provides general information and specifications. See **Table 1** at the end of this chapter. It also discusses equipment and tools useful both for preventive maintenance and troubleshooting.

Chapter Two provides methods and suggestions for quick and accurate diagnosis and repair of problems. Troubleshooting procedures discuss typical symptoms and logical methods to pinpoint the trouble.

Chapter Three explains all periodic lubrication and routine maintenance necessary to keep your bike running well. Chapter Three also includes recommended tune-up procedures, eliminating the need to constantly consult chapters on the various assemblies.

Subsequent chapters describe specific systems such as the engine, transmission, and electrical system. Each chapter provides disassembly, repair, and assembly procedures in simple step-by-step form. If a repair is impractical for a home mechanic, it is so indicated. It is usually faster and less expensive to take such repairs to a dealer or competent repair shop. Specifications concerning a particular system are included at the end of the appropriate chapter.

Some of the procedures in this manual specify special tools. In all cases, the tool is illustrated either in actual use or alone. A well-equipped mechanic may find that he can substitute similar tools already on hand or fabricate his own.

All dimensions and capacities are expressed in English units familiar to U.S. mechanics as well as in metric units.

The terms NOTE, CAUTION, and WARNING have specific meanings in this manual. A NOTE provides additional information to make a step or procedure easier or clearer. Disregarding a NOTE could cause inconvenience, but would not cause damage or personal injury.

A CAUTION emphasizes areas where equipment damage could result. Disregarding a CAUTION could cause permanent mechanical damage; however, personal injury is unlikely.

A WARNING emphasizes areas where personal injury or even death could result from negligence. Mechanical damage may also occur. WARNINGS *are to be taken seriously.* In some cases, serious injury or death has resulted from disregarding similar warnings.

Throughout this manual, keep in mind two conventions. "Front" refers to the front of the bike. The front of any component, such as the engine, is the end which faces toward the front of the bike. The "left" and "right" sides refer to a person sitting on the bike facing forward. For example, the shift lever is on the left side. These rules are simple, but even experienced mechanics occasionally become disoriented.

SERVICE HINTS

Most of the service procedures covered are straightforward and can be performed by anyone reasonably handy with tools. It is suggested, however, that you consider your own capabilities carefully before attempting any operation involving major disassembly of the engine.

Some operations, for example, require the use of a press. It would be wiser to have these performed by a shop equipped for such work than to try to do the job yourself with makeshift equipment. Other procedures require precise measurements. Unless you have the skills and equipment required, it would be better to have a qualified repair shop make the measurements for you.

Repairs go much faster and easier if your machine is clean before you begin work. There are special cleaners, like Gunk Cycle Degreaser, for washing the engine and related parts. Just brush or spray on the cleaning solution, let it stand, then rinse it away with a garden hose. Clean all oily or greasy parts with cleaning solvent as you remove them.

WARNING
Never use gasoline as a cleaning agent. It presents an extreme fire hazard. Be sure to work in a well-ventilated area when using cleaning solvent. Keep a fire extinguisher, rated for gasoline fires, handy in any case.

Special tools are required for some repair procedures. These may be purchased at a dealer, rented from a tool rental dealer, or fabricated by a mechanic or machinist, often at a considerable savings.

Much of the labor charge for repairs made by dealers is for removal and disassembly of other parts to reach the defective unit. It is frequently possible to perform preliminary operations yourself and then take the defective unit to the dealer for repair at considerable savings.

Once you have decided to tackle the job yourself, read the entire section in this manual which pertains to it, making sure you have identified the proper one. Study the illustrations and text until you have a good idea of what is involved in completing the job satisfactorily. If special tools are required, make arrangements to get them before you start. It is frustrating and time-consuming to get partly into a job and then be unable to complete it.

Simple wiring checks can be easily made at home; but knowledge of electronics is almost a necessity for performing tests with complicated electronic testing gear.

During disassembly of parts, keep a few general cautions in mind. Force is rarely needed to get things apart. If parts are a tight fit, like a bearing in a case, there is usually a tool designed to separate them. Never use a screwdriver to pry apart parts with machined surfaces such as crankcase halves and cam cover. You will mar the surfaces and end up with leaks.

Make diagrams wherever similar-appearing parts are found. For instance, case cover screws are often not the same length. You may think you can remember where everything came from — but mistakes are costly. There is also the possibility you may be sidetracked and not return to work for days, or even weeks, in which interval, carefully laid out parts may have become disturbed.

Tag all similar internal parts for location and mark all mating parts for position. Record number and thickness of any shims as they are removed. Small parts, such as bolts, can be identified by placing them in plastic sandwich bags. Seal and label the bags with masking tape.

Wiring should be tagged with masking tape and marked as each wire is removed. Again, do not rely on memory alone.

Disconnect battery ground (negative) cable before working near electrical connections and before disconnecting wires. Never run the engine with the battery disconnected; the alternator could be seriously damaged.

Protect finished surfaces from physical damage or corrosion. Keep gasoline and brake fluid off painted surfaces.

Frozen or very tight bolts and screws can often be loosened by soaking with penetrating oil, like WD-40 or Liquid Wrench, then sharply striking the bolt head a few times with a hammer and punch (or screwdriver for screws). Avoid heat unless absolutely necessary, since it may melt, warp, or remove the temper from many parts.

Avoid flames or sparks when working near a charging battery or flammable liquids such as brake fluid or gasoline.

No parts, except those assembled with a press fit, require unusual force during assembly. If a part is hard to remove or install, find out why before proceeding.

Cover all openings after removing parts to keep dirt, small tools, etc., from falling in.

When assembling two parts, start all fasteners, then tighten evenly.

Clutch plates, wiring connections, and brake pads and discs should be kept clean and free of grease and oil.

When assembling parts, be sure all shims and washers are replaced exactly as they came out.

Whenever a rotating part butts against a stationary part, look for a shim or washer. Use new gaskets if there is any doubt about the condition of old ones. Generally, you should apply gasket cement to one mating surface only so the parts may be easily disassembled in the future. A thin coat of oil on gaskets helps them seal effectively.

Heavy grease can be used to hold small parts in place if they tend to fall out during assembly. However, keep grease and oil away from electrical components or brake pads and discs.

High spots may be sanded off a piston with sandpaper, but emery cloth and oil do a much more professional job.

Carburetors are best cleaned by disassembling them and soaking the parts in a commercial carburetor cleaner. Never soak gaskets and rubber parts in these cleaners. Never use wire to clean out jets and air passages; they are easily damaged. Use compressed air to blow out the carburetor only if the float has been removed first.

A baby bottle makes a good measuring device for adding oil to forks and transmissions. Get one that is graduated in ounces and cubic centimeters.

Take your time and do the job right. Do not forget that a newly rebuilt motorcycle engine must be broken in the same as a new one. Keep rpm within the limits given in your owner's manual when back on the road.

SAFETY FIRST

Professional motorcycle mechanics can work for years and never sustain a serious injury. If you observe a few rules of common sense and safety, you can enjoy many hours servicing your own machine. You could hurt yourself or damage the bike if you ignore these rules.

1. Never use gasoline as a cleaning solvent.

2. Never smoke or use a torch in the vicinity of flammable liquids such as cleaning solvent in open containers.

3. Never smoke or use a torch in an area where batteries are being charged. Highly explosive hydrogen gas is formed during the charging process.

4. If welding or brazing is required on the machine, remove the fuel tank to a safe distance, at least 50 feet away. Welding on gas tanks requires special safety procedures and must be performed by someone skilled in the process.

5. Use the proper sized wrenches to avoid damage to nuts and injury to yourself.

6. When loosening a tight or stuck nut, be guided by what would happen if the wrench should slip. Protect yourself accordingly.

7. Keep your work area clean and uncluttered.

8. Wear safety goggles during all operations involving drilling, grinding, or use of a cold chisel.

9. Never use worn tools.

10. Keep a fire extinguisher handy and be sure it is rated for gasoline and electrical fires.

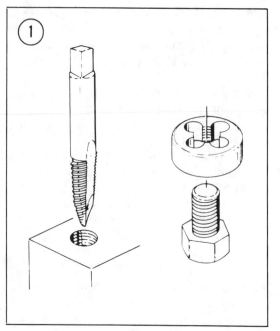

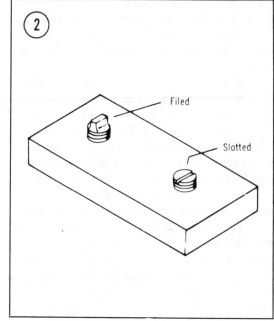

MECHANIC'S TIPS

Removing Frozen Nuts and Screws

When a fastener rusts and cannot be removed, several methods may be used to loosen it. First, apply penetrating oil such as Liquid Wrench or WD-40 (available at any hardware or auto supply store). Apply it liberally. Rap the fastener several times with a small hammer; do not hit it hard enough to cause damage.

For frozen screws, apply penetrating oil as described, then insert a screwdriver in the slot and rap the top of the screwdriver with a hammer. This loosens the rust so the screw can be removed in the normal way. If the screw head is too chewed up to use a screwdriver, grip the head with Vise-Grip pliers and twist screw out.

Remedying Stripped Threads

Occasionally, threads are stripped through carelessness or impact damage. Often the threads can be cleaned up by running a tap (for internal threads on nuts) or die (for external threads on bolts) through threads. See **Figure 1**.

Removing Broken Screws or Bolts

When the head breaks off a screw or bolt, several methods are available for removing the remaining portion.

If a large portion of the remainder projects out, try gripping it with Vise Grips.If the projecting portion is too small, try filing it to fit a wrench or cut a slot in it to fit a screwdriver. See **Figure 2**.

If the head breaks off flush, try using a screw extractor. To do this, centerpunch the exact center of the remaining portion of the screw or bolt. Drill a small hole in the screw and tap the extractor into the hole. Back the screw out with a wrench on the extractor. See **Figure 3**.

PARTS REPLACEMENT

Yamaha makes frequent changes during a model year — some minor, some relatively major. When you order parts from the dealer or other parts distributor, always order by engine and frame number. Write the numbers down and carry them with you. Compare new parts to old before purchasing them. If they are not alike, have the parts manager explain the difference to you.

EXPENDABLE SUPPLIES

Certain expendable supplies are also required. These include grease, oil, gasket cement, wiping rags, cleaning solvent, and distilled water. Ask your dealer for the special

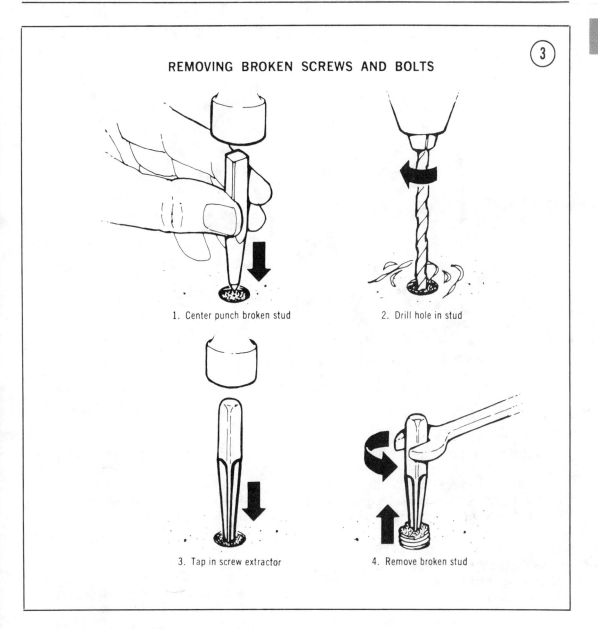

REMOVING BROKEN SCREWS AND BOLTS ③

1. Center punch broken stud

2. Drill hole in stud

3. Tap in screw extractor

4. Remove broken stud

locking compounds, silicone lubricants, and lube products which make motorcycle maintenance simpler and easier. Solvent is available at most service stations and distilled water for the battery is available at most supermarkets.

TOOLS

To properly service your motorcycle, you will need an assortment of ordinary tools. As a minimum, these include:

a. Combination wrench
b. Socket wrenches
c. Plastic mallet
d. Small hammer
e. Snap ring pliers
f. Phillips screwdrivers
g. Slot screwdrivers
h. Impact driver
i. Pliers
j. Feeler gauges
k. Spark plug gauge
l. Spark plug wrench
m. Drift

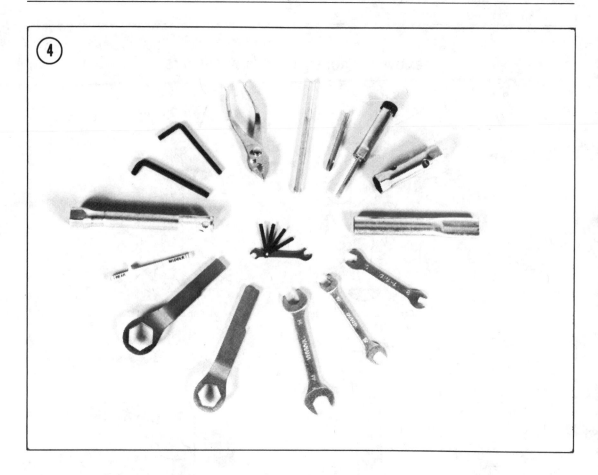

④

An original equipment tool kit, like the one shown in **Figure 4**, is available through most Yamaha dealers and is suitable for most minor servicing.

Engine tune-up and troubleshooting procedures require a few more tools, described in the following sections.

Hydrometer

This instrument measures state of charge of the battery, and tells much about battery condition. Such an instrument is available at any auto parts store and through most larger mail order outlets. See **Figure 5**.

Multimeter or VOM

This instrument (**Figure 6**) is invaluable for electrical system troubleshooting and service. A few of its functions may be duplicated by locally fabricated substitutes, but for the serious hobbyist, it is a must. Its uses are

described in the applicable sections of this book. Multimeters are available at electronics hobbyist stores and mail order outlets.

Compression Gauge

An engine with low compression cannot be properly tuned and will not develop full power. A compression gauge measures engine compression. The one shown in **Figure 7** has a flexible stem, which enables it to reach cylinders where there is little clearance between the cylinder head and frame. These are available at auto accessory stores or by mail order from large catalog order firms.

Impact Driver

This tool makes removal of engine components easy and eliminates damage to bolt heads. Good ones are available at larger hardware stores. See **Figure 8**.

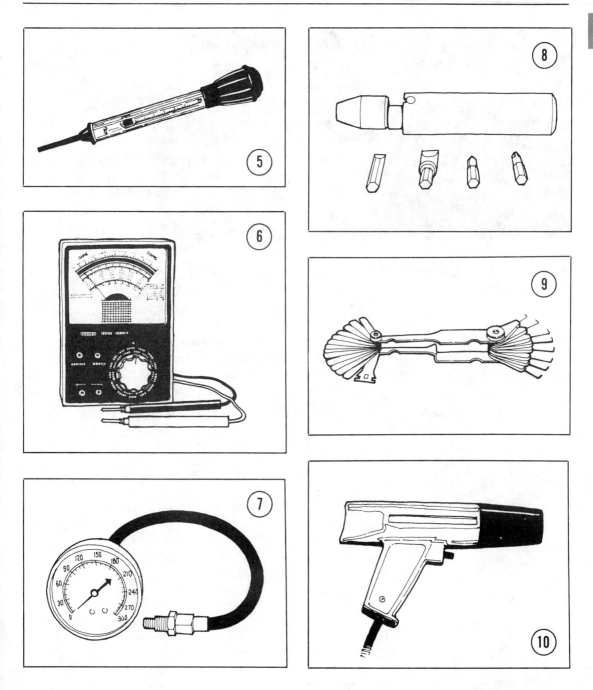

Ignition Gauge

This tool has round wire gauges for measuring spark plug gap. See **Figure 9**.

Strobe Timing Light

This instrument is necessary for tuning. By flashing a light at the precise instant the cylinder fires, the position of the flywheel at that instant can be seen. Marks on the ignition governor plate and the stationary scale on the crankcase must align.

Suitable lights range from inexpensive neon bulb types to powerful xenon strobe lights. See **Figure 10**. Neon timing lights are difficult to see and must be used in dimly lit areas. Xenon strobe timing lights can be used outside in bright sunlight. Both types work on this mo-

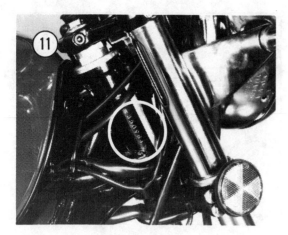

torcycle: use according to the manufacturer's instructions.

Other Special Tools

A few other special tools may be required for major service. These are described in the appropriate chapters and are available from Yamaha dealers.

SERIAL NUMBERS

You must know the model serial number for registration purposes and when ordering special parts.

The frame serial number is stamped on the right side of the steering head. (**Figure 11**) and on the VIN plate on the steering head. The engine number is stamped on the top right-hand side of the crankcase (**Figure 12**).

Table 1 GENERAL SPECIFICATIONS

Engine type	Air-cooled, 4 stroke, DOHC, inline triple
Bore and stroke	2.677 x 2.701 in. (68 x 68.6 mm)
Displacement	45.58 cu. in. (747 cc)
Compression ratio	
Models D and 2D	8.5 to 1
Models E, SE, F and SF	9.2 to 1
Carburetion	3 Mikuni, constant velocity, 34 mm
Models D and 2D	Model BS34/1J701
Models E and F	Model BS34/2F3-00
Models SE and SF	Model BS34/2G2-00
Ignition	
Models D and 2D	Contact breaker point
Models E, SE, F and SF	Fully transistorized
Lubrication	Wet sump, filter, oil pump
Clutch	Wet, multi-plate (6)
Transmission	5-speed, constant mesh
Transmission ratios	
1st	2.461
2nd	1.588
3rd	1.300
4th	1.095
5th	0.956
Starting system	Manual kick and electric
Wheelbase	
Models D, 2D and E	57.7 in. (1,465 mm)
Models SE and SF	59.1 in. (1,500 mm)
Model F	57.1 in. (1,450 mm)
Steering head angle	
Models D, 2D, E and F	26° 30'
Models SE and SF	28°
Trail	
Models D, 2D and E	4.3 in. (109 mm)
Models SE and SF	3.94 in. (100 mm)
Model F	4.8 in. (122 mm)
Front suspension	Telescopic fork, 6.9 in. (175 mm) travel
Rear suspension	Swing arm, adjustable shock aborbers
Model F	4.1 in. (104 mm) travel
All others	3.2 in. (80 mm) travel
Front tire	3.25 H 19-4PR*
Rear tire	4.00 H 18-4PR*
Ground clearance	
Models D, 2D, E and F	5.5 in. (140 mm)
Models SE and SF	6.3 in. (160 mm)
Seat height	
Models D, 2D, E and F	32.3 in. (820 mm)
Models SE and SF	32.1 in. (815 mm)

(continued)

Table 1 GENERAL SPECIFICATIONS (continued)

Overall height	
Models D, 2D, E and F	46.3 in. (1,175 mm)
Models SE and SF	48.8 in. (1,240 mm)
Overall width (handlebars)	
Models D, 2D, E and F	35.4 in. (900 mm)
Models SE and SF	34.3 in. (870 mm)
Overall length	
Models D, 2D and E	84.8 in. (2,155 mm)
Models SE and SF	85.4 in. (2,170 mm)
Model F	84.3 in. (2,140 mm)
Fuel capacity	4.5 U.S. gal. (17 liters; 3.7 Imp. gal.)
Oil capacity	
Oil change	3.4 U.S. qt. (3.1 liters; 2.8 Imp. qt.)
Oil and filter change	3.7 U.S. qt. (3.5 liters; 3.0 Imp. qt.)
Weight (dry)	
Model D	505 lb. (229 kg)
Models 2D and E	512 lb. (232 kg)
Models SE and SF	507 lb. (230 kg)
Model F	522 lb. (237 kg)

*Model F uses tubeless type tires.

NOTE: If you own a 1980 or later model, first check the Supplement at the back of the book for any new service information.

CHAPTER TWO

TROUBLESHOOTING

Diagnosing mechanical problems is relatively simple if you use orderly procedures and keep a few basic principles in mind.

The troubleshooting procedures in this chapter analyze typical symptoms, and show logical methods of isolating causes. These are not the only methods. There may be several ways to solve a problem, but only a systematic, methodical approach can guarantee success.

Never assume anything. Do not overlook the obvious. If you are riding along and the bike suddenly quits, check the easiest, most accessible problem spots first. Is there gasoline in the tank? Are the shut-off valves in the ON or RESERVE position? Has a spark plug wire fallen off? Check ignition switch. Sometimes the weight of keys on a key ring may turn the ignition off suddenly.

If nothing obvious turns up in a cursory check, look a little further. Learning to recognize and describe symptoms will make repairs easier for you or a mechanic at the shop. Describe problems accurately and fully. Saying that "it won't run" isn't the same as saying "it quit on the highway at high speed and wouldn't start," or that "it sat in my garage for three months and then wouldn't start."

Gather as many symptoms together as possible to aid in diagnosis. Note whether the engine lost power gradually or all at once, what color smoke (if any) came from the exhaust, and so on. Remember that the more complicated a machine is, the easier it is to troubleshoot because symptoms point to specific problems.

After the symptoms are defined, areas which could cause the problems are tested and analyzed. Guessing at the cause of a problem may provide the solution, but it can easily lead to frustration, wasted time, and a series of expensive, unnecessary part replacements.

You do not need fancy equipment or complicated test gear to determine whether repairs can be attempted at home. A few simple checks could save a large repair bill and time lost while the bike sits in a dealer's service department. On the other hand, be realistic and do not attempt repairs beyond your abilities. Service departments tend to charge heavily for putting together a disassembled engine that may have been abused. Some won't even take on such a job — so use common sense, don't get in over your head.

OPERATING REQUIREMENTS

An engine needs three basics to run properly: correct gas/air mixture, compression, and a spark at the right time. If one or more are missing, the engine won't run. The electrical system is the weakest link of the three basics. More problems result from electrical breakdowns than from any other source. Keep that in mind before you begin tampering with carburetor adjustments and the like.

If a bike has been sitting for any length of time and refuses to start, check the battery for a charged condition first, and then look to the gasoline delivery system. This includes the tank, fuel shut-off valves, lines, and the carburetors. Rust may have formed in the tank, obstructing fuel flow. Gasoline deposits may have gummed up carburetor jets and air passages. Gasoline tends to lose its potency after standing for long periods. Condensation may contaminate it with water. Drain old gas and try starting with a fresh tankful.

TROUBLESHOOTING INSTRUMENTS

Chapter One lists many of the instruments needed and detailed instructions on their use.

EMERGENCY TROUBLESHOOTING

When the bike is difficult to start or won't start at all, it does not help to grind away at the starter or kick the tires. Check for obvious problems even before getting out your tools. Go down the following list step-by-step. Do each one; you may be embarrassed to find your kill switch off, but that is better than wearing out your leg or wearing your battery down with the starter. If the bike still will not start, refer to the appropriate troubleshooting procedures which follow in this chapter.

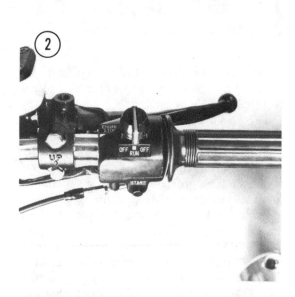

1. Is there fuel in the tank? Remove the filler cap and rock the bike; listen for fuel sloshing around.

> **WARNING**
> *Do not use an open flame to check in the tank. A serious explosion is certain to result.*

2. Are both fuel shut-off valves on? Turn both to RESERVE **(Figure 1)** to be sure that you get the last remaining gas. Make sure that the vacuum lines are attached and are tight. Without engine vacuum the shut-off valves will not operate.

3. Is the kill switch in RUN position **(Figure 2)**?

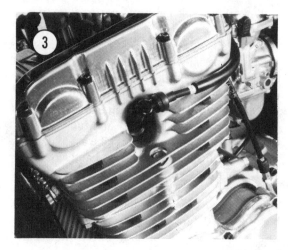

4. Are spark plug wires on tight? See **Figure 3**.

5. Is the choke lever in the right position? It should be pulled out for a cold engine (**Figure 4**) and pushed in for a warm engine.

6. Is the battery dead? Check it with a hydrometer.

7. Has the main fuse (**Figure 5**) blown? Replace it with a good one.

8. Is the transmission in neutral or the clutch lever pulled in? The bike will not start in gear without pulling in the clutch.

STARTER

Starter system troubles are relatively easy to isolate. The following are common symptoms and cures.

1. *Engine cranks very slowly or not at all* — If the headlight is very dim or not lighting at all,

most likely the battery or its connecting wires are at fault. Check the battery condition using the procedures described in Chapter Seven. Check the wiring for breaks, shorts, and dirty connections.

If the battery and connecting wires check good, the trouble may be in the starter, starter solenoid or wiring. To isolate the trouble, short the 2 large starter solenoid terminals together (not to ground): if the starter cranks normally, check the starter solenoid wiring. If the starter still fails to crank properly, remove the starter and test it. Refer to Chapter Seven.

2. *Loud grinding noises when starter runs* — This may mean the teeth are not meshing properly, or it may mean the starter drive mechanism is damaged. In the first case, remove the starter and examine the gear teeth. In the latter case, remove the starter and replace the starter drive mechanism.

3. *Starter engages, but will not disengage when ignition switch is released* — This trouble is usually caused by a sticking starter solenoid.

CHARGING SYSTEM

Troubleshooting an alternator system is somewhat different from troubleshooting a generator. For example, *never* short any terminals to ground on the alternator or the voltage regulator/rectifier. The following symptoms are typical of alternator charging system troubles.

1. *Battery requires frequent charging* — The charging system is not functioning or is undercharging the battery. Test the alternator and voltage regulator/rectifier as described in Chapter Seven.

2. *Battery requires frequent additions of water, or lamps require frequent replacement* — The alternator is probably overcharging the battery. Check voltage regulator/recitfer as described in Chapter Seven.

ENGINE

These procedures assume that the starter cranks the engine over normally. If not, refer to *Starter* section in this chapter.

Poor Performance

1. *Engine misses erratically at all speeds* — Intermittent trouble like this can be difficult to find. The fault could be in the ignition system, exhaust system (exhaust restriction), or fuel system. Follow troubleshooting procedures for these systems carefully to isolate the trouble.

2. *Engine misses at idle only* — Trouble could exist anywhere in ignition system. Refer to *Ignition System* in Chapter Seven. Trouble could exist in the carburetor idle circuits.

3. *Engine misses at high speed only* — Trouble could exist in the fuel system or ignition system. Check the fuel lines, etc., as described under *Fuel System Troubleshooting.* Also check spark plugs and wires. Refer to *Ignition System* in Chapter Seven.

4. *Poor performance at all speeds, lack of acceleration* — Trouble usually exists in ignition or fuel system. Check each with the appropriate troubleshooting procedure.

5. *Excessive fuel consumption* — This can be caused by a wide variety of seemingly unrelated factors. Check for clutch slippage, brake drag, and defective wheel bearings. Check ignition and fuel system as described later.

ENGINE NOISES

1. *Valve clatter* — This is a light to heavy tapping sound from under cam cover. It is usually caused by excessive valve clearance. Adjust clearance as described under *Valve Clearance Adjustment* in Chapter Three. If noise persists, disassemble the cam and valve mechanism as described under *Camshaft and Valve Assemblies* in Chapter Four. Look for broken springs, worn cams and bearings.

2. *Knocking or pinging during acceleration* — Caused by using a lower octane fuel than recommended. May also be caused by poor fuel available at some "discount" gasoline stations. Pinging can also be caused by spark plugs of the wrong heat range. Refer to *Correct Spark Plug Heat Range* in Chapter Three.

3. *Slapping or rattling noises at low speed or during acceleration* — May be caused by piston

slap, i.e., excessive piston-cylinder wall clearance.

4. *Knocking or rapping while decelerating* — Usually caused by excessive rod bearing clearance.

5. *Persistent knocking and vibration* — Usually caused by excessive main bearing clearance.

6. *Rapid on-off squeal* — Compression leak around cylinder head gasket or spark plugs.

EXCESSIVE VIBRATION

This can be difficult to find without disassembling the engine. Usually this is caused by loose engine mounting hardware or worn engine or transmission bearings.

LUBRICATION TROUBLES

1. *Excessive oil consumption* — May be caused by worn rings and bores. Overhaul is necessary to correct this; see Chapter Four. May also be caused by worn valve guides or defective valve guide seals. Also check for exterior leaks.

2. *Oil pressure lamp does not light when ignition switch is on* — The oil pressure sending unit is located on the front lower right-hand side of the engine (**Figure 6**). Remove cover plate (**Figure 7**) to gain access to it. Check that the wire is connected to the sender and makes good contact. Pull off wire and ground it. If the lamp lights, replace the sender. If the lamp does not light, replace the lamp.

3. *Oil pressure lamp lights or flickers when engine is running*—This indicates low or

complete loss of oil pressure. Stop the engine immediately; coast to a stop with the clutch disengaged or transmission out of gear. This may simply be caused by a low oil level, or an overheating engine. Check the oil level. Check for a shorted oil pressure sender with an ohmmeter or other continuity tester. Do not restart the engine until you know why the light went on and have corrected the problem. If necessary, start the engine and listen for unusual noises indicating bad bearings, etc.

FUEL SYSTEM

Fuel system troubles must be isolated to the carburetor, fuel tank, fuel shut-off valve, or fuel lines. These procedures assume that the ignition system has been checked and properly adjusted.

1. *Engine will not start* — First, determine that the fuel is being delivered to the carburetor.

Turn the fuel shut-off valves to the ON position and remove the flexible fuel lines to the carburetor. Place the loose end into a small container and turn the shut-off valves to the PRIME position. Fuel should run out of the tube. If it does not, remove the shut-off valves and check for restrictions within them or the fuel tank. Refer to Chapters Three and Six.

2. *Rough idle or engine miss with frequent stalling* — Check carburetor adjustment. See Chapter Three.

3. *Stumbling when accelerating from idle* — Check idle speed adjustment. See Chapter Three.

4. *Engine misses at high speed or lacks power* — This indicates possible fuel starvation. Clean main jets and float needle valves.

5. *Black exhaust smoke* — Black exhaust smoke means a badly overrich mixture. Check that manual choke disengages. Check idle speed. Check for leaky floats or worn float needle valves. Also check that jets are proper size.

CLUTCH

All clutch troubles except adjustments require partial engine disassembly to identify and cure the problem. Refer to Chapter Five for procedures.

1. *Slippage* — This is most noticeable when accelerating in a high gear at relatively low speed. To check slippage, shift to second gear and release the clutch as if riding off. If the clutch is good, the engine will slow and stall. If the clutch slips, continued engine speed will give it away. Slippage results from insufficient clutch lever free play, worn discs or pressure plate, or weak springs.

2. *Drag or failure to release* — This trouble usually causes difficult shifting and gear clash, especially when downshifting. The cause may be excessive clutch lever free play, warped or bent pressure plate or clutch disc, or broken or loose linings.

3. *Chatter or grabbing* — A number of things can cause this trouble. Check tightness of engine mounting bolts. Also check lever free play.

TRANSMISSION

Transmission problems are usually indicated by one or more of the following symptoms:

    a. Difficulty shifting gears

    b. Gear clash when downshifting

    c. Slipping out of gear

    d. Excessive noise in neutral

    e. Excessive noise in gear

Transmission symptoms are sometimes hard to distinguish from clutch symptoms. Be sure that the clutch is not causing the trouble before working on the transmission. Refer to Chapter Five.

BRAKES

1. *Brake lever or pedal goes all the way to its stop* — There are numerous causes for this including excessively worn pads, air in the hydraulic system, leaky brake lines, leaky calipers, or leaky or worn master cylinder. Check for leaks and thin brake pads. Bleed the brakes. If this does not cure the trouble, rebuild the calipers and/or master cylinder.

2. *Spongy lever* — Normally caused by air in the system; bleed the brakes.

3. *Dragging brakes* — Check for swollen rubber parts due to improper brake fluid or contamination, and obstructed master cylinder bypass port. Clean or replace defective parts.

4. *Hard lever or pedal* — Check brake pads for contamination. Also check for restricted brake line and hose and brake pedal needing lubrication.

5. *High speed fade* — Check for glazed or contaminated brake pads. Ensure that recommended brake fluid is installed. Drain entire system and refill if in doubt.

6. *Pulsating lever or pedal* — Check for excessive brake disc runout. Undetected accident damage is also a frequent cause of this.

FRONT SUSPENSION AND STEERING

1. *Too stiff or too soft* — Make sure forks have not been leaking and oil is correct. If in doubt, drain and refill as described under *Front Fork Oil Change.*

2. *Leakage around seals* — There should be a light film of oil on fork tubes. However, large amounts of oil on tubes means the seals are leaking. Replace seals as described under *Front Fork Seal Replacement* in Chapter Eight.

3. *Fork action is rough* — Check for bent tube.

4. *Steering wobbles* — Check for correct steering head bearing tightness as described under *Steering Head Adjustment* in Chapter Eight.

ELECTRICAL PROBLEMS

Bulbs which continuously burn out may be caused by excessive vibration, loose connections that permit sudden current surges, poor battery connections, installation of the wrong type bulb, or a faulty voltage regulator.

A dead battery or one which discharges quickly may be caused by a faulty alternator or rectifier. Check for loose or corroded terminals. Shorted battery cells or broken terminals will keep a battery from charging. Low water level will decrease a battery's capacity. A battery left uncharged after installation will sulphate, rendering it useless.

A majority of light and horn or other electrical accessory problems are caused by loose or corroded ground connections. Check those first, and then substitute known good units for easier troubleshooting.

NOTE: If you own a 1980 or later model, first check the Supplement at the back of the book for any new service information.

CHAPTER THREE

3

PERIODIC MAINTENANCE, LUBRICATION, AND TUNE-UP

Regular maintenance is the best guarantee for a safe, troublefree, good performing, long lasting motorcycle. An afternoon spent now — cleaning, inspecting, and adjusting — can prevent costly mechanical problems in the future and unexpected breakdowns on the road.

The procedures presented in this chapter can be easily carried out by anyone with average mechanical skills. The operations are presented step-by-step. If they are followed, it is difficult to go wrong.

ROUTINE CHECKS

The following simple checks should be performed at each stop at a service station for gas.

Engine Oil Level

Refer to *Checking Engine Oil Level* under *Periodic Lubrication* in this chapter.

General Inspection

1. Quickly examine the engine for signs of oil or fuel leakage.
2. Check the tires for imbedded stones. Pry them out with your ignition key.
3. Make sure all lights work.

NOTE: *At least check the brakelight. It can burn out anytime. Motorists cannot stop as quickly as you and need all the warning you can give.*

Tire Pressure

Tire pressure must be checked with the tires cold. Correct tire pressure depends a lot on the load you are carrying. See **Table 1**.

Battery

Hinge the seat open and check the battery electrolyte level. The level must be between the upper and lower marks on the case (**Figure 1**). For complete details see *Battery, Checking Electrolyte Level* in this chapter.

Check the level more frequently in hot weather.

Exhaust System

Check for leakage at all fittings. Do not forget the bolt (**Figure 2**) on the crossover pipe. Tighten all bolts and nuts; replace any gaskets as necessary.

Crankcase Breather Hose

Inspect the hose for cracks and deterioration and make sure that the hose clamps are tight (**Figure 3**).

Table 1   TIRE PRESSURES

Load	Pressure
Up to 198 lb. (90 kg)	
Front	26 psi (1.8 kg/cm^2)
Rear	28 psi (2.0 kg/cm^2)
198-410 lb. (90-186 kg)	
Front	28 psi (2.0 kg/cm^2)
Rear	32 psi (2.3 kg/cm^2)
Maximum Load Limit*	
Front — 470 lb. (214 kg)	40 psi (2.8 kg/cm^2)
Rear — 615 lb. (280 kg)	40 psi (2.8 kg/cm^2)

*Maximum load includes the total weight of motorcycle with accessories, rider(s), and luggage.

Final Checks

Inspect the entire motorcycle for loose fasteners, oil and fuel leaks, cracks in the frame and wheels, worn insulation on electrical wires, or anything else which might create unsafe riding conditions.

SERVICE INTERVALS

The services and intervals shown in **Table 2** are recommended by the factory. Strict adherence to these recommendations will go a long way toward insuring long service from your Yamaha XS750.

For convenience of maintaining your motorcycle, most of the services shown in the table are described in this chapter. However, some

Table 2　SERVICE INTERVALS

Every month	• Check tire pressure
Every 2,500 miles (4,000km) or 6 months	• Check engine oil level. • Lubricate all control cables with oil. • Adjust free play of front brake hand lever and rear brake lever. • Examine disc brake pads for wear. • Lubricate rear brake pedal arm and shift lever shaft. • Lubricate side and centerstand pivots. • Inspect front steering assembly for looseness. • Check wheel bearings for smooth operation. • Check battery condition. • Check ignition timing. • Inspect exhaust system for leaks. • Synchronize carburetors. • Check and adjust idle speed. • Check clutch lever free play. • Clean fuel shutoff valves and filters. • Lubricate speedometer gear housing. • Lubricate contact breaker point cam lubrication wicks.
Every 4,000 miles (6,400km)	• Complete engine tune-up.
Every 5,000 miles (8,000km) or 12 months	• Clean air filter element. • Inspect spark plugs: regap if necessary. • Adjust cam chain tensioner. • Check and adjust valve clearance. • Inspect all fuel lines for chafed, cracked, or swollen ends. • Inspect throttle operation. • Inspect crankcase ventilation hose for cracks, deterioration, or loose hose clamps. • Check engine mounts for side play. • Check all suspension components.
Every 8,000 miles (12,000km)	• Dismantle carburetors and clean. • Replace spark plugs. • Change oil in front forks. • Inspect and repack steering head bearings. • Inspect and repack rear swing arm bushings. • Inspect and repack wheel bearings.
Every 2 years	• Change brake fluid. • Replace master cylinder and caliper cylinder internal seals.
Every 4 years	• Replace all brake hoses.

3

procedures which require more than minor disassembly or adjustment are covered elsewhere in the appropriate chapter.

TIRES

Pressure

Tire pressure should be checked and adjusted to accommodate rider and luggage weight. A simple, accurate gauge (**Figure 4**) can be purchased for a few dollars and should be carried in your motorcycle tool kit. The appropriate tire pressures are shown in **Table 1**.

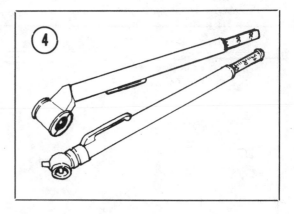

Inspection

Check tread for excessive wear, deep cuts, imbedded objects such as stones, nails, etc. If you find a nail in a tire, mark its location with a light crayon before pulling it out. This will help locate the hole in the inner tube. Refer to *Tire Changing* in Chapter Eight.

Check local traffic regulations concerning minimum tread depth. Measure with a tread depth gauge (**Figure 5**) or small ruler. Yamaha recommends replacement when the tread depth is 0.03 in. (0.8mm) or less. Tread wear indicators appear across the tire when tread reaches minimum safe depth. Replace the tire at this point.

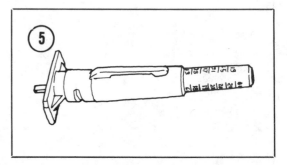

WHEELS

Check the aluminum wheels for cracks, bends, or warpage. These wheels cannot be serviced, except for balancing, and if found to be damaged they must be replaced. Refer to Chapter Eight for complete wheel inspection and balancing procedures.

Prior to 1979, the stock XS750 wheel was not designed to be used with tubeless tires. For models D, 2D, E, SE and SF always use a tube type tire. For model F or custom wheels, check the instructions on the tire's sidewall.

Check both axle nuts for tightness. Refer to **Table 3** for the correct torque values.

BATTERY

Checking Electrolyte Level

The battery is the heart of the electrical system. It should be checked and serviced as indicated. The majority of electrical system

troubles can be attributed to neglect of this vital component.

The electrolyte level may be checked with the battery installed. However it is necessary to hinge the seat up. The electrolyte level should be maintained between the two marks on the battery case (**Figure 1**). If the electrolyte level is low, it's a good idea to remove the battery so that it can be thoroughly serviced and checked.

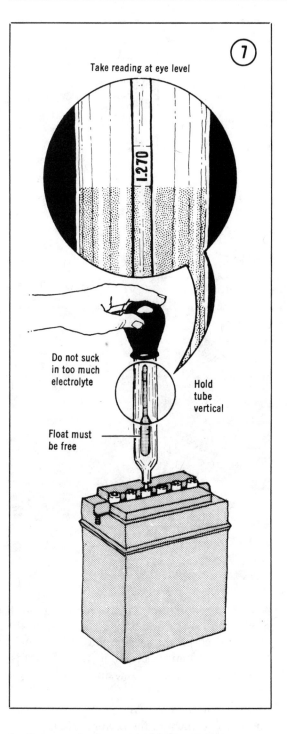

Take reading at eye level

1.270

⑦

Do not suck in too much electrolyte

Hold tube vertical

Float must be free

Table 3   AXLE NUT TORQUE VALUES

Item	Foot-pounds	Newton Meters
Front axle nut		
Model D	61	82
Models 2D and E	76	103
Models SE and SF	76	103
Front axle holding nuts		
Models D, 2D and E	16	22
Front axle pinch bolt		
Models E, SE and SF	15	20
Rear axle nut		
All models	108	147
Rear axle pinch bolt		
All models	4	5

3

CAUTION
Be careful not to spill battery electrolyte on painted or polished surfaces. The liquid is highly corrosive and will damage the finish. If it is spilled, wash it off immediately with soapy water and thoroughly rinse with clean water.

4. Remove the caps from the battery cells and add distilled water to correct the level. Never add electrolyte (acid) to correct the level.

5. After the level has been corrected and the battery allowed to stand for a few minutes, check the specific gravity of the electrolyte in each cell with a hydrometer (**Figure 7**). Follow the manufacturer's instructions for reading the instrument.

Testing

Hydrometer testing is the best way to check battery condition. Use a hydrometer with numbered graduations from 1.100 to 1.300 rather than one with color-coded bands. To use the hydrometer, squeeze the rubber ball, insert the tip into the cell and release the ball. Draw enough electrolyte to float the weighted float inside the hydrometer. Note the number in line with surface of the electrolyte; this is the specific gravity for this cell. Return the electrolyte to the cell from which it came.

The specific gravity of the electrolyte in each battery cell is an excellent indication of that cell's condition. A fully charged cell will read

1. Remove the battery hold-down strap.

2. Disconnect both the negative (black) and positive (red) electrical cables (**Figure 6**). Remove the breather tube.

3. Lift up and pull out the battery and rubber boot. Remove the battery from the boot.

Table 4   STATE OF CHARGE

Specific Gravity	State of Charge
1.110 - 1.130	Discharged
1.140 - 1.160	Almost discharged
1.170 - 1.190	One-quarter charged
1.200 - 1.220	One-half charged
1.230 - 1.250	Three-quarters charged
1.260 - 1.280	Fully charged

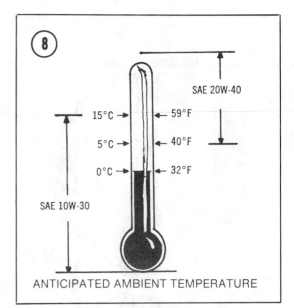

ANTICIPATED AMBIENT TEMPERATURE

1.260-1.280, while a cell in fair condition reads from 1.230-1.250. A weak cell reads from 1.200-1.220 and anything below 1.140 is discharged.

Specific gravity varies with temperature. For each 10° the electrolyte exceeds 80° F, add 0.004 to readings indicated on the hydrometer. Subtract 0.004 for each 10° below 80° F.

If the cells test in the poor range, the battery requires recharging. The hydrometer is useful for checking the progress of the charging operation. **Table 4** shows approximate state of charge.

Charging

> CAUTION
> *Always remove the battery from the motorcycle before connecting charging equipment.*

> WARNING
> *During charging, highly explosive hydrogen gas is released from the battery. The battery should be charged only in a well-ventilated area, and open flames and cigarettes should be kept away. Never check the charge of the battery by arcing across the terminals; the resulting spark can ignite the hydrogen gas.*

1. Connect the positive (+) charger lead to the positive battery terminal and the negative (−) charger lead to the negative battery terminal.

2. Remove all vent caps from the battery, set the charger at 12 volts, and switch it on. If the output of the charger is variable, it is best to select a low setting — 1½ to 2 amps.

3. After battery has been charged for about 8 hours, turn off the charger, disconnect the leads and check the specific gravity. It should be within the limits specified in **Table 4**. If it is, and remains stable after one hour, the battery is charged.

4. Clean the battery terminals, case, and tray and reinstall them in the motorcycle, reversing the removal steps. Coat the terminals with Vaseline or silicone spray to retard decomposition of the terminal material. install the breather tube without any kinks or sharp bends. It must be clear in order to dissipate the gas normally given off by the battery.

PERIODIC LUBRICATION

Checking Engine Oil Level
Models D and 2D

Engine oil level is checked with the dipstick, located on the top of the crankcase on the right-hand side (**Figure 3**).

1. Place the bike on the centerstand on a level surface.

2. Stop the engine and allow the oil to settle. Remove the dipstick, wipe it clean, and rest it on the case threads; do not screw it in. Remove it and check the level. The motorcycle must be level for the correct reading.

3. The level should be between the 2 lines but not above the upper one. If necessary, add the recommended weight of oil (**Figure 8**) to correct the level; do not overfill. Install the dipstick and tighten it securely.

Checking Engine Oil Level
Models E, F, SE and SF

Engine oil level is checked by viewing the oil level window located on the lower right-hand side of the crankcase cover.

1. Place the bike on the centerstand on a level surface.

2. Start the engine and allow it to run for a couple of minutes.

3. Shut off engine and allow the oil to settle.

4. Check the oil level through the oil level window (**Figure 9**).

5. The oil level should be between the maximum and minimum marks to the left of the window. If necessary, add the recommended weight of oil (**Figure 8**) to correct the level; do not overfill. Add oil through the filler hole located on the top right-hand side of the crankcase.

Changing Engine Oil and Filter

The factory-recommended oil change interval is 2,500 miles (4,000 km). The filter should be changed every other oil change. This assumes that the motorcycle is operated in moderate climates. In extremely cold climates, oil should be changed every 30 days. The time interval is more important than the mileage interval because acids formed by gasoline and water vapor from combustion will contaminate the oil even if the motorcycle is not run for several months. If motorcycle is operated under dusty conditions, the oil will get dirty more quickly and should be changed more frequently than recommended.

Use only a detergent oil with an API rating of SE or better. The quality rating is stamped on top of can (**Figure 10**). Try always to use same brand of oil. Use of oil additives is not recommended. Refer to **Figure 8** for correct weight of oil to use under different temperatures.

1. Place the motorcycle on the centerstand.

2. Start the engine and run it until it is at normal operating temperature, then turn it off.

3. Place a drip pan under the crankcase and remove the drain plug (A, **Figure 11**). Remove the dipstick (**Figure 12**) or oil filler cap; this will speed up the flow of oil.

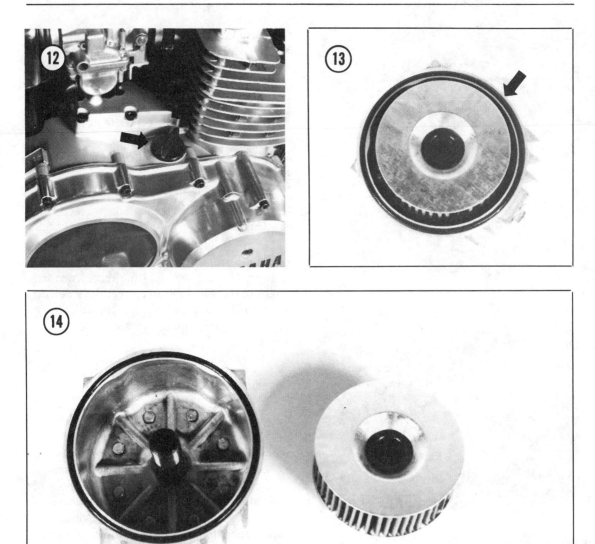

Table 5   MIDDLE AND FINAL GEAR OIL SPECIFICATIONS

Item	Type	Quantity
Middle gear case	Hypoid gear oil	12.7 U.S. oz. (375 cc; 10.56 Imp. oz.)
Final gear case	Hypoid gear oil	10.0 U.S. oz. (300cc; 8.45 Imp. oz.)
Temperature		
All weather	SAE 80W-90/GL4	
Above 40°F (5°C)	SAE 90/GL4	
Below 40°F (5°C)	SAE 80/GL4	

4. Let it drain for at least 15-20 minutes during which time, kick the starter a couple of times to help drain any remaining oil.

CAUTION
Make sure the ignition switch is in the OFF *position.*

NOTE: *Before removing filter cover, thoroughly clean off all road dirt and oil around it.*

5. To remove the oil filter, unscrew the bolt securing the filter cover (B, **Figure 11**) to the crankcase.

6. Remove the cover and the filter, discard the old filter and clean out the cover and the bolt with cleaning solvent and dry thoroughly. Remove all solvent residue.

7. Inspect the O-ring (**Figure 13**) on the cover. Replace it if deteriorated or damaged. Make sure it is properly positioned within the cover, prior to installation.

8. Insert the bolt into the cover and install the spring and washer (**Figure 14**). Insert the filter and reinstall into the crankcase.

9. Tighten the filter cover bolt to 20-25 ft.-lb. (29-32 N•m). Install the drain plug and tighten it to 31 ft.-lb. (43 N•m).

10. Fill the crankcase with the correct weight (**Figure 8**) and quantity of oil.

NOTE
The capacity with a filter change is approximately 3.3 qt. (3.1 liters; 2.66 Imp qt.).

11. Screw in the dipstick and start the engine; let it idle at moderate speed and check for leaks.

12. Turn off the engine and check for correct oil level.

13. Start the engine; the oil light should go off within 1-2 seconds. If it stays on, shut off the engine immediately and locate the problem. Do not run the engine with the light on.

Checking Middle Gear Oil Level

Check the middle gear oil with the level gauge furnished in the owner's tool kit. The engine and gear case should be cool. If the bike has been run, allow it to cool down (10-15 minutes), then check the oil level.

1. Place the bike on the centerstand on a level surface.

2. Wipe the area around the filler cap clean, and unscrew the cap. Do not allow any dirt or foreign matter to enter the gear case opening.

3. Insert the end of the gauge marked MIDDLE into the hole until it rests on the filler opening.

4. Remove the gauge. The correct oil level is between the two lines on the end of the gauge (**Figure 15**).

5. Add oil to maintain correct level. Refer to **Table 5** for recommended type and weight oil.

6. Install the filler cap and tighten it securely.

Changing Middle Gear Oil

The factory-recommended oil change interval is every 5,000 miles (8,000km).

1. Start the engine and let it run for a couple of minutes.

2. Shut it off and place bike on centerstand.

3. Place drip pan under the crankcase below the drain plug.

4. Wipe the area around the drain plug clean of all road dirt and remove drain plug (**Figure 16**). Loosen the filler cap as this will speed up the draining process.

5. Allow the oil to drain for at least 10-15 minutes.

6. Install the drain plug and tighten it to 33 ft.-lb. (45 N•m).

7. Remove filler cap and refill the case with 12.7 oz. (375cc) of the recommended type and weight oil. See **Table 5**.

Checking Final Drive Oil Level

Final drive gear oil is checked using the level gauge furnished in the owner's tool kit. The gear case should be cool. If the bike has been run, allow it to cool down, then check the oil level. When checking or changing the final drive gear oil, do not allow any dirt or foreign matter to enter the gear case opening.

1. Place the bike on the centerstand on a level surface.

2. Wipe the area around the filler cap clean and unscrew the cap.

3. Insert the end of the level gauge marked REAR into the hole until it rests on the filler opening. Remove the gauge.

4. The correct oil level is between the two marks on the end of the gauge (**Figure 17**).

5. Add oil to maintain the correct level. Refer to **Table 5** for the recommended type and weight oil. Install the filler cap and tighten it securely.

Changing Final Drive Gear Oil

The factory-recommended oil change interval is every 5,000 miles (8,000km).

1. Place the bike on the centerstand.

2. Place a drip pan under the final drive gear housing drain plug.

3. Wipe the area around the drain plug clean of all road dirt and remove drain plug (**Figure 18**). Loosen the filler cap as this will speed up the flow of oil.

4. Allow the oil to drain for at least 10-15 minutes.

> CAUTION
> *Do not allow any of the oil to come in contact with any of the brake components or drip onto the rear tire.*

5. Install the drain plug and tighten it to 17 ft.-lb. (23 N•m).

6. Remove the filler cap and refill the case with 10 U.S. oz. (300cc; 8.45 Imp. qt.) of the recommended type and weight oil. See **Table 5**.

Front Fork Oil Change

The factory-recommended fork oil change interval is every 10,000 miles (16,000km).

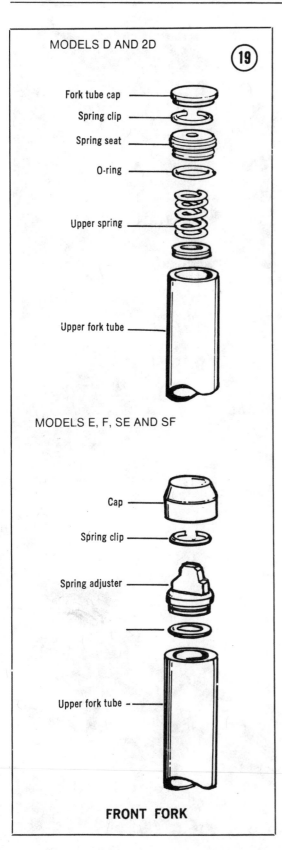

MODELS D AND 2D   (19)

Fork tube cap

Spring clip

Spring seat

O-ring

Upper spring

Upper fork tube

MODELS E, F, SE AND SF

Cap

Spring clip

Spring adjuster

Upper fork tube

FRONT FORK

(20)

(21)

Refer to **Figure 19** for this procedure.

1. Remove the front wheel as described under *Front Wheel Removal/Installation* in Chapter Eight.

2. Remove the cap (**Figure 20**) at the top of each fork.

3. Depress the spring seat (**Figure 21**) and fork spring. Remove the spring wire circlip with a small screwdriver.

4. Place a drip pan under the fork and remove the drain screw (**Figure 22**). Allow the oil to drain for at least 5 minutes.

CAUTION
Do not allow the fork oil to come in contact with any of the brake components.

5. *On Models D and 2D*: Remove the spring seat and O-ring and the upper spring. *On Models E, SE, and SF*: Remove the spring seat, spring adjuster, and O-ring.

6. After most of the oil has drained out, carefully move the outer fork tube up and down pumping out any remaining oil.

7. Install the drain screw; make sure the screw gasket is in good condition prior to installation. Replace if necessary.

8. Repeat Steps 4-7 for the other fork.

9. Refill each tube with SAE 20 fork oil. Refer to **Table 6** for specific capacity.

10. Slowly pump the outer fork tubes to distribute the oil.

11. Inspect all components removed in Step 5. If the O-ring needs replacement, replace the spring seat or spring adjuster also. They should always be replaced as a set. Install new spring wire clips upon assembly.

12. Install all components that were removed.

13. Road test the bike and check for leaks.

Swing Arm Bearings

Repack the rear swing arm bearings every 10,000 miles (16,000km), with a lithium-base, waterproof wheel bearing grease.

Refer to *Swing Arm, Removal/Installation* in Chapter Nine for complete details.

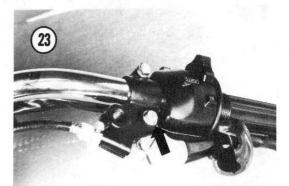

Miscellaneous Lubrication Points

Lubricate the clutch lever (**Figure 23**), front brake lever (**Figure 24**), rear brake pedal lever, center and side stand pivot points (**Figure 25**), and footrest pivot points with SAE 10W/30 motor oil.

PERIODIC MAINTENANCE

Disc Brakes — Front and Rear

The hydraulic fluid level in the disc brake master cylinders should be checked every month or 1,000 miles and the brake pads should be checked for wear. Bleeding the hydraulic system, servicing the master cylinder, caliper, and disc and replacing brake pads are covered in Chapter Ten.

Table 6   FRONT FORK OIL CAPACITY

Model	Type	Quantity - each fork
Model D	SAE 20 fork oil	5.75 U.S. oz (170 cc; 4.9 Imp. oz.)
Models 2D, E	SAE 20 fork oil	6.8 U.S. oz. (200cc; 5.6 Imp. oz.)
Models SE, F	SAE 20 fork oil	6.2 U.S. oz. (190 cc; 5.35 Imp. oz.)
Models SF	SAE 20 fork oil	7.91 U.S. oz. (234cc; 6.59 Imp. oz.)

Disc Brake Fluid Level

1. Clean the outside of the reservoir cap thoroughly with a dry rag and remove the screws securing the cap. Remove the cap, gasket, and diaphragm.

2. The fluid level in the reservoir should be up to the upper level line. See **Figure 26** for the front brake and **Figure 27** for the rear brake. If it is necessary, correct the level by adding fresh brake fluid.

WARNING
Use brake fluid clearly marked DOT 3 only and specified for disc brakes. Others may vaporize and cause brake failure.

CAUTION
Be careful not to spill brake fluid on painted or plated surfaces as it will destroy the surface. Wash immediately with soapy water and thoroughly rinse it off.

3. Reinstall the washer, diaphragm, and cap; make sure that the cap is screwed on tightly.

Disc Brake Lines

Check brake lines between the master cylinders and the brake calipers. If there is any leakage, tighten the connections and bleed the brakes as described under *Bleeding the System* in Chapter Ten. If this does not stop the leak, or if a line is obviously damaged, cracked, or chafed, replace the line and bleed the brake.

Brake lines should be replaced every four years or earlier if cracked or damaged.

Disc Brake Pad Wear

Inspect the brake pads for excessive or uneven wear, scoring, and oil or grease on the friction surface. If the pads are worn to the red line, they must be replaced.

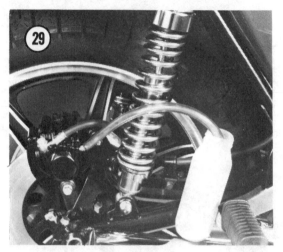

NOTE: *Always replace both pads at the same time.*

If any of these conditions exist, replace the pads as described under *Brake Pad Replacement* in Chapter Ten.

Disc Brake Fluid Change

Every time you remove the reservoir cap a small amount of dirt and moisture enters the brake fluid. The same thing happens if a leak occurs, or any part of the hydraulic system is loosened or disconnected. Dirt can clog the system and cause unneccessary wear. Water in the fluid vaporizes at high temperatures, impairing the hydraulic action and reducing brake performance.

To maintain peak performance, change the brake fluid every 10,000 miles (16,000km) or two years.

1. Remove dust cap from the caliper bleeder valve. Connect a small clear hose to the valve and place the free end into a container. Refer to **Figure 28** for the front wheel and **Figure 29** for the rear wheel.

2. Open the bleeder valve with a wrench about ½ turn.

3. Squeeze the brake lever several times to force out as much brake fluid as possible. Close the bleeder valve.

4. Fill the reservoir with new brake fluid, install the cap and bleed the system as described under *Bleeding the System* in Chapter Ten.

WARNING
Use brake fluid clearly marked DOT 3 only. Others may vaporize and cause brake failure.

Front Brake Lever Adjustment

The front brake lever should be adjusted every 2,500 miles (4,000km).

The clearance between the pads and discs are automatically adjusted as the pads wear. The free play of the hand grip should be maintained to avoid brake drag.

WARNING
Do not reuse brake fluid which has been drained from a brake system. Contaminated fluid can cause brake failure.

3

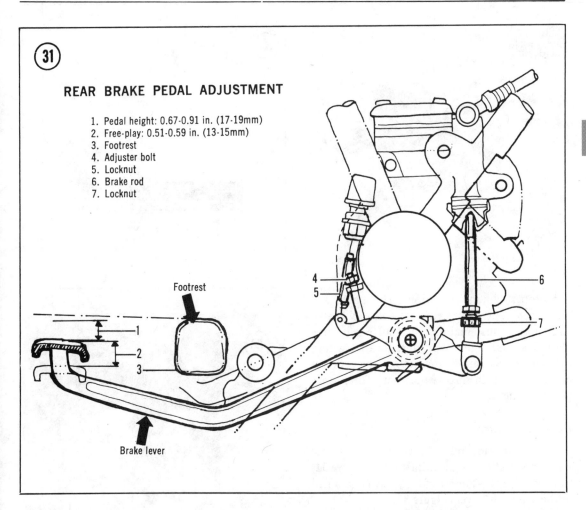

(31)

REAR BRAKE PEDAL ADJUSTMENT

1. Pedal height: 0.67-0.91 in. (17-19mm)
2. Free-play: 0.51-0.59 in. (13-15mm)
3. Footrest
4. Adjuster bolt
5. Locknut
6. Brake rod
7. Locknut

Footrest

Brake lever

Loosen the locknut (A, **Figure 30**) and turn the adjusting screw (B, **Figure 30**) in or out. The proper amount of free play is 0.2-0.3 in. (5-8mm) measured at the end of the lever. After adjustment is completed, tighten the locknut.

Rear Brake Height and Free Play Adjustment

The rear brake should be adjusted every 2,500 miles (4,000km).

Refer to **Figure 31** for this procedure.

1. Place the motorcycle on the centerstand.

2. Check to be sure that the brake pedal is in the "at-rest" position.

3. Loosen pedal height adjuster locknut (5).

4. Turn adjuster bolt (4) so that the top of pedal is approximately 0.67-0.91 in. (17-23mm) below the footrest.

5. Tighten the adjuster locknut (5).

6. Loosen the brake rod adjuster locknut (7).

7. Screw the brake rod (6) down and away from the master cylinder until there is noticeable free play.

8. Turn the brake rod (6) upward until it lightly touches the master cylinder. Back it off 1⅓ turns for the correct free play, approximately 0.50-0.59 in. (13-15mm).

CAUTION
The punch mark on the brake rod (6) is not to show above the top surface of the adjuster locknut (7) after final tightening. If this happens, check for excessive brake pad wear and/or low brake fluid level in the master cylinder.

Clutch Adjustment

The clutch should be adjusted every 2,500 miles (4,000km).

There are two different clutch adjustment procedures. Both must be properly maintained

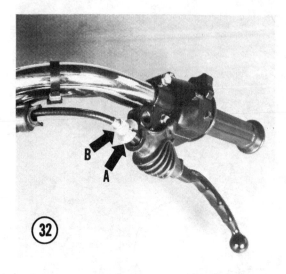

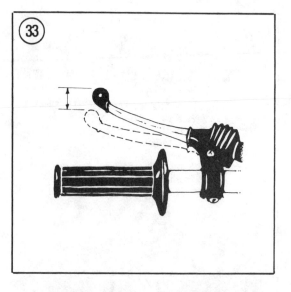

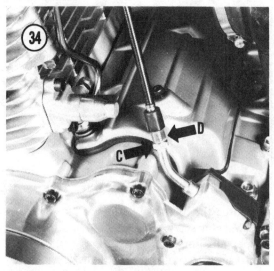

for proper clutch operation. The cable adjustments take up slack, caused by cable stretching, thus maintaining sufficient free play. The mechanism adjuster, located within the clutch assembly maintains the correct amount of clutch throw, necessary for proper disengagement.

Cable Adjustment

Loosen the locknut (A, **Figure 32**) at the hand grip and rotate the adjuster (B, **Figure 32**) until ½-1 in. (13-26mm) of free play is obtained at the end of the lever (**Figure 33**).

If sufficient free play cannot be obtained at the hand grip, additional adjustment may be made at the cable length adjuster located on the left-hand side of the engine. Loosen the locknut (C, **Figure 34**) and rotate the adjuster (D, **Figure 34**) until the proper free play is obtained.

If proper amount of free play cannot be achieved by using these two adjustment procedures the cable has stretched to the point that it needs replacing. Refer to *Clutch Cable Removal/Installation* in Chapter Five for the complete procedure.

Mechanism Adjustment

Remove the mechanism adjuster cover (**Figure 35**). Loosen the locknut (A, **Figure 36**) and rotate the setscrew (B, **Figure 36**) in until it seats against the clutch pushrod. Back the screw out ¼ turn and tighten the locknut. Install the cover.

After completing this adjustment, recheck the free play adjustment at the hand grip, readjust if necessary.

Road test the bike to make sure the clutch fully disengages when the lever is pulled in; if it does not, the bike will creep in gear when stopped. Also, make sure the clutch fully engages; if it does not, the clutch will slip, particularly when accelerating in high gear.

Air Cleaner

A clogged air cleaner can decrease the efficiency and life of the engine. Never run the bike without the air cleaner installed; even minute particles of dust can cause severe internal wear.

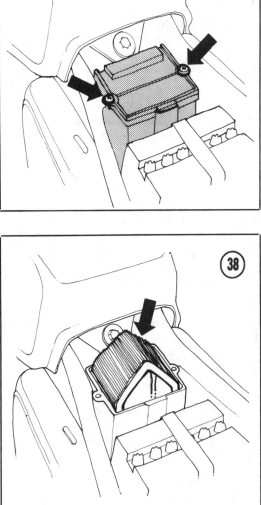

Clean the air cleaner every 1,000 miles (1,600km), or more often if ridden in dusty areas.

Removal/Installation
(Models D and 2D)

Hinge the seat open and remove the 2 screws (**Figure 37**) securing the air filter case cap. Pull out the element (**Figure 38**). Tap the element lightly to remove most of the dust and dirt; then apply compressed air to the inside surface of the element.

Inspect the element; make sure it is in good condition. Replace it if necessary.

Reinstall the element making sure it is seated against the case properly.

Removal/Installation
(Models E, SE, and SF)

Remove the wing nut (**Figure 39**) securing the filter case. Remove case and pull element out of it (**Figure 40**). Remove most of the dirt and dust by tapping it, then apply compressed air to the inside surface of the element.

Inspect the element; make sure it is in good condition. Replace if necessary.

Insert the element into the case and install the case onto the air box.

Throttle Operation/Adjustment

The throttle grip should have 10-15° rotational play (**Figure 41**). Make sure there is free play in the cable so the carburetors will be able to close completely when the throttle is turned off. If adjustment is necessary, loosen the cable locknut (A, **Figure 42**) and turn the adjuster (B, **Figure 42**) in or out to achieve the proper play. Tighten the locknut (A).

Check the throttle cable from grip to carburetors. Make sure they are not kinked or chafed. Replace them if necessary.

Make sure that the throttle grip rotates smoothly from fully closed to fully open. Check at center, full left, and full right position of the steering.

Fuel Shut-off Valve Cleaning

NOTE
If equipped with more than one valve, use the same procedure for each.

1. Turn the valve to the ON or RESERVE position (**Figure 43**).

2. Remove the fuel and vacuum lines to the carburetors.

3. Remove the screws securing the drain cover and remove the cover. Clean it with solvent and reinstall it.

> NOTE: *On models SE and SF, it is necessary to hinge up the seat and remove the fuel tank bolt (**Figure 44**). Pull up on the fuel tank and remove the fuel line. Remove the drain bolt and clean it with solvent. Inspect the gasket and replace if necessary.*

Fuel Shut-off Valve/Filter Removal/Installation

The fuel filter removes particles which might otherwise enter into the carburetors and may cause the float needle to remain in the open position.

1. Turn the valve to the ON or RESERVE position (**Figure 43**).

2. Remove the fuel line and vacuum line to the valve.

> NOTE: *There is no OFF position on the valve. Fuel will not flow through the valve in the ON or RESERVE position without engine vacuum to open the valve.*

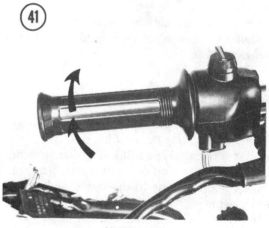

10-15° rotation

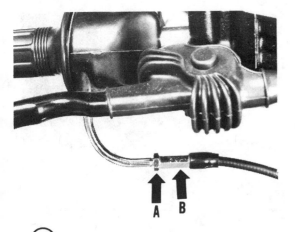

3

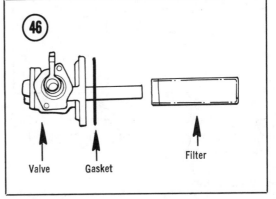

3. Install a longer piece of fuel line to the valve, place the loose end into a clean, sealable metal container. This fuel can be reused if it is kept clean.

4. Turn the valve to the PRIME position and open the fuel filler cap. This will speed up the flow of fuel. Drain the tank completely.

5. Remove the screws (**Figure 45**) securing the valve to the tank.

6. Remove the valve, gasket and filter assembly (**Figure 46**).

7. After removing the valve, insert a corner of a clean shop rag into the opening in the tank to stop the dribbling of fuel onto the engine and frame.

8. Slide the filter off the valve. Clean it with a medium soft toothbrush and blow out with compressed air. Replace it if defective.

9. Repeat Steps 5-8 for the other valve.

10. Inspect the diaphragm and gasket, replace if necessary.

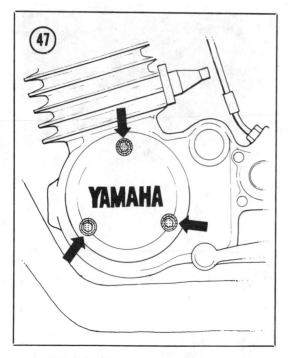

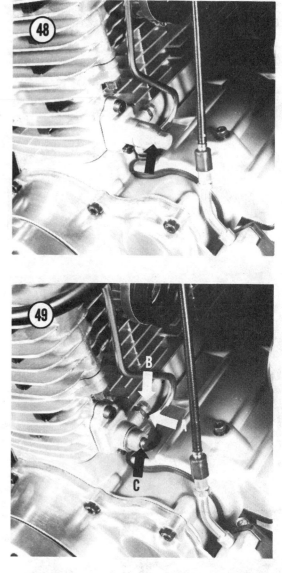

11. Install by reversing the removal steps. Do not forget the gasket between the valve body and the fuel tank.

Wheel Bearings

The wheel bearings should be cleaned and repacked every 8,000 miles (12,000km) or after crossing or riding small rivers or creeks. Refer to Chapters Eight and Nine for complete service procedures.

Cam Chain Tensioner Adjustment

The cam chain should be adjusted every 3,000 miles (4,800km) or when it becomes noisy.

1. Remove the spark plugs (this will make it easier to turn the engine over by hand).

2. Remove the screws securing the ignition cover (**Figure 47**).

3. Remove the cam chain tensioner cover (**Figure 48**).

4. Loosen the tensioner holder locknut (A, **Figure 49**).

5. Loosen tensioner holder bolt (B, **Figure 49**).

6. Slowly rotate the crankshaft *counterclockwise* several times with a wrench on the nut at the left-hand end of the crankshaft (**Figure 50**).

Observe the in and out movement of the tensioner during crankshaft rotation.

7. Continue to rotate the crankshaft until the tensioner travels the deepest into the holder (C, **Figure 49**). At this point, stop turning the crankshaft and tighten the holder bolt and locknut.

8. Install the tensioner cover, ignition cover, and spark plugs.

Steering Head Adjustment Check

The steering head is fitted with two tapered bearings and should be checked for looseness at least every 2,500 miles (4,000km).

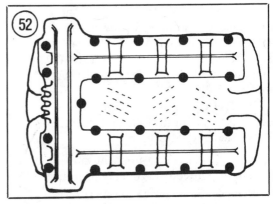

Jack up the bike so that the front wheel is off the ground.

Hold onto the front fork tubes and gently rock the fork assembly back and forth. If you can feel looseness refer to *Steering Head Adjustment* in Chapter Eight.

TUNE-UP

A complete tune-up should be performed every 4,000 miles (6,400km) of normal riding. More frequent tune-ups may be required if the bike is ridden primarily in stop-and-go traffic. The purpose of the tune-up is to restore the performance lost due to normal wear and deterioration of parts.

The spark plugs should be routinely replaced at every other tune-up or if the electrodes show signs of erosion. In addition, this is a good time to clean the air cleaner element. Have the new parts on hand before you begin.

Because different systems in an engine interact, the procedures should be done in the following order:

a. Tighten cylinder head nuts and bolts

b. Adjust valve clearances

c. Run a compression test

d. Check and adjust ignition components and timing

e. Synchronize carburetors and set idle speed

Cylinder Head Nuts and Bolts

The engine must be at room temperature for this procedure.

1. Place the bike on the centerstand and remove the seat.

2. Turn the fuel shut-off valves to the ON or RESERVE position (**Figure 51**) and remove the fuel lines to the carburetors. Also remove the vacuum lines to the intake manifolds.

3. Remove the bolt securing the fuel tank at the rear. Slide the tank to the rear and remove it.

4. On Models D and 2D, remove the 6 Allen bolts securing the cam cover air scoop and remove it.

5. Remove the 21 Allen bolts (**Figure 52**) securing the cam cover in place. Remove the cam cover and the 3 air scoop brackets (Models 2 and 2D only).

NOTE
Do not forget the inner left-hand bolt.

6. Tighten the cylinder head nuts and bolts in the sequence shown in **Figure 53**. Torque the 10mm nuts (No. 1-8) to 25 ft.-lb. (34 N•m), the 8mm bolts (No. 9 and 10) to 14 ft.-lb. (19 N•m) and the 2 holder nuts (No. 11 and 12) to 14 ft.-lb. (19 N•m).

The fuel tank and cam cover should be left off at this time for the following procedures.

Valve Clearance Measurement

Valve clearance measurement must be made with the engine cool, at room temperature.

1. Remove the screws (**Figure 54**) securing the ignition cover.

2. Remove the spark plugs (this makes it easier to turn over the engine by hand).

3. Rotate the cam by turning the crankshaft. Use a wrench on the nut located on the left-hand end of the crankshaft (**Figure 50**). In order to obtain a correct measurement, the cam lobe must be directly opposite the lifter surface (**Figure 55**).

4. Insert a feeler gauge between the cam and the lifter surface (**Figure 56**). The clearance is measured correctly when there is a slight drag on the feeler gauge when it is inserted and withdrawn.

> *NOTE*
> *The correct valve clearance is 0.21-0.24 mm for the exhaust valve (front) and 0.16-0.20 mm for the intake valve (rear). For best performance, adjust to the smaller dimension. Measure the valve clearance with a **metric** feeler gauge as it will be easier to calculate pad replacement described later in this section.*

5. To correct the clearance, the pad on top of the valve lifter must be replaced with one of the correct thickness. These pads are available in 25 different thicknesses from No. 200 (2.00 mm) to No. 320 (3.20 mm) in increments of 0.05 mm. These pads are available from Yamaha dealers. The thickness is marked on the pad face that contacts the lifter body, not the cam.

6. Measure all valves and record the clearance. They must be measured very accurately.

Valve Clearance Adjustment

A special tool, Yamaha No. 90890-01223-00/ Valve Adjusting Tool, **Figure 57** is necessary

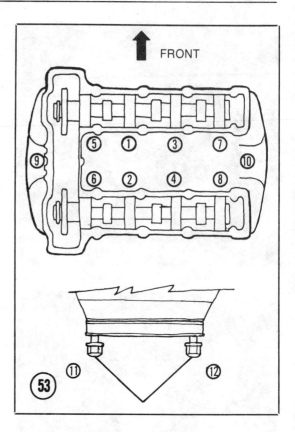

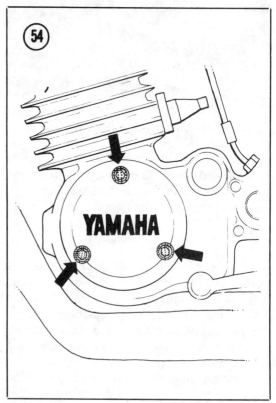

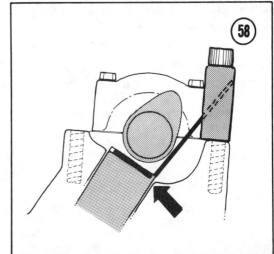

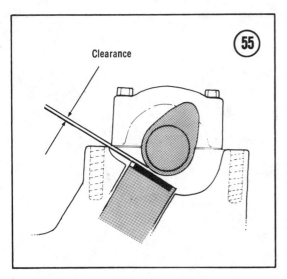

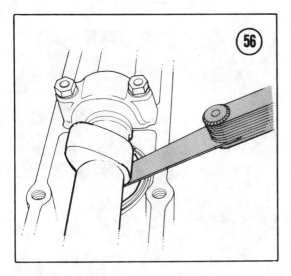

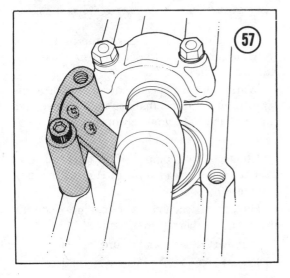

for this procedure. It is attached to the cylinder head, next to the valve being adjusted, with one of the Allen bolts used to secure the cylinder head cover. This tool holds the valve lifter down so the adjusting pad can be removed and replaced.

There is no set order to follow but it is suggested that you start with the No. 1 cylinder and do all exhaust valves, then return to No. 1 cylinder and do all intake valves.

1. The top of the valve lifter has a slot. This slot must be turned opposite the blade of the valve adjusting tool prior to installing the tool.

2. Turn the cam by rotating the crankshaft until the cam lobe fully depresses the valve lifter (valve in the completely open position).

3. Install the adjusting tool, using one of the cylinder head cover Allen bolts, as shown in **Figure 58**. Make sure the tool blade touches only the lifter body (**Figure 58**), not the pad.

CAUTION
Do not allow the cam lobe to come in contact with the valve adjusting tool as it may fracture the cylinder head. To avoid cam contact with the tool, rotate the cams as follows: intake — **clockwise** *and exhaust —* **counterclockwise**, *as viewed from the left-hand side looking directly at No. 1 cylinder.*

4. Carefully rotate the cam lobe off of the pad so it can be removed. Remove the pad from the lifter (**Figure 59**) with a small screwdriver, nee-

dle nose pliers, or magnetic tool. Turn the pad over and note the number.

5. For correct pad selection proceed as follows:

> NOTE: *For calculations use the midpoint of the specified clearance tolerance — e.g., intake valve 0.16 – 0.22mm = **0.19mm** and exhaust valve 0.21 – 0.25mm = **0.23mm**.*

> NOTE: *The following numbers are for examples only.*

EXAMPLES:	Intake	Exhaust
Actual measured clearance	0.50mm	0.41mm
Subtract specified clearance	– 0.19	– 0.23
Equals excess clearance	= 0.31	= 0.18
Existing pad number	220	245
Add excess clearance	+ 31	+ 18
Equals new pad number	= 251	= 263
(round off to the nearest pad number)	250	265

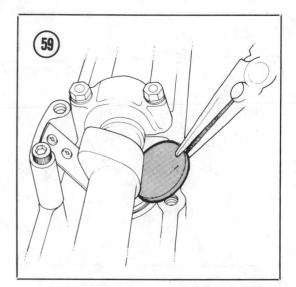

6. Install the new pad into the lifter with the number facing down. Make sure the pad is positioned correctly into the lifter.

7. Carefully rotate the cam until the lobe comes in contact with the new pad and lifter. Remove the adjusting tool.

8. Rotate the cam a couple of times to make sure the pad has properly seated into the lifter.

9. Recheck valve clearance as described under *Valve Clearance Measurement*. If clearance is incorrect, repeat these steps until proper clearance is obtained.

10. Discard all old pads removed. They are worn and their numbers are no longer accurate.

11. Install the cam cover (make sure the gasket is in good condition; replace if necessary), air scoop, spark plugs, fuel tank, and seat.

Compression Test

Every 4,000 miles (6,400km) check cylinder compression. Record the results and compare them at the next 4,000 mile (6,400km) check. A running record will show trends in deterioration so that corrective action can be taken before complete failure.

The results, when properly interpreted, can indicate general cylinder, piston ring, and valve condition.

1. Warm the engine to normal operating temperature. Ensure that the choke valve and throttle valve are completely open.

2. Remove the spark plugs.

3. Connect the compression tester to one cylinder following manufacturer's instructions (**Figure 60**).

4. Have an assistant crank the engine over until there is no further rise in pressure.

5. Remove the tester and record the reading.

6. Repeat Steps 3-5 for the other cylinders.

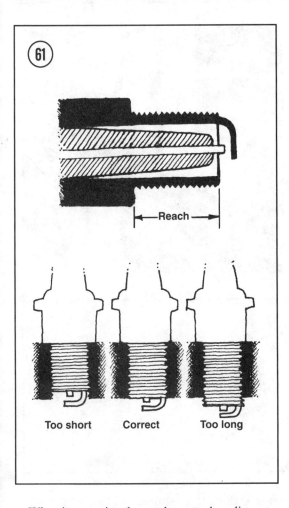

Reach

Too short Correct Too long

cantly, the valves are good but the rings are defective on that cylinder. If compression does not increase, the valves require servicing. A valve could be hanging open but not burned or a piece of carbon could be on a valve seat.

Correct Spark Plug Heat Range

Spark plugs are available in various heat ranges, hotter or colder than plugs originally installed at the factory.

Select plugs of a heat range designed for the loads and temperature conditions under which the bike will run. Use of incorrect heat ranges can cause seized pistons, scored cylinder walls, or damaged piston crowns.

In general, use a hot plug for low speeds, low loads, and low temperatures. Use a cold plug for high speeds, high engine loads, and high temperatures.

In areas where seasonal temperature variations are great, the factory recommends a "two-plug system" — a cold plug for hard summer riding and a hot plug for slower winter operation.

The reach (length) of a plug is also important. A longer than normal plug could interfere with the valves and pistons causing permanent and severe damage. Refer to **Figure 61**.

The standard heat range spark plugs are NGK BP-7ES or Champion N-7Y.

Spark Plug Cleaning/Replacement

1. Grasp the spark plug leads (**Figure 62**) as near to the plug as possible and pull them off the plugs.
2. Blow away any dirt that has accumulated in the spark plug wells.

CAUTION
The dirt could fall into the cylinders when the plugs are removed, causing serious engine damage.

3. Remove spark plugs with a spark plug wrench.

NOTE: *If plugs are difficult to remove, apply penetrating oil, like WD-40 or Liquid Wrench, around base of plugs and let it soak in about 10-20 minutes.*

When interpreting the results, actual readings are not as important as the difference between the readings. At sea level, the standard compression pressure is 142 psi (10 kg/cm^2). Minimum pressure is 128 psi (9 kg/cm^2) and maximum 156 psi (11 kg/cm^2). Pressure should not vary from cylinder to cylinder by more than 14 psi (1 kg/cm^2). Greater differences indicate worn or broken rings, leaky or sticky valves, blown head gasket or a combination of all.

If compression reading does not differ between cylinders by more than 10 psi, the rings and valves are in good condition.

If a low reading (10% or more) is obtained on one of the cylinders, it indicates valve or ring trouble. To determine which, pour about a teaspoon of engine oil through the spark plug hole onto the top of the piston. Turn the engine over once to distribute the oil, then take another compression test and record the reading. If the compression increases signifi-

4. Inspect spark plugs carefully. Look for plugs with broken center porcelain, excessively eroded electrodes, and excessive carbon or oil fouling. Replace such plugs. If deposits are light, plugs may be cleaned in solvent with a wire brush or cleaned in a special spark plug sandblast cleaner.

5. Gap plugs to 0.02-0.03 in. (0.6-0.7mm) with a wire feeler gauge. See **Figure 63**.

6. Install plugs with a new gasket. First, apply a small drop of oil to threads. Tighten plugs finger-tight, then tighten with a spark plug wrench an additional ½ turn. If you must reuse an old gasket, tighten only an additional ¼ turn.

> NOTE: *Do not overtighten. This will only squash the gasket and destroy its sealing ability.*

Reading Spark Plugs

Much information about engine and spark plug performance can be determined by careful examination of the spark plugs. This information is more valid after performing the following steps.

1. Ride bike a short distance at full throttle in any gear.
2. Turn off kill switch before closing throttle, and simultaneously, pull in clutch and coast to a stop.
3. Remove spark plugs and examine them. Compare them to **Figure 64**.

If the insulator is white or burned, the plug is too hot and should be replaced with a colder one.

A too-cold plug will have sooty deposits ranging in color from dark brown to black. Replace with a hotter plug and check for too rich carburetion or evidence or oil blow-by at the piston rings.

If any one plug is found unsatisfactory, discard all three.

Breaker Point Inspection and Cleaning
Models D and 2D

Through normal use, the surfaces of the breaker points gradually pit and burn. If they are not too badly pitted, they can be dressed with a few strokes of a clean point file or Flex-

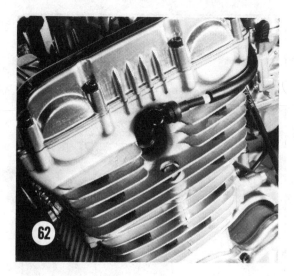

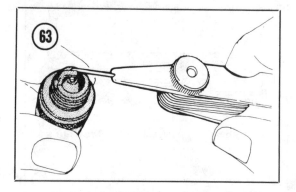

stone (available at most auto parts stores). Do not use emery cloth or sandpaper, as particles remain on the points and cause arcing and burning. If a few strokes of the file do not smooth the points completely, replace them.

If points are still serviceable after filing, remove all residue with lacquer thinner or electrical contact cleaner. Close the points on a piece of clean white paper such as a business card. Continue to pull the card through the closed points until no particles or discoloration are transferred to the card. Finally, rotate the engine and observe the points as they open and close. If they do not meet squarely (**Figure 65**) replace them as described under *Breaker Point Replacement* in this chapter.

Breaker Point Replacement
Models D and 2D

Breaker points should be replaced only when the point gap exceeds the maximum tolerance

SPARK PLUG CONDITION ⑥⁴

NORMAL

- Identified by light tan or gray deposits on the firing tip.
- Can be cleaned.

GAP BRIDGED

- Identified by deposit buildup closing gap between electrodes.
- Caused by oil or carbon fouling. If deposits are not excessive, the plug can be cleaned.

OIL FOULED

- Identified by wet black deposits on the insulator shell bore and electrodes.
- Caused by excessive oil entering combustion chamber through worn rings and pistons, excessive clearance between valve guides and stems, or worn or loose bearings. Can be cleaned. If engine is not repaired, use a hotter plug.

CARBON FOULED

- Identified by black, dry fluffy carbon deposits on insulator tips, exposed shell surfaces and electrodes.
- Caused by too cold a plug, weak ignition, dirty air cleaner, too rich a fuel mixture, or excessive idling. Can be cleaned.

LEAD FOULED

- Identified by dark gray, black, yellow, or tan deposits or a fused glazed coating on the insulator tip.
- Caused by highly leaded gasoline. Can be cleaned.

WORN

- Identified by severely eroded or worn electrodes.
- Caused by normal wear. Should be replaced.

FUSED SPOT DEPOSIT

- Identified by melted or spotty deposits resembling bubbles or blisters.
- Caused by sudden acceleration. Can be cleaned.

OVERHEATING

- Identified by a white or light gray insulator with small black or gray brown spots and with bluish-burnt appearance of electrodes.
- Caused by engine overheating, wrong type of fuel, loose spark plugs, too hot a plug, or incorrect ignition timing. Replace the plug.

PREIGNITION

- Identified by melted electrodes and possibly blistered insulator. Metallic deposits on insulator indicate engine damage.
- Caused by wrong type of fuel, incorrect ignition timing or advance, too hot a plug, burned valves, or engine overheating. Replace the plug.

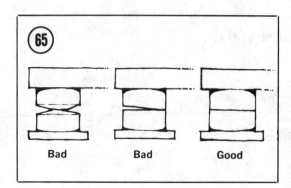

Bad   Bad   Good

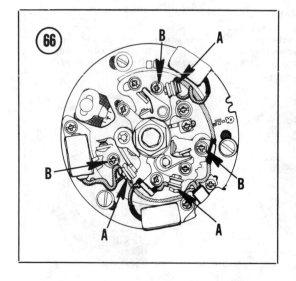

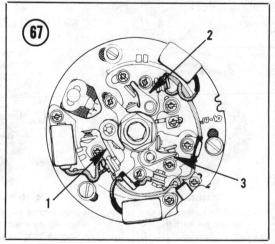

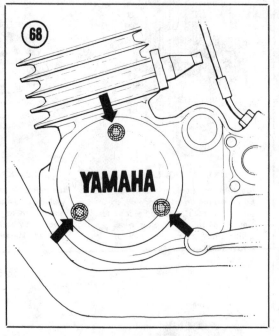

or when the points surface becomes pitted or burned. Each cylinder has its own set of breaker points.

Remove the nut (A, **Figure 66**) securing the electrical terminal and the attachment screw (B, **Figure 66**), securing the breaker assembly to the backing plate.

Install the new set and adjust as described under *Breaker Point Adjustment* in this chapter. Apply a few drops of lightweight oil to the point cam lubricators.

Breaker Point Adjustment
Models D and 2D

Each cylinder has its own set of breaker points: the No. 1 (left-hand cylinder), No. 2 (center cylinder), and No. 3 (right-hand cylinder). These numbers relate to the numbers on the backing plate (**Figure 67**).

1. Remove the 3 screws securing the ignition cover (**Figure 68**), and remove it.

2. Rotate the crankshaft with a wrench on the crankshaft nut until the No. 1 cylinder point gap is open to the maximum setting.

3. Check gap with a flat feeler gauge. The correct gap is 0.012-0.016 in. (0.3-0.4mm).

4. Adjust the gap by loosening the securing screw and moving the adjustable point using a screwdriver and the adjusting slots in the backing plate (**Figure 67**). After correct gap is achieved, tighten the securing screw and recheck the gap setting. Reset if necessary.

5. Repeat Steps 2-4 for the other 2 cylinders.

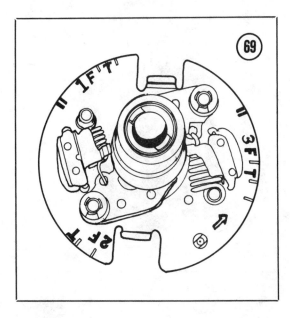

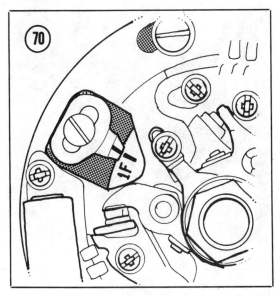

Ignition Timing
Models D and 2D

Prior to checking ignition timing, the contact breaker point gap must be adjusted properly as described earlier.

Timing is set by using a timing light and observing the alignment of the stationary pointer in relation to the marks on the governor plate. The marks on the governor plate (**Figure 69**) indicate the following:

a. 1F — retarded firing point for left-hand cylinder

b. 2F — retarded firing point for center cylinder

c. 3F — retarded firing point for right-hand cylinder

d. T — top dead center (TDC) for each cylinder

e. II — parallel lines indicating full advance for that specific cylinder

NOTE: *Before starting on this procedure, check all electrical connections related to the ignition system. Make sure all connections are tight and free of corrosion and that all ground connections are tight.*

1. Place the bike on the centerstand.

2. Connect a portable tachometer following the manufacturer's instructions. The bike's tach is not accurate enough in the low rpm range for this adjustment.

3. Connect a timing light to the No. 1 cylinder (left-hand side) following the manufacturer's instructions.

NOTE: *Timing must be set first on the No. 1 cylinder, then the two remaining cylinders.*

4. Start the engine and let it warm up to normal operating temperature. Let the engine idle (1,100-1,500 rpm) and aim the timing light toward the timing marks on the breaker point backing plate.

5. The stationary pointer should align with the 1F mark on the governor plate (**Figure 70**). If not, proceed as follows.

6. Shut off the engine and loosen the 3 breaker point backing plate screws (**Figure 71**). Slightly rotate the backing plate in either direction. Tighten the screws, restart the engine and recheck the timing. Continue this procedure until the timing marks align. Be sure the 3 screws are tightened securely.

7. Increase engine speed to 3,000 rpm and check the alignment of the stationary pointer and the 2 parallel lines (**Figure 72**). If the idle speed timing is correct but the full advance is incorrect, refer to *Ignition Advance Mechanism* in Chapter Seven.

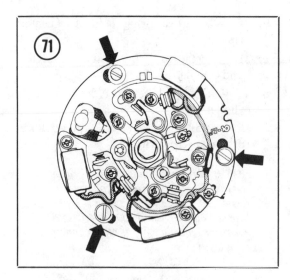

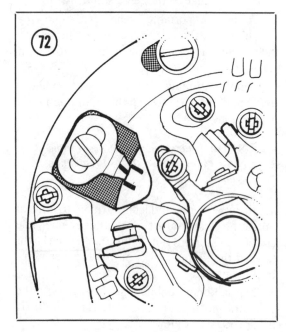

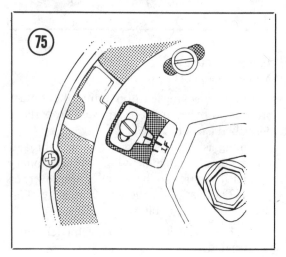

8. Repeat Steps 3-7 for the No. 2 (center cylinder) then the No. 3 (right-hand cylinder).

> NOTE: *In Step 6, loosen the individual point assembly plate screw — not the backing plate assembly screws — to change alignment for that cylinder. Refer to* **Figure 67** *for the specific cylinder number to point assembly number.*

9. Make sure the point assembly screws are tightened securely; after tightening, recheck the timing for each cylinder.

Ignition Timing
Models E, SE, and SF

Timing is set by using a timing light and observing the alignment of the stationary pointer in relationship to the marks on the governor plate. The marks on the governor plate (**Figure 73**) indicate the following:

a. 1F — retarded firing point for left-hand cylinder

b. T — top dead center (TDC) for left-hand cylinder

c. III — full advance marks for left-hand cylinder

It is only necessary to check and adjust the timing on the No. 1 cylinder. Once it is adjusted correctly, the other two cylinders will automatically be correct.

> NOTE: *Before starting on this procedure, check all electrical connections related to the ignition system. Make sure all connections are tight and free of corrosion and that all ground connections are tight.*

1. Place the bike on the centerstand.

2. Connect a portable tachometer following the manufacturer's instructions. The bike's tach is not accurate enough in the low rpm range for this adjustment.

3. Connect a timing light to the No. 1 cylinder (left-hand side) following the manufacturer's instructions (**Figure 74**).

4. Start the engine and let it warm up to normal operating temperature. Let the engine idle (1,000 ± 100 rpm) and aim the timing light toward the timing marks on the pick-up base plate.

5. The stationary pointer should align with the 1F mark on the governor plate (**Figure 75**). If not, proceed as follows.

6. Shut off the engine and loosen the 3 pick-up base plate screws (**Figure 76**). Slightly rotate the plate in either direction. Tighten the screws. Restart the engine and recheck the timing. Continue this procedure until the timing marks align. Be sure 3 screws are tightened securely.

7. Increase engine speed to slightly above 5,000 rpm and check the alignment of the stationary

pointer and the full advance marks (**Figure 77**). If the idle speed timing is correct but the full advance is incorrect, refer to *Automatic Timing Unit Inspection* in Chapter Seven.

Carburetor Idle Mixture

Idle mixture (**Figure 78**) is preset at the factory and it *is not to be reset*.

Carburetor Sychronization

Prior to sychronizing the carburetors, the ignition timing and valve clearance must be properly adjusted.

This procedure requires a special tool to measure the manifold vacuum for all three cylinders simultaneously.

1. Place the bike on the centerstand and turn the fuel shut-off valves to the ON position.

2. Remove the vacuum lines from the right- and left-hand carburetor manifolds (A, **Figure 79**).

3. Remove the cap from the center carburetor manifold (B, **Figure 79**).

> NOTE: *The carburetor assembly has been removed for clarity only — do not remove it.*

4. Connect the vacuum lines from the sychronizing tool, following the manufacturer's instructions, to the manifolds.

5. Turn the fuel shut-off valves to the PRIME position, start the engine and let it reach normal operating temperature. Let the engine idle.

6. The carburetors are sychronized if all have the same gauge readings. If not, proceed as follows.

7. The center carburetor has no sychronizing screw, so the outer two carburetors must be aligned to it. Turn the left-hand carburetor sychronizing screw (**Figure 80**) until the gauge reading is the same as the center carburetor.

> NOTE: *Figure 80 is shown with the carburetor assembly removed for clarity only. Do not remove it.*

8. Repeat for the right-hand carburetor.

9. Remove the vacuum gauge hoses and install the cap on the center carburetor and vacuum lines onto the right- and left-hand carburetors.

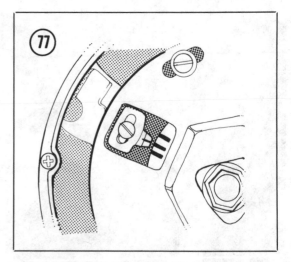

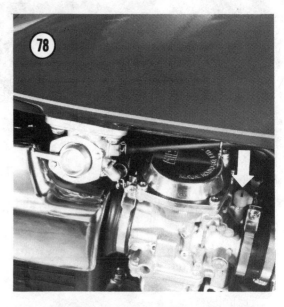

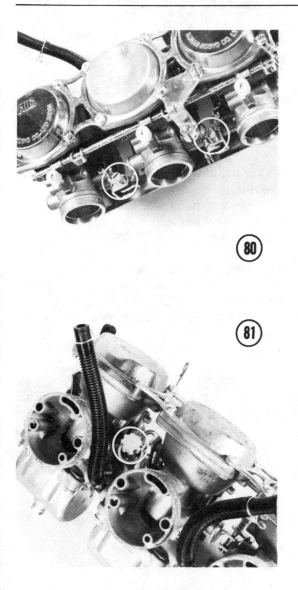

3. Set the idle speed by turning the idle speed stop screw (**Figure 81**) in to increase or out to decrease idle speed.

> NOTE: *Figure 81 is shown with the carburetor assembly removed for clarity only.*

4. The correct idle speed is:

   a. Models D and 2D—1,050-1,150 rpm
   b. Models E, F, SE and SF—950-1,050 rpm

STORAGE

Several months of inactivity can cause serious problems and general deterioration of your bike. This is especially important in areas with extremely cold winters. During the winter, you should prepare your bike carefully for "hibernation."

Selecting a Storage Area

Most cyclists store their bikes in their home garage. If you do not have a garage, there are other facilities for rent or lease in most areas. When selecting an area, consider the following points.

1. The storage area must be dry; there should be no dampness or excessive humidity. A heated area is not necessary, but the area should be insulated to minimize extreme temperature variations.

2. Avoid buildings in industrial areas where factories are liable to emit corrosive fumes. Also avoid buildings near large bodies of salt water.

3. Avoid buildings with large window areas. If this is not possible, mask the window to keep direct sunlight off the bike.

4. Select an area where there is a minimum risk of fire, theft, or vandalism. Check with your insurance agent to make sure that your insurance covers the bike where it is stored.

Preparing Bike for Storage

Careful preparation will minimize deterioration and make it easier to restore the bike to service later. Use the following procedure.

1. Wash the bike completely. Make certain to remove any road salt which may have ac-

Carburetor Idle Speed Adjustment

Before making this adjustment, the air cleaner must be clean, the carburetors must be synchronized and the engine must have adequate compression (see *Compression Test* in this chapter). Otherwise this procedure cannot be done properly.

1. Attach a portable tachometer following the manufacturer's instructions.

> NOTE: *The bike's tach is not accurate enough in the low rpm range for this adjustment.*

2. Start the engine and let it warm up to normal operating temperature.

cumulated during the first weeks of winter. Wax all painted and polished surfaces, including any chromed areas.

2. Run the engine for 20-30 minutes to stabilize oil temperature. Drain oil, regardless of mileage since last oil change. Replace the oil filter and fill engine with normal quantity of fresh oil.

3. Remove battery and coat cable terminals with petroleum jelly. If there is evidence of acid spillage in the battery box, neutralize with baking soda, wash clean, and repaint the damaged area. Store the battery in a warm area and recharge it every 2 weeks.

4. Drain all gasoline from fuel tank, interconnecting hoses, and carburetors. Leave fuel petcock in the RESERVE position. As an alternative, a fuel preservative may be added to the fuel.

This preservative is available from many motorcycle shops and marine equipment suppliers.

5. Remove spark plugs and add a small quantity of oil to each cylinder. Turn the engine a few revolutions by hand to distribute the oil and install the spark plugs.

6. Check tire pressures. Move machine to storage area and store it on the centerstand.

After Storage

Before starting the engine after storage, remove the spark plugs and squirt a small amount of fuel into the cylinders to help remove the oil coating. Install the spark plugs but do not connect the spark plug wires. Drain and refill the fuel system if a preservative was used. Turn the engine over a few times, then reconnect the spark plug wires and start the engine.

NOTE: If you own a 1980 or later model, first check the Supplement at the back of the book for any new service information.

CHAPTER FOUR

4

ENGINE

The engine is an air-cooled, four-stroke, in-line three-cylinder with chain driven double overhead camshafts. The counterbalanced crankshaft is supported by four main bearings, one of which is a special side thrust bearing.

The oil pump supplies oil under pressure throughout the engine and is driven by the starter clutch assembly shaft and gear.

This chapter provides complete service and overhaul procedures for the Yamaha XS750 Models D, 2D, E, SE, and SF. **Table 1**, at the end of this chapter, provides complete specifications for the engine. Although the clutch and transmission are mounted within the crankcase, they are covered separately in Chapter Five to simplify the presentation of this material.

Service procedures for the engine are virtually the same for all models. Where differences occur, they are identified.

Prior to removing the engine or any major assembly, clean the entire engine and frame with a good grade commercial degreaser, like Gunk Cycle Degreaser, or equivalent. It is easier to work on a clean engine and you will do a better job.

Make certain you have the necessary tools available, especially any special tools, and purchase any known faulty parts prior to disassembly. Also make sure you have a clean place to work.

It is a good idea to identify and mark parts as they are removed so that errors will be avoided during assembly and installation. Clean all parts thoroughly upon removal, then place them in trays or boxes together with their associated mounting hardware. Make certain all parts related to a particular cylinder, piston, connecting rod, and/or valve assembly are identified for installation in the proper place. Do not rely on memory alone as it may be days or weeks before you complete the job.

ENGINE PRINCIPLES

Figure 1 explains how the engine works. This will be helpful when troubleshooting or repairing your engine.

SERVICING ENGINE IN FRAME

Many components can be serviced while the engine is mounted in the frame:

a. Cylinder head and camshafts
b. Cylinder and pistons
c. Gearshift mechanism
d. Clutch

① **4-STROKE OPERATING PRINCIPLES**

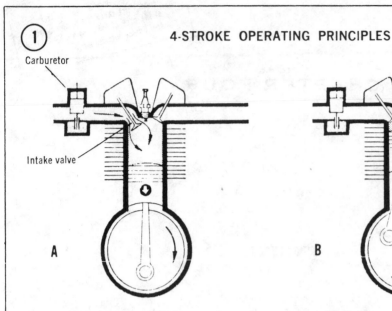

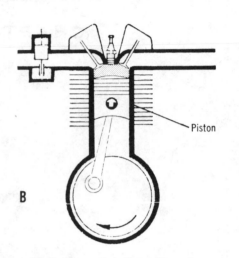

Carburetor

Intake valve

Piston

A

B

As the piston travels downward, the exhaust valve is closed and the intake valve opens, allowing the new fuel/air mixture from the **carburetor** to be drawn into the cylinder. When the piston reaches the bottom of its travel (BDC), the **intake valve** closes and remains closed for the next revolution-and-a-half of the crankshaft.

While the crankshaft continues to rotate, the **piston** moves upward, compressing the fuel/air mixture.

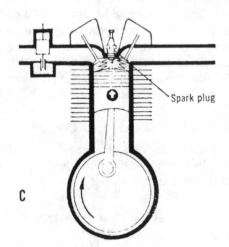

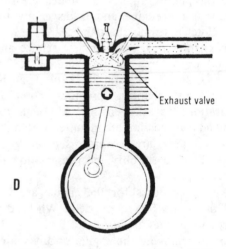

Spark plug

Exhaust valve

C

D

As the piston almost reaches the top of its travel, the **spark plug** fires, igniting the compressed fuel/air mixture. The piston continues to top dead center (TDC) and is pushed downward by the expanding gases.

When the piston almost reaches BDC, the **exhaust valve** opens and remains open until the piston is near TDC. The upward travel of the piston causes the exhaust gases to be pushed out of the cylinder. After the piston has reached TDC, the exhaust valve closes and the cycle starts all over again.

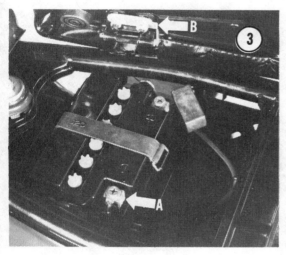

e. Carburetors

f. Starter motor and gears

g. Alternator and electrical systems

It is recommended that prior to engi
removal and disassembly the majority of par
be removed from the engine while it is in tl
frame. By doing so it will reduce the weight
the engine considerably and make engi
removal easier and safer.

ENGINE

Removal/Installation

1. Place the bike on the centerstand; rem
the right- and left-hand side covers (**Figure**
and accessories such as fairings and crash ba

2. Hinge up the seat and disconnect the bat
negative lead (A, **Figure 3**).

3. Loosen the inboard hinge nuts (B, **Figur**
Pivot hinge pin retainers up and remove
hinge pins. Remove the seat.

4. Remove the rear bolt (**Figure 4**) securin
fuel tank.

5. Turn both fuel shutoff valves to the
RES position. Lift up on the rear of the tank
remove the fuel lines to the carburetors
vacuum lines to the intake manifolds.

6. Pull the fuel tank to the rear and remove

7. Drain the engine oil as described u
Changing Oil and Filter in Chapter T
(leave the oil filter housing off).

8. Disconnect the spark plug wires (**Figu**
and tie them up out of the way.

9. Remove tachometer drive cable (**Figure 6**) from the cylinder head. Remove the drive gear from the cable.

10. Remove the exhaust system as described under *Exhaust System Removal/Installation* in Chapter Six.

11. Loosen the clutch cable at the hand grip (**Figure 7**).

12. Lift up on the cable retaining clip (**Figure 8**) and remove the cable (**Figure 9**).

13. Remove the chrome trim panels on the air box. Remove the four bolts (A, **Figure 10**) securing the air cleaner box.

14. Remove the carburetor assembly as described under *Carburetor Removal/Installation* in Chapter Six.

15. Remove the electrical leads from the alternator to the electrical connector (B, **Figure 10**).

16. Remove the cylinder head and cylinder as described under *Cylinder Removal/Installation* in this chapter.

17. Remove the ignition governor assembly as described under *Ignition Governor Removal/Installation* in Chapter Seven.

18. Remove starter gears as described under *Starter Gears Removal/Installation* in this chapter.

19. Remove the two Allen bolts (**Figure 11**) securing the starter cover and remove it.

20. Remove the starter electrical cable (A, **Figure 12**) and two Allen bolts (B, **Figure 12**) securing the motor. Pull the starter motor to the right; carefully disengage the gears and remove it.

21. Remove the clutch assembly as described under *Clutch Removal/Installation* in Chapter Five.

22. Pull back the rubber boot and remove the four bolts (A. **Figure 13**) securing the drive shaft coupling.

> NOTE: *Have an assistant apply the rear brake to keep the shaft from turning.*

23. Remove the coil spring retainer (**Figure 14**).

24. Remove the engine ground strap (B. **Figure 13**).

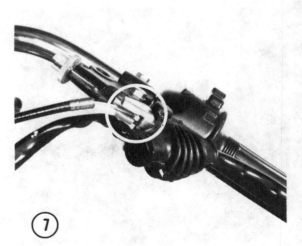

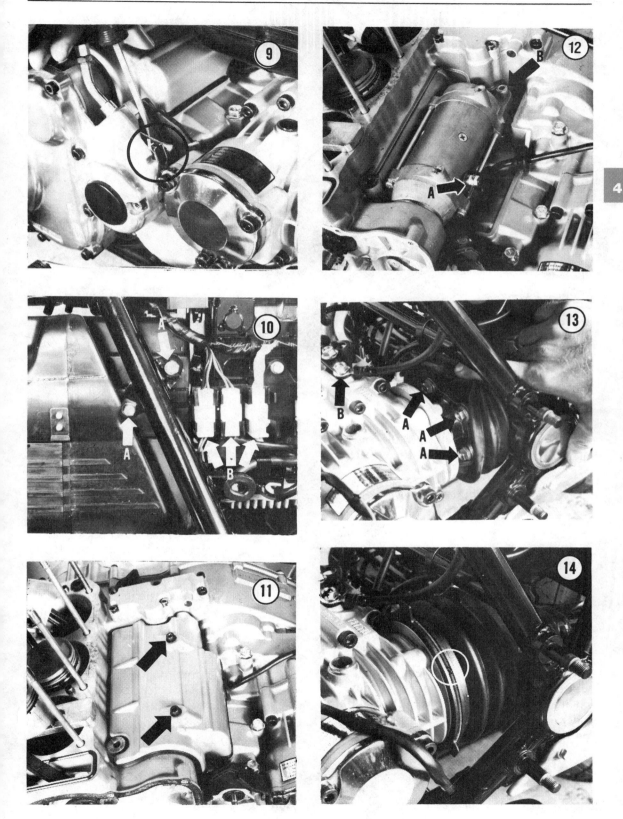

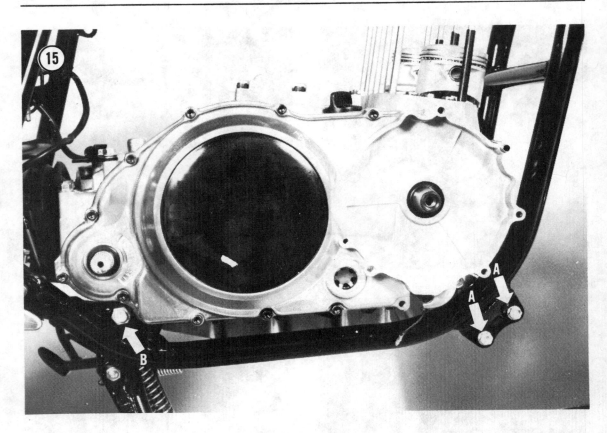

25. Take a final look all over the engine to make sure everything has been disconnected.

> NOTE: *Place wooden blocks under the crankcase to support the engine after mounting bolts have been removed.*

26. Loosen all engine mounting bolts one to two turns only. Remove the front bolts, nuts, and mounting plates (A, **Figure 15**). Remove the locknut and nut on the rear through-bolt (B, **Figure 15**). Withdraw the through-bolt from the left-hand side.

> NOTE: *Do not lose the two rubber spacers between the frame and engine on the rear through-bolt.*

27. Have an assistant help you remove the engine from the frame through the right-hand side.

28. Install by reversing the removal steps.

> NOTE: *Due to the weight of the complete engine assembly it is suggested that all components removed in the preceding procedure be left off until the*

> *crankcase and middle gear assembly are reinstalled into the frame. If you choose to install a completed engine assembly it requires a **minimum of three people**. It must be installed into the frame from the right-hand side and the oil filter housing must be removed.*

29. After the engine is positioned correctly, install the rear through-bolt from the left-hand side and install the two front bolts and plates. Start the nuts but *do not tighten now*.

> NOTE: *Do not forget to install the two rubber spacers between the frame and engine on the rear through-bolt.*

30. Install the four bolts securing the drive shaft coupling and tighten them evenly in two stages.

31. Tighten the rear through-bolt nuts to 69 ft.-lb. (94 N•m) and the front nuts to 40 ft.-lb. (54 N•m).

32. Install the oil filter and housing and fill the crankcase with the recommended type and quantity of engine oil. Refer to Chapter Three.

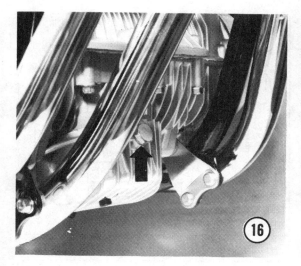

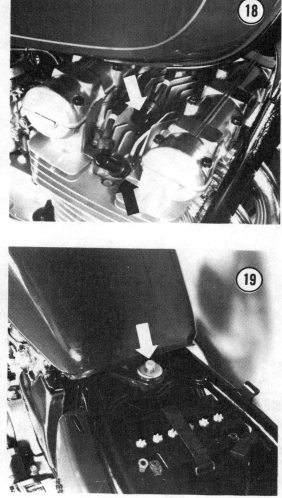

CAUTION
*If the engine has been overhauled, the oil filter must be filled with approximately one pint (½ liter) of engine oil in order to prime the oil pump. Use the filler cap on filter housing (**Figure 16**) for this purpose.*

33. Start the engine and check for leaks.

CYLINDER HEAD

Removal

The cylinder head can be removed with the engine in the frame.

1. Place the bike on the centerstand; remove the right- and left-hand side covers, and accessories such as fairings and crash bars.

2. Hinge up the seat and disconnect the battery negative lead (A, **Figure 17**).

3. Loosen the hinge nuts (B, **Figure 17**), pivot the hinge pin retainers up and remove the hinge pins. Remove the seat.

4. Disconnect the spark plug wires (**Figure 18**) and tie them up and out of the way.

5. Remove the rear bolt (**Figure 19**) securing the fuel tank.

6. Turn both fuel shutoff valves to the ON or RES position.

7. Lift up on the rear of the tank and remove the fuel lines to the carburetors and the vacuum lines to the intake manifolds (**Figure 20**).

8. Pull the fuel tank to the rear and remove it.

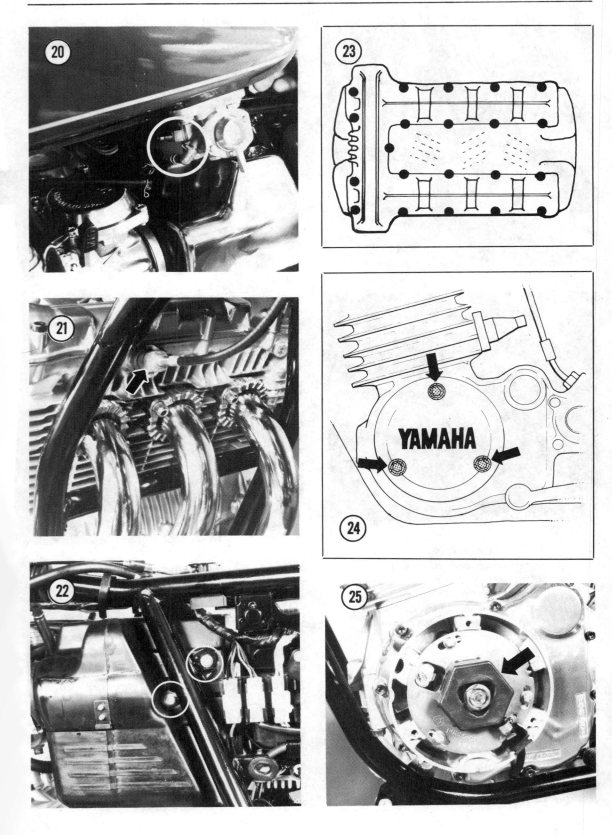

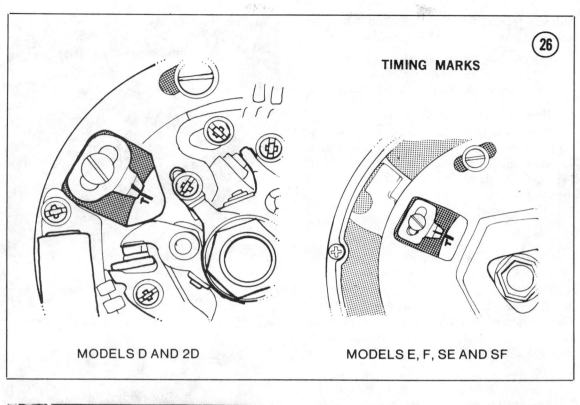

MODELS D AND 2D   MODELS E, F, SE AND SF

9. Remove tachometer drive cable (**Figure 21**) from the cylinder head. Pull the drive gear out of the cable; do not let it drop onto the floor.

10. Remove the exhaust system as described under *Exhaust System Removal/Installation* in Chapter Six.

11. Remove the chrome trim panels on the air cleaner box. Remove the 4 bolts (**Figure 22**) securing the air cleaner box.

12. Remove the carburetor assembly as described under *Carburetor Removal/Installation* in Chapter Six.

13. Remove the air scoop from the front of the cam cover on models so equipped.

14. Remove the 21 Allen bolts (**Figure 23**) securing the cam cover and remove it.

> NOTE: *Do not forget the inner bolt on the left-hand side.*

15. Remove the ignition cover (**Figure 24**) and rotate the crankshaft with a wrench on the nut (**Figure 25**) until the No. 1 cylinder (left-hand side) is at top dead center (TDC) on the compression stroke.

> NOTE: *The cylinder is at TDC when the "T" mark on the governor plate aligns with the stationary pointer (Figure 26) and both valves are completely closed on the compression stroke (cam lobes off both valve lifters).*

16. Remove the cam chain guide (**Figure 27**).

17. Attach a chain splitter to the cam chain and tie each end of the chain to the frame with wire.

This will prevent the chain from falling into the left-hand crankcase cover (**Figure 28**).

> NOTE: *Place a clean shop rag under the chain prior to splitting the chain to catch any small pieces that may fall out.*

18. Remove the chain link (**Figure 29**).

19. Rotate the intake cam *counterclockwise* ⅙ turn and the exhaust cam *clockwise* ⅙ turn as viewed from the left-hand side of the engine. See **Figure 30**. This will take all cam tension off the valve lifters.

> CAUTION
> *Severe damage can be caused to the cams, valves, and cylinder head if the cams are rotated other than the specified direction and amount described in Step 19.*

20. Remove all nuts, flat washers, and cam bearing caps (**Figure 31**). The bearing caps must be loosened, then removed from the right to left (No. 4,3,2,1) for both cams.

> NOTE: *The cam bearing caps are numbered 1-4 from left to right, and with an I (intake) and E (exhaust).*

21. Carefully lift out the cams one at a time (**Figure 32**).

> NOTE
> *The front (exhaust) camshaft has the tachometer drive gear (**Figure 33**).*

22. Remove the 2 Allen bolts (**Figure 34**) securing the cam chain tensioner and remove it.

23. Remove the upper and lower union bolts (**Figure 35**) securing the oil pipe and remove it. Note the location of the copper washers — do not lose them.

24. Remove the valve lifters and pads at this time to avoid the accidental mix up if they should come out while removing the head. Remove them one cylinder at a time and place them into a container (like an egg carton, see **Figure 36**) marked with the specific cylinder and intake and exhaust. No. 1 cylinder is on the left-hand side.

> CAUTION
> *The lifters must be reinstalled into their original cylinder positions upon assembly.*

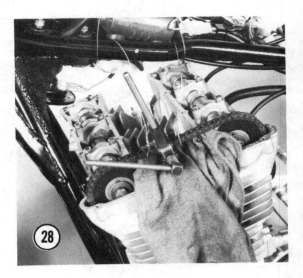

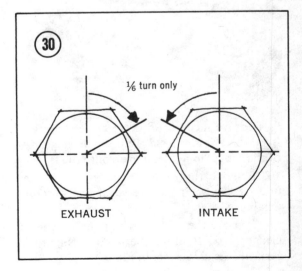

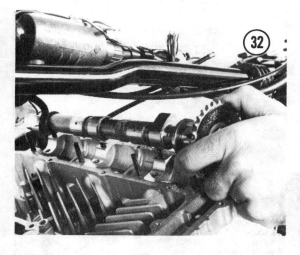

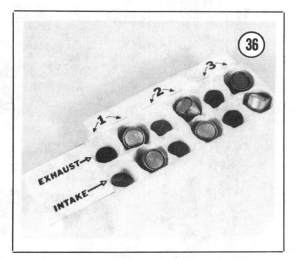

25. Remove the 12 cylinder head nuts and bolts in the following order:

a. Loosen all nuts and bolts ½ turn in the sequence shown in **Figure 37**. Do not forget numbers 11 and 12 **(Figure 38)** under the left-hand side of the head.

b. Remove the nuts first; note the washers under the two center exhaust nuts.

c. Remove the remaining nuts and bolts; note the 2 bolts have washers under them.

26. Loosen the head by tapping around the perimeter with a rubber or plastic mallet. If necessary, *gently* pry the head loose with a broad tipped screwdriver only in the ribbed areas of the fins.

CAUTION
Remember the cooling fins are fragile and may be damaged if tapped or pryed on too hard. Never use a metal hammer.

NOTE: *Sometimes it is possible to loosen the head with engine compression. Rotate the engine with the kickstarter (make sure the spark plugs*

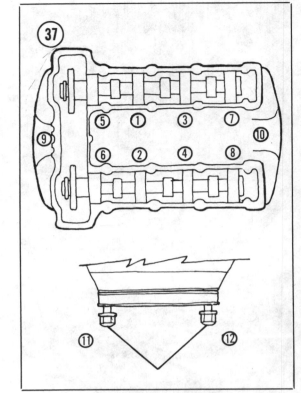

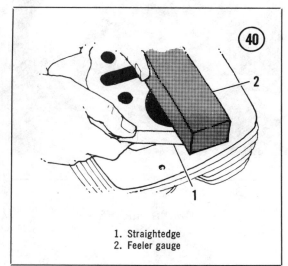

1. Straightedge
2. Feeler gauge

are installed but the wires are not attached). As the pistons reach TDC *on the compression stroke, they will pop the head loose.*

27. Remove the head by pulling straight up and off the cylinder. Place a clean shop rag into the cam chain opening in the cylinder to prevent the entry of foreign matter (**Figure 39**).

Inspection

1. Remove all traces of gasket from head and cylinder mating surface.

2. Without removing the valves, remove all carbon deposits from the combustion chambers with a wire brush. A blunt screwdriver or chisel may be used if care is taken not to damage the head, valves, and spark plug threads.

3. After all carbon is removed from combustion chambers and valve intake and exhaust ports, clean the entire head in solvent.

4. Clean away all carbon on the piston crowns. Do not remove carbon ridge at the top of the cylinder bore.

5. Check for cracks in the combustion chamber and exhaust ports. A cracked head must be replaced.

6. After the head has been thoroughly cleaned, place a straightedge across the gasket surface at several points (**Figure 40**). Measure warp by inserting a feeler gauge between the straightedge and cylinder head at each location. There should be no warpage; if a small amount is present, it can be resurfaced by a Yamaha dealer or qualified machine shop.

7. Check the cam cover mating surface using the procedure in Step 6. There should be no warpage.

8. Check the condition of the valves and valve guides as described under *Valve and Valve Components* in this chapter.

9. Check condition of the end seals (**Figure 41**). Make sure they fit tight; if not, replace them.

Installation

1. Install a new head gasket with the tab (A, **Figure 42**) facing forward and a new upper cylinder seal (B, **Figure 42**) around the cam chain opening.

2. Make sure the small locating dowel (C, **Figure 42**) is in position.

3. Install new dowel and O-ring seals (A, **Figure 43**).

> NOTE: *Make sure the rounded side of the rubber seal is installed **down into the cylinder**. If installed incorrectly, there will be a guaranteed oil leak.*

4. Make sure the small locating dowel is in position (B, **Figure 43**).

5. Rotate the engine until No. 1 cylinder (left-hand side) is at top dead center (TDC).

> NOTE: *The cylinder is at TDC when the "T" mark on the governor plate aligns with the stationary pointer (**Figure 44**) and the piston is at its uppermost travel (**Figure 45**).*

6. Carefully slide the cylinder head onto the cylinder. Place the 2 flat washers onto the 2 center exhaust studs, oil the threads on the

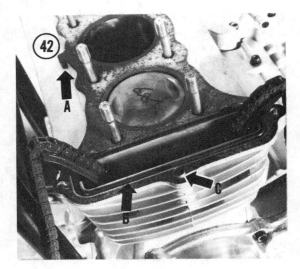

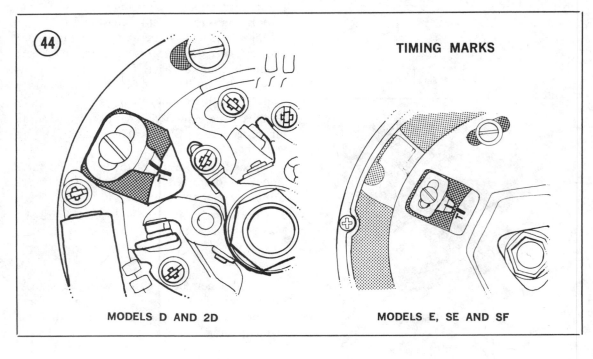

TIMING MARKS

MODELS D AND 2D

MODELS E, SE AND SF

studs, and install all 8 top acorn nuts and 2 bolts, finger-tight only.

7. Tighten the top 8 nuts and 2 bolts, in the sequence shown in **Figure 37**, in 2 stages. In the first stage, tighten them to 11 ft.-lb. (15 N•m) and in the second stage to 25 ft.-lb. (34 N•m).

8. Install the 2 holding nuts and washers **(Figure 38)** on the lower left-hand side of the cylinder. Tighten to 14 ft.-lb. (19 N•m).

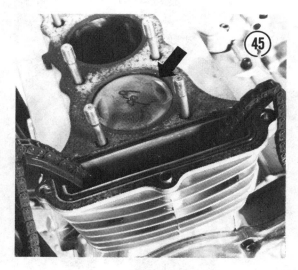

9. Install the oil pipe. Make sure the copper washers are placed on each side of each end of the pipe. The shorter union bolt is installed into the crankcase.

10. Install the valve lifters and pads.

CAUTION
The lifters must be installed into their original positions (Figure 36) as removed in Step 24 in the removal sequence.

11. Lubricate all cam bearing surfaces in the cylinder head **(Figure 46)** and bearing caps with assembly oil.

12. Make sure the No. 1 cylinder is still at TDC as set up in Step 5.

13. Install the exhaust cam; it has the tachometer drive gear **(Figure 47)**. Position the cam so that the pin on the front of the cam, below the rubber damper, is at approximately the 11 o'clock position **(Figure 48)**. The cam in this position *will not* be pressing on any valve lifter.

CAUTION
If the cam is positioned other than this, it may cause damage to either the cam or to the bearing caps.

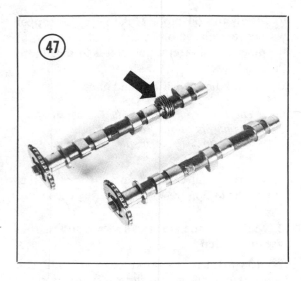

14. Install the cam bearing caps in this correct number sequence. From left to right: E1, E2, E3, and E4 with the arrows pointing to the left-hand side (**Figure 49**).

15. Install all flat washers and nuts to the studs and tighten from left to right gradually to 7 ft.-lb. (9 N•m). Carefully rotate the cam 1/6 turn *clockwise* (as viewed from the left-hand side) and back to the original position to help seat the cam to the bearings midway through the tightening steps.

> **CAUTION**
> *Do not rotate the cam other than specified as it will cause severe damage to the cam, valves, and cylinder head.*

16. Install the intake cam (**Figure 47**). Position the pin on the front of the cam, below the rubber damper, at approximately the 2 o'clock position. The cam in this position *will not* be pressing on any valve lifter.

> **CAUTION**
> *If the cam is positioned other than this, it may cause damage to either the cam or to the bearing caps.*

17. Install the cam bearing caps in this correct number sequence. From left to right: I1, I2, I3, and I4 with the arrows pointing to the left-hand side.

18. Install all flat washers and nuts to the studs and tighten from left to right gradually to 7 ft.-lb. (9 N•m). Carefully rotate the cam ⅙ turn *counterclockwise* and back to the original posi-

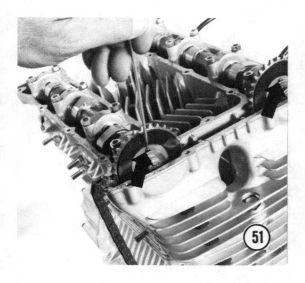

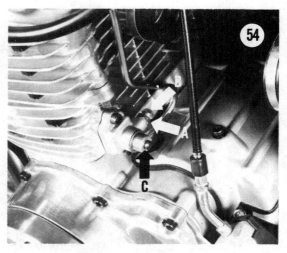

tion to help seat the cam to the bearings midway through the tightening steps.

CAUTION
Do not rotate the cam other than specified as it will cause severe damage to the cam, valves, and cylinder head.

19. Rotate the exhaust cam *clockwise approximately ⅙ turn* until the dot on the cam, behind the chain sprocket, aligns with the arrow on the No. 1 cam bearing cap (**Figure 50**). Also check that the pin on the front of the cam (**Figure 51**) is at the 12 o'clock position.

20. Repeat Step 19 for the intake cam, except rotate the cam *counterclockwise approximately ⅙ turn.*

21. Check once more that No. 1 cylinder is still at TDC.

22. Position the chain onto the sprockets and push down on the chain midway between the 2 sprockets. This will allow slack in the chain for ease of installing the new link. Insert the new master link from the backside. Make sure the master link pins are properly peened over (**Figure 52**) and that the link plates are running true to the rest of the links. Also make sure that both pins on the cam sprockets are still located at the 12 o'clock position (**Figure 51**).

23. Install the chain guide (**Figure 53**).

24. Remove the tensioner cover and loosen the tensioner locknut (A, **Figure 54**).

25. Loosen the tensioner holder bolt (B, **Figure 54**).

26. Slowly rotate the crankshaft *counterclockwise* several times. Use a wrench on the nut on the left-hand end of the crankshaft (**Figure 55**). Observe the in and out movement of the tensioner during crankshaft rotation.

27. Continue to rotate the crankshaft until the tensioner travels the deepest into the holder (C, **Figure 54**). At this point, stop turning the crankshaft and tighten the holder bolt and locknut. Install the cover.

28. Continue installation by reversing *Cylinder Head Removal*, Steps 1-14.

29. Start the engine and check for leaks.

VALVES AND VALVE COMPONENTS

Refer to **Figure 56** for this procedure.

1. Remove the cylinder head as described under *Cylinder Head Removal* in this chapter.

2. Remove the valve lifters and adjustment pads.

3. Compress springs with a valve spring compression tool (**Figure 57**); remove the valve keepers and release compression.

4. Remove the valve spring caps, springs, and valves (**Figure 58**).

> *CAUTION*
> *Remove any burrs from the valve stem grooves before removing the valve. Otherwise the valve guides will be damaged.*

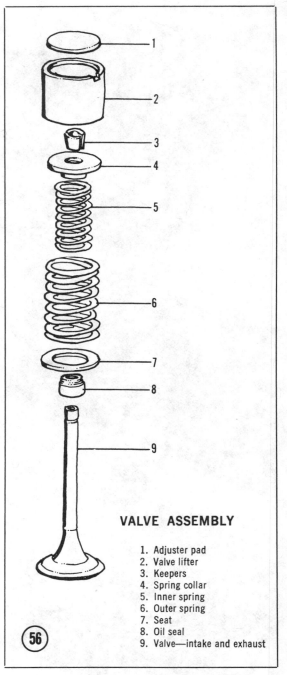

VALVE ASSEMBLY

1. Adjuster pad
2. Valve lifter
3. Keepers
4. Spring collar
5. Inner spring
6. Outer spring
7. Seat
8. Oil seal
9. Valve—intake and exhaust

Inspection

1. Clean valves with a wire brush and solvent.

2. Inspect the contact surface of each valve for burning (**Figure 59**). Minor roughness and pitting can be removed by lapping the valve as described under *Valve Lapping* in this chapter.

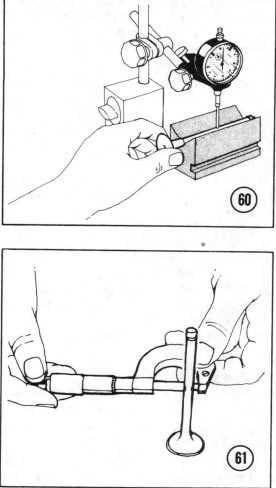

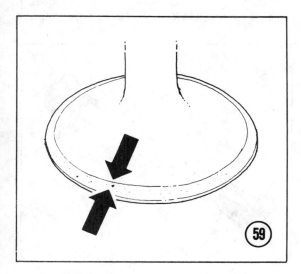

Excessive unevenness to the contact surface is an indication that the valve is not serviceable. The contact surface of the valve may be ground on a valve grinding machine, but it is best to replace a burned or damaged valve with a new one.

Inspect the valve stems for wear and roughness and measure the vertical runout of the valve stem as shown in **Figure 60**. The runout should not exceed 0.0012 in. (0.03mm).

3. Measure valve stems for wear (**Figure 61**). Compare with specifications in **Table 1** at the end of the chapter.

4. Remove all carbon and varnish from the valve guides with a stiff spiral wire brush.

5. Insert each valve in its guide. Hold the valve just slightly off its seat and rock it sideways. If

it rocks more than slightly, the guide is probably worn and should be replaced. As a final check, take the head to a dealer and have the valve guides measured.

6. Measure the valve spring heights with a vernier caliper (**Figure 62**). All should be the length specified in **Table 1** with no bends or other distortion. Replace defective springs.

7. Measure the tilt of all valve springs as shown in **Figure 63**. Compare with specifications shown in **Table 1**.

8. Check the valve spring retainer and valve keepers. If they are in good condition, they may be reused.

9. Inspect valve seats. If worn or burned, they must be reconditioned. This could be performed by your dealer or local machine shop, although the procedure is described later in this section. Seats and valves in near perfect condition can be reconditioned by lapping with fine carborundum paste. Lapping, however, is always inferior to precision grinding.

Installation

1. Coat the valve stems with molybdenum disulphide paste and insert into cylinder head.

2. Install bottom spring retainers and new seals.

3. Install valve springs with the narrow pitch end (end with coils closest together) facing the head, and install upper valve spring retainers.

4. Push down on upper valve spring retainers with the valve spring compressor and install valve keepers.

Valve Guide Replacement

When guides are worn so that there is excessive stem-to-guide clearance or valve tipping, they must be replaced. Replace all, even if only one is worn. This job should only be done by a Yamaha dealer as special tools are required.

Valve Seat Reconditioning

This job is best left to your dealer or local machine shop. They have the special equipment and knowledge for this exacting job. You can still save considerable money by removing the

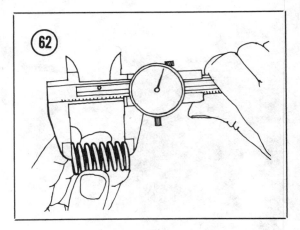

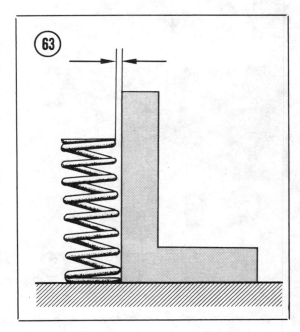

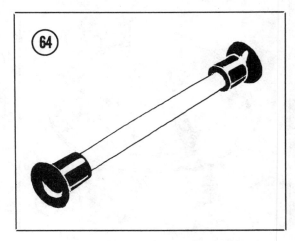

tinue lapping until the contact surfaces of the valve and the valve seat are a uniform grey. Stop as soon as they are, to avoid removing too much material.

4. Thoroughly clean the valves and cylinder head in solvent to remove all grinding compound. Any compound left on the valves or the cylinder head will end up in the engine and will cause damage.

After the lapping has been completed and the valve assemblies have been reinstalled into the head the valve seal should be tested. Check the seal of each valve by pouring solvent into each of the intake and exhaust ports. There should be no leakage past the seat. If fluid leaks past any of the seats, disassemble that valve assembly and repeat the lapping procedure until there is no leakage.

Valve Lifters and Pads

Inspect the sides of the lifter body for scratches and scoring. If it is damaged in any way, inspect the lifter cavity in the cylinder head in which it travels. If the damage is severe the cylinder head may have to be replaced. The lifter will also have to be replaced.

Check the top ridge that retains the lifter pad. Make sure the pad seats correctly into the recess but is not too loose. Replace any parts as necessary.

> CAUTION
> *The lifters and pads must be reinstalled into their original cylinder positions upon assembly. Refer to **Cylinder Head Removal** Step No. 24 in this chapter.*

cylinder head and taking just the head to the shop.

Valve Lapping

Valve lapping is a simple operation which can restore the valve seal without machining if the amount of wear or distortion is not too great.

1. Coat the valve seating area in the head with a lapping compound such as Carborundum or Clover Brand.

2. Insert the valve into the head.

3. Wet the suction cup of the lapping stick (**Figure 64**) and stick it onto the head of the valve. Lap the valve to the seat by rotating the lapping stick in both directions. Every 5 to 10 seconds, rotate the valve 180° in the seat, con-

CAMSHAFT

Removal/Installation

The camshafts can be removed with the engine in the frame.

1. Place the bike on the centerstand; remove the right- and left-hand side covers (**Figure 65**), and accessories such as fairings and crash bars.

2. Hinge up the seat and disconnect the battery negative lead (A, **Figure 66**).

3. Loosen the hinge nuts (B, **Figure 66**), pivot the hinge pin retainers up and remove the hinge pins. Remove the seat.

4. Disconnect the spark plug wires (**Figure 67**) and tie them up and out of the way.

5. Remove the rear bolt (**Figure 68**) securing the fuel tank.

6. Turn both fuel shut-off valves to the ON or RES position.

7. Lift up on the rear of the tank and remove the fuel lines to the carburetors and the vacuum lines to the intake tubes (**Figure 69**).

8. Pull the tank to the rear and remove it.

9. Remove tachometer drive cable (**Figure 70**) from the cylinder head. Pull the drive gear out of the cable, do not let it drop on the floor.

10. Remove the air scoop from the front of the cam cover on models so equipped.

11. Remove the 21 Allen bolts (**Figure 71**) securing the cam cover and remove it.

> NOTE: *Do not forget the inner bolt on the left-hand side.*

12. Remove the ignition cover (**Figure 72**) and rotate the crankshaft with a wrench on the nut (**Figure 73**) until the No. 1 cylinder (left-hand side) is at top dead center (TDC) on the compression stroke.

> NOTE: *The cylinder is at TDC when the "T" mark on the governor plate aligns with the stationary pointer (**Figure 74**) and both valves are completely closed on the compression stroke (cam lobes off both valve lifters).*

> NOTE: *Figures 75 and 76 are shown with the exhaust system and carburetor assembly removed. It is not necessary to remove them for this procedure.*

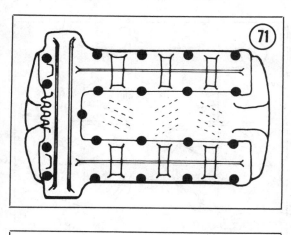

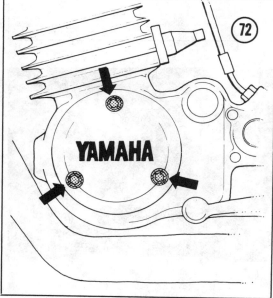

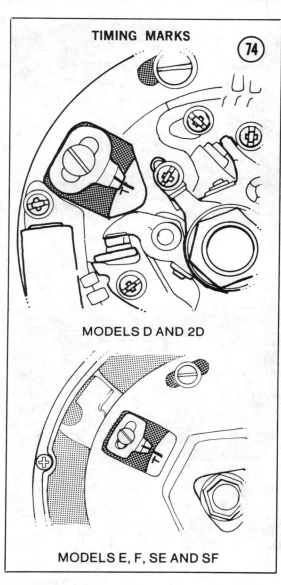

TIMING MARKS

MODELS D AND 2D

MODELS E, F, SE AND SF

13. Remove the cam chain guide (**Figure 75**).

14. Attach a chain splitter to the cam chain (**Figure 76**) and tie each end of the chain to the frame with wire. This will prevent the chain from falling into the left-hand side crankcase cover.

> NOTE: *Place a clean rag under the chain prior to splitting the chain to catch any small pieces that may fall out.*

15. Remove the chain link (**Figure 77**).

16. Rotate the intake cam *counterclockwise* ⅙ turn and the exhaust cam *clockwise* ⅙ turn as

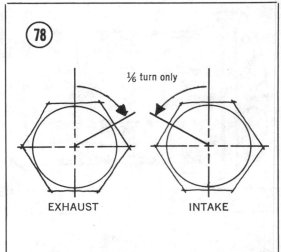

⅙ turn only

EXHAUST   INTAKE

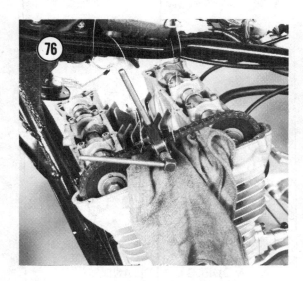

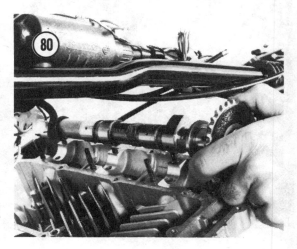

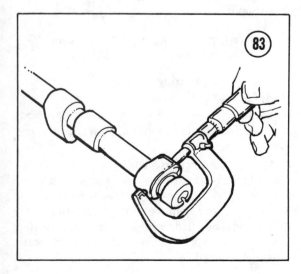

viewed from the left-hand side of the engine. See **Figure 78**. This will take all cam tension off the valve lifters.

> CAUTION
> *Severe damage can be caused to the cams, valves, and the cylinder head if the cams are rotated other than the specified direction and amount described in Step 16.*

17. Remove all nuts, flat washers, and cam bearing caps (**Figure 79**). The bearing caps must be loosened, then removed from right to left (No. 4, 3, 2, 1) for both cams.

> *NOTE*
> *The cam bearing caps are numbered 1-4 from left to right, and are marked with an I (intake) or E (exhaust).*

18. Carefully lift out the cams one at a time (**Figure 80**).

> NOTE: *The exhaust cam has the tachometer drive gear on it (Figure 81).*

19. Remove the 2 Allen bolts (**Figure 82**) securing the cam chain tensioner and remove it.

20. Install the cams. Perform Steps 11-30, *Cylinder Head Installation* in this chapter.

Camshaft Inspection

1. Check the bearing journals for wear and scoring.

2. Check cam lobes for wear. The lobes should not be scored and the edges should be square. Slight damage may be removed with a silicon carbide oilstone. Use No. 100-120 grit initially, then polish with a No. 280-320 grit.

> NOTE: *The exhaust cam is darker in color due to the manufacturing hardening process. It is not caused by lack of oil pressure or excessive engine heat.*

3. Even though the cam lobe surface appears to be satisfactory, with no visible signs of wear, they must be measured with a micrometer as shown in **Figure 83**. Replace the shaft(s) if worn beyond the service limits (measurements less than those given in **Table 1** at the end of this chapter).

4. Check the bearing bores in the cylinder head and bearing caps. They should not be scored or excessively worn.

5. Inspect the sprockets for wear, replace if necessary. Check the condition of the damping rubber on each side of the sprocket (**Figure 84**). If it is starting to disintegrate it must be replaced, otherwise the bits of rubber will contaminate the engine oil and may cause excess engine noise.

6. Check the condition of the chain guide. If it is worn or disintegrating it must be replaced. This may indicate a worn chain or improper chain adjustment.

Camshaft Bearing Clearance

This procedure requires the use of a Plastigage set.

1. Install both cams into the head. Position the exhaust cam so the pin on the front of the cam, below the rubber damper, is at approximately the 11 o'clock position (**Figure 85**) and the intake cam with its pin is at approximately the 2 o'clock position. In these positions, the cam lobes *will not* be pressing on any valve lifter.

> **CAUTION**
> *If the cam is positioned other than this, it may cause damage to either the cam or to the bearing caps.*

2. Place a strip of Plastigage between the cam and cam bearing cap, parallel to the cam, as shown in **Figure 86**.

3. Install the cam bearing caps in the correct number sequence. From left to right: E1-4 (exhaust cam) and I1-4 (intake cam) with the arrows pointing to the left-hand side (**Figure 87**).

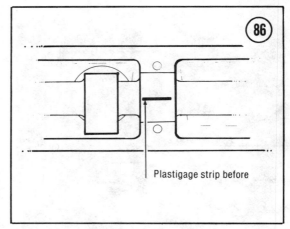

Plastigage strip before

4. Install the flat washers and nuts to the studs and tighten from left to right gradually to 7 ft.-lb. (9 N•m).

> NOTE: *Do not rotate either cam with the Plastigage material in place.*

5. Remove the bearing caps from right to left (4, 3, 2, 1) for both cams.

6. Measure the width of the flattened Plastigage according to manufacturer's instructions (**Figure 88**).

7. If the clearance exceeds the wear limit in **Table 1**, measure the cam bearing journals with a micrometer and compare to the wear limits in **Table 1**. If the cam bearing is less than the dimension specified, replace the cam. If the cam is within specifications, the cylinder head must be replaced.

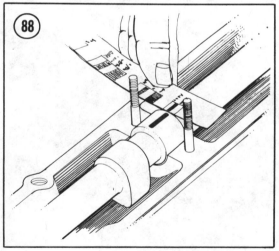

Chain Guide

Check the condition of the top surface of the guide. If it is worn or disintegrating it must be replaced. This may indicate a worn chain or improper chain adjustment.

If its condition is very bad, check the condition of the two vertical chain dampers by looking into the chain cavity with a flashlight. If they look bad they should be replaced. Refer to *Cylinder Removal* in this chapter for removal procedures.

CAMSHAFT CHAIN AND DAMPERS

Replacement

The cam chain and dampers can be removed with the engine in the frame.

1. Drain the engine oil as described under *Changing Engine Oil and Filter* in Chapter Three.

2. Remove the cylinder head and cylinder as described under *Cylinder Removal/Installation* in this chapter.

3. Remove the ignition governor assembly as described under *Ignition Governor Assembly Removal/Installation* in this chapter.

4. Loosen the bolt securing the shift lever and remove the lever.

5. Remove the left-hand front peg.

6. Remove the 11 Allen bolts (**Figure 89**) securing left-hand crankcase cover and remove it.

7. Remove the idler gear and shaft (**Figure 90**).

8. Remove the nut (**Figure 91**) securing the oil pump drive gear. To hold the gear while loosening the nut, place a rag between it and the starter gear assembly (**Figure 92**). Remove the gear (**Figure 93**).

9. Remove the cam chain (**Figure 94**) from the crankshaft gear.

10. Remove the 2 Allen bolts and washers (**Figure 95**) and remove the 2 chain dampers.

11. Assemble and install by reversing the disassembly and removal steps.

> NOTE: *The front (exhaust) chain damper is the longer of the two.*

12. When installing the left-hand cover be sure to install 2 washers (A, **Figure 89**) under the 2 indicated bolts. This will help prevent an oil leak. Be sure to install the electrical wire clamps (**Figure 96**) as indicated.

13. Fill the crankcase with the recommended type and quantity of engine oil. Refer to Chapter Three.

Cam Chain Tensioner Adjustment

After cam chain replacement, adjust the chain as described under *Cam Chain Tensioner Adjustment* in Chapter Three.

CYLINDER

Removal

1. Remove the cylinder head as described under *Cylinder Head Removal* in this chapter.

2. Remove cylinder head gasket (A, **Figure 97**), upper cylinder seal (B, **Figure 97**) and small locating dowel (C, **Figure 97**). Also remove the small locating dowel (D, **Figure 98**) and 2 locating dowels and rubber O-rings (E, **Figure 98**).

3. Loosen the cylinder by tapping around the perimeter with a rubber or plastic mallet. If necessary, *gently* pry the cylinder loose with a broad tipped screwdriver only in the ribbed areas of the fins.

> CAUTION
> *Remember cooling fins are fragile and may be damaged if tapped or pryed on too hard. Do not use a metal hammer.*

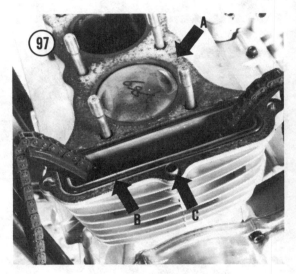

4. Pull the cylinder straight up and off the pistons and cylinder studs.

> NOTE: *Be sure to keep the cam chain wired up to prevent it from falling into the left-hand crankcase cover.*

5. Remove lower cylinder seal (A, **Figure 99**) and locating dowel (B, **Figure 99**). Also remove the 2 locating dowels and rubber O-ring seals and small locating dowel (**Figure 100**).

Inspection

1. Measure the cylinder bores, with a cylinder gauge or inside micrometer (**Figure 101**) at the points shown in **Figure 102**.

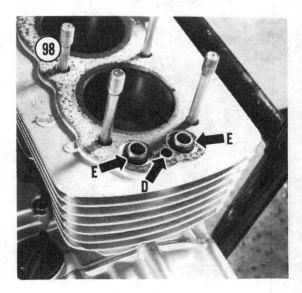

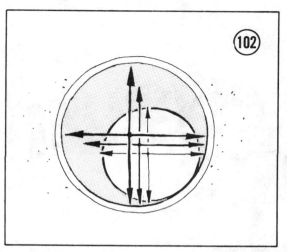

2. Measure in 2 axes — in line with the wrist pin and at 90° to the pin. If the taper or out-of-round is greater than 0.002 in. (0.05mm), the cylinders must be rebored to the next oversize and new pistons and rings installed. Rebore all cylinders even though only one may be faulty.

> NOTE: *The new pistons should be obtained first before the cylinders are bored so that pistons can be measured; slight manufacturing tolerances must be taken into account to determine the actual size and the working clearance. Piston-to-cylinder clearance should be 0.0020-0.0022 in. (0.050-0.055mm).*

3. Check the cylinder walls for scratches; if evident the cylinders should be rebored.

> *NOTE*
> *The maximum wear limit on a cylinder is 2.681 in. (68.10 mm). If any cylinder is worn to this limit, the cylinder assembly must be replaced. Never rebore a cylinder if the finished rebore diameter will be this dimension or larger.*

Installation

1. Check that the top surface of the crankcase and the bottom surface of the cylinder are clean prior to installing new gaskets.

2. Install a new cylinder base gasket (**Figure 103**) to the cylinder. Make sure all holes align.

3. Install a new lower cylinder seal (A, **Figure 104**) and locating dowel (B, **Figure 104**).

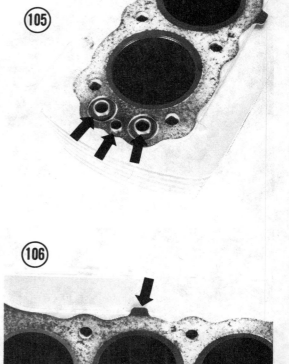

NOTE: *Be sure to install the lower cylinder seal with the flat side down into the crankcase.*

NOTE: *On early models of Model D, refer to* **Lower Cylinder Seal Selection (Model XS750-D)** *in this chapter, for correct seal number.*

4. Install 2 locating dowels and rubber O-ring seals and small locating dowel (**Figure 105**).

NOTE: *Make sure the round side of the rubber seals are installed into the crankcase, flat side up. If installed incorrectly there will be a guaranteed oil leak.*

5. Install a new head gasket with the tab (**Figure 106**) facing forward.

6. Install a piston holding fixture under the pistons protruding out of the crankcase opening (**Figure 107**).

NOTE: *These fixtures may be purchased or may be homemade units of wood. See* **Figure 108** *for dimensions.*

7. Carefully install the cylinder onto the cylinder studs (**Figure 109**) and slide it down over the pistons. Compress each piston ring, with your fingers, as the cylinder starts to slide over it.

NOTE: *Guide the front 4 black vinyl tubes through the holes in the fins as the cylinder is lowered. Do not let them bunch up as they may prevent the cylinder from seating completely.*

8. Remove the piston holding fixture and push the cylinder down all the way.

9. Install the cylinder head as described under *Cylinder Head Installation* in this chapter.

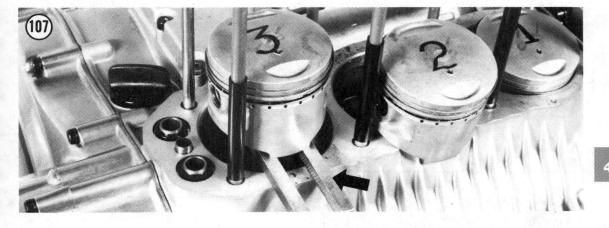

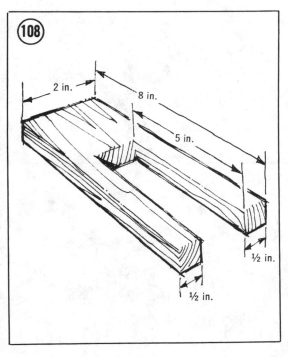

Lower Cylinder Seal Selection
(Model XS750-D)

The depth of the groove in the upper crankcase half, for the lower cylinder seal, was manufactured with a large variation in depth. This is true only in the early production run of the XS750-D. In order to maintain the proper seal in this area, there are two different size seals available.

There should be a letter (A, B or C) stamped on the rear short vertical wall of the crankcase, just behind the seal (**Figure 110**). A number of engines manufactured between engine serial No. 000101 and 000780 were not stamped with a letter. On these engines and on engines where the letter is illegible the groove will have to be measured (**Figure 111**).

NOTE
Do not measure the depth at the corners of the groove.

Engine serial No. 000781 and later uses the standard seal if there is no letter stamped in place.

Measure the seal depth and/or establish the letter designation and compare to **Table 2** for the correct seal part number.

PISTONS AND
CONNECTING RODS

The pistons may be removed with the engine in the frame by removing the cylinder head and the cylinder. To remove the rods, the crankcase has to be split in order to gain access to the rod bearing caps.

Table 2   LOWER CYLINDER SEAL SELECTION — MODEL D

Letter	Groove Depth	Yamaha Part Number
A	0.075-0.102 in. (1.90-2.60mm)	Standard 1J7-11356-00-00
B	0.067-0.075 in. (1.70-1.89mm)	Alternate No. 1 1J7-11356-10-00
C	0.059-0.067 in. (1.50-1.69mm)	Alternate No. 2*

*Not available at time of printing. Use alternate No. 1.

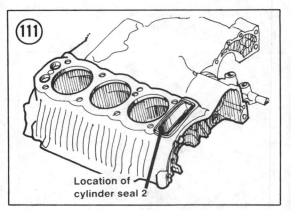

Location of cylinder seal 2

Piston Removal

1. Remove the cylinder head and cylinder as described under *Cylinder Removal/Installation* in this chapter.

2. Lightly mark top of the piston with a 1, 2 and 3 (**Figure 112A**) so that they will be installed into the correct cylinder. Remember No. 1 is on the left-hand side.

3. Remove the top ring first by spreading the ends with your thumbs just enough to slide it up over the piston (**Figure 112B**). Repeat for the remaining rings.

4. Before removing the piston, hold the rod tightly and rock piston as shown in **Figure 113**. Any rocking motion (do not confuse with the normal sliding motion) indicates wear on the piston pin, rod bushing, pin bore or, more likely, a combination of all three. Mark the piston, pin and rod so that they will be reassembled into the same set.

5. Remove the circlips from the the piston pin bores (**Figure 114**). Wrap a clean shop cloth under the piston so that the clips will not fall into the crankcase.

6. Heat the piston and pin with a small butane torch. The pin will probably drop right out. If it doesn't, heat the piston to about 140° F (60° C), i.e., until it is too warm to touch, but not excessively hot. If the pin is still difficult to push out, use a homemade tool as shown in **Figure 115**.

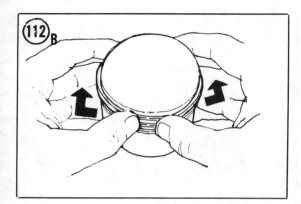

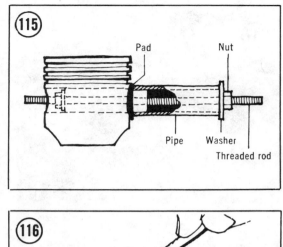

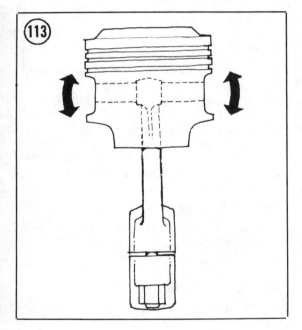

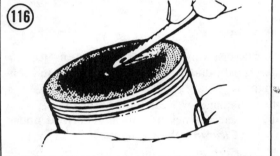

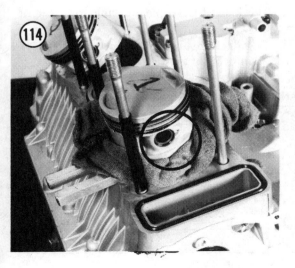

Piston Inspection

1. Carefully clean the carbon from the piston crown with a chemical remover or with a soft scraper (**Figure 116**). Do not remove or damage the carbon ridge around the circumference of the piston above the top ring. If the pistons, rings and cylinders are found to be dimensionally correct and can be reused, removal of the carbon ring from the tops of pistons or the carbon ridges from the tops of cylinders will promote excessive oil consumption.

> *WARNING*
> *The rail portions of the oil scraper can be very sharp. Be careful when handling them to avoid cut fingers.*

> *CAUTION*
> *Do not wire brush piston skirts.*

2. Examine each ring groove for burrs, dented edges and wide wear. Pay particular attention to the top compression ring groove, as it usually wears more than the others.

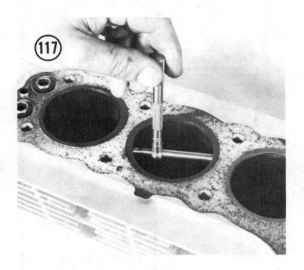

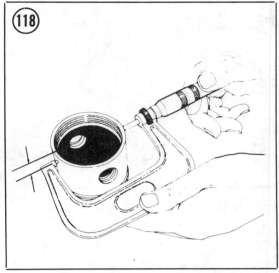

3. Measure piston-to-cylinder clearance as described under *Piston Clearance* in this chapter.

4. If damage or wear indicate piston replacement, select a new piston as described under *Piston Clearance* in this chapter.

5. Measure all parts marked in Step 4 of the *Piston Removal* procedure with a micrometer and dial bore gauge to determine which part or parts are worn. Check against measurements given in **Table 1**. Any machinist can do this for you if you do not have micrometers. Replace piston/pin set as a unit if either or both are worn.

Piston Clearance

1. Make sure the piston and cylinder walls are clean and dry.

2. Measure the inside diameter of the cylinder bore at a point ½ in. (13mm) from the upper edge with a bore gauge (**Figure 117**).

3. Measure the outside diameter of the piston at a point 3/8 in. (10 mm) from the lower edge of the piston 90 degrees to piston pin axis (**Figure 118**). Check against measurement given in **Table 1**. Refer to **Table 3** for piston oversize numbers and dimensions.

Connecting Rod Removal

In order to remove the rods, the crankcase has to be split. Refer to *Crankcase Disassembly* in this chapter.

Connecting Rod Inspection

1. Check each rod for obvious damage such as cracks and burns.

2. Check the piston pin bushing for wear or scoring.

3. Take the rods to a machine shop and check the alignment for twisting and bending.

Table 3   PISTON AND RING SIZES

Piston Size	Piston Diameter	Compression Rings*
Standard	2.6755 in. (67.96mm)	—
	2.6759 in. (67.97mm)	—
Oversize 1	2.6870 in. (68.25mm)	0.0098 in. (0.25mm)
Oversize 2	2.6968 in. (68.50mm)	0.0196 in. (0.50mm)
Oversize 3	2.7067 in. (68.75mm)	0.0295 in. (0.75mm)
Oversize 4	2.7165 in. (69.00mm)	0.0394 in. (1.00mm)
*Oversize number is stamped on the top of the ring.		

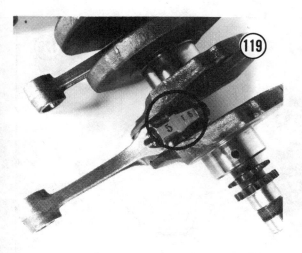

4. Examine the bearing inserts for wear, scoring, or burning. They are reusable if in good condition. Make a note of the bearing size (if any) stamped on the back of the insert if the bearing is to be discarded; a previous owner may have used undersize bearings.

5. Check bearing clearance and connecting rod side play as described under *Connecting Rod Bearing and Crankpin Inspection.*

Connecting Rod Bearing and Crankpin Inspection

Disassembly

1. Split crankcase as described under *Crankcase Disassembly/Assembly* in this chapter.

2. Remove the rods from crankshaft if not already removed. Install bearing inserts in rod and cap.

> CAUTION
> *If the old bearings are reused, be sure that they are installed in their exact original locations.*

3. Wipe bearing inserts and crankpins clean. Check again that inserts and crankpins are in good condition.

4. Place a piece of Plastigage on one crankpin parallel to the crankshaft.

5. Install rod cap and tighten nuts to 27 ft.-lb. (36 N•m).

> CAUTION
> *Do not rotate crankshaft while Plastigage is in place.*

6. Remove rod cap.

7. Measure width of flattened Plastigage according to the manufacturer's instructions. Measure at both ends of the strip. A difference of 0.001 in. (0.025mm) or more indicates a tapered crankpin, indicating that the crankshaft must be reground or replaced.

8. If the crankpin taper is within tolerance, measure the bearing clearance with the same strip of Plastigage. Used bearing clearance must not exceed 0.003 in. (0.08mm). New bearing clearance should be 0.0008-0.0017 in. (0.020-0.044mm). Remove the Plastigage strips.

9. If the bearing clearance is greater than specified, use the following steps for new bearing selection.

10. The connecting rods and caps are marked with number 4, 5, or 6 (**Figure 119**). The crankshaft is marked on the left-hand counterbalancer with number 1, 2, or 3 (**Figure 120**). The group of 3 numbers relates to the crankshaft connecting rod journals (the group of 4 numbers relates to the crankshaft main bearing journals; *DO NOT* refer to these 4 numbers).

11. To select the proper bearing insert number, subtract the crankshaft connecting rod journal number from the connecting rod and cap number.

Example:

Connecting rod and cap No.	4
Crankshaft connecting rod journal No.	− 2
New bearing insert No.	2

12. After new bearings have been installed, recheck clearance to the specifications given in Step 8.

13. Repeat Steps 3-12 for the other 2 cylinders.

14. Measure the inside diameter of the small ends of the connecting rods with an inside dial gauge (**Figure 121**). Check against measurments given in **Table 1** at the end of this chapter.

15. Insert the bearing shells into each connecting rod and cap. Make sure they are locked in place correctly.

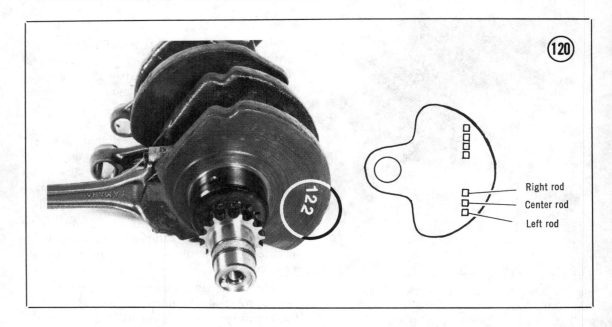

Right rod
Center rod
Left rod

CAUTION
If the old bearings are reused, be sure they are installed in their exact original positions.

16. Lubricate the bearings and crankpins with assembly oil and install the rods. Apply molybdenum disulfide grease to the threads of the connecting rods. Install the caps and tighten the cap nuts evenly, in a couple of steps, to 27 ft.-lb. (36 N•m).

CAUTION
*On the final sequence, if a torque of 24 ft.-lb. (33 N•m) is reached, **do not stop** until the final torque value is achieved. If the tightening is interrupted between 24-27 ft.-lb. (33-36 N•m), loosen the nut to less than 24 ft.-lb. (33 N•m), start again and tighten to the final torque value.*

17. Rotate the crankshaft a couple of times to make sure the bearings are not too tight.

Assembly

1. Coat the connecting rod bushing, piston pin, and piston holes with assembly oil.

CAUTION
Be sure to install the correct piston onto the same rod from which it was removed, No. 1, 2, or 3 (Figure 122).

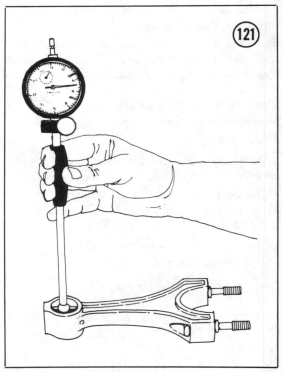

2. Place the piston over the connecting rod. If you are reusing the same piston and connecting rods, match the piston to the rod from which it came and orient it in the same way. Make sure the arrow on the piston (**Figure 123**) is pointing forward in the engine.

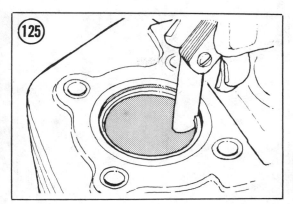

so that the rod does not have to take any shock. Otherwise, it may be bent. Drive the pin in until it is centered in the rod. If pin is still difficult to install, use the homemade tool (**Figure 115**) but eliminate the piece of pipe.

4. Install rings as described in Steps 5-8 under *Piston Ring Replacement*.

PISTON RINGS

Replacement

1. Remove old rings with a ring expander tool or by spreading the ring ends with your thumbs and lifting the rings up evenly (**Figure 124**).

2. Carefully remove all carbon from the ring grooves. Inspect grooves carefully for burrs, nicks, or broken and cracked lands. Recondition or replace piston if necessary.

> *WARNING*
> *The rail portions of the oil scraper ring can be very sharp. Be careful when handling them to avoid cut fingers.*

3. Check end gap of each ring. To check ring, insert the ring into the bottom of the cylinder bore and square it with the wall by tapping with the piston. The ring should be in about $5/8$ in. (15mm). Insert a feeler gauge as shown in **Figure 125**. Compare gap with **Table 1**. If the gap is smaller than specified, hold a small file in a vise, grip the ends of the ring with your fingers, and enlarge the gap. See **Figure 126**.

4. Roll each ring around its piston groove as shown in **Figure 127** to check for binding. Minor binding may be cleaned up with a fine cut file.

> NOTE: *Install all rings with their markings facing up.*

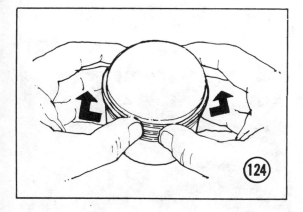

3. Insert the piston pin and tap it with a plastic mallet until it starts into the connecting rod bushing. If it does not slide in easily, heat the piston until it is too warm to touch but not excessively hot (140° F or 60° C). Continue to drive the piston pin in while holding the piston

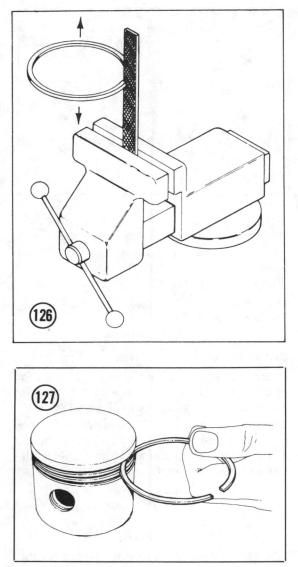

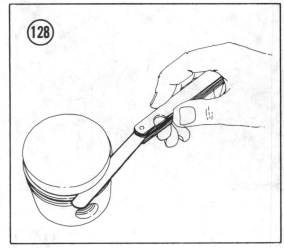

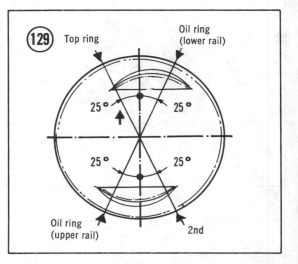

Oil ring (lower rail)

Top ring

25°   25°

25°   25°

Oil ring (upper rail)   2nd

5. Install oil ring in oil ring groove with a ring expander tool or spread the ends with your thumbs.

6. Install 2 compression rings carefully with a ring expander tool or spread the ends with your thumbs.

7. Check side clearance of each ring as shown in **Figure 128**. Compare with specifications in **Table 1**.

8. Distribute ring gaps around piston as shown in **Figure 129**. The important thing is that the ring gaps are not aligned with each other when installed.

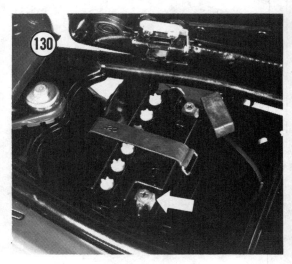

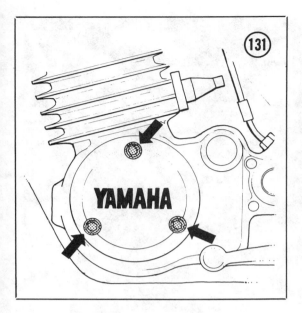

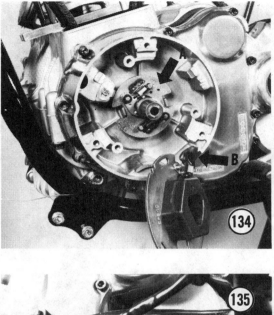

4

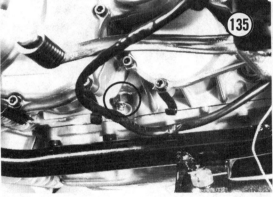

IGNITION GOVERNOR ASSEMBLY

Removal/Installation

1. Disconnect the negative battery lead from the battery (**Figure 130**).

2. Remove the 3 bolts (**Figure 131**) securing the cover and remove it.

3. Remove the center bolt (**Figure 132**) and 3 attachment screws (**Figure 133**) securing the ignition timing plate (contact breaker point or transistor type) and let it hang down carefully.

4. Remove the ignition advance governor plate (A, **Figure 134**).

5. Pull the rubber grommet (B, **Figure 134**) and wires out of the side cover notch. Loosen all clamps securing the wires to the crankcase.

6. Disconnect the electrical wire to the neutral safety switch (**Figure 135**).

7. Disconnect the electrical connectors to the ignition unit (**Figure 136**) located under the right-hand side cover. On models with contact breaker ignition, disconnect the electrical terminal adjacent to the housing.

> NOTE: *Make a drawing of the routing of electrical cable so it will be installed in the same position.*

8. Install by reversing the removal steps. Tighten the center bolt (**Figure 132**) to 17 ft.-lb. (23 N•m).

9. Be sure to route the electrical wires in the same location especially in the clips shown in **Figure 137**.

> NOTE: *Figure 137 is shown with the engine removed for clarity only.*

ALTERNATOR

Removal/Installation

This procedure is shown with the cylinder and cylinder head removed. It is not necessary to remove them.

1. Remove the exhaust system as described under *Exhaust System Removal/Installation* in Chapter Six.

2. Loosen the bolt securing the kickstarter arm (**Figure 138**) to the shaft and remove the arm.

3. Loosen 3 bolts and straps (A, **Figure 139**) securing the alternator electrical cable to the crankcase. Disconnect the oil pressure sending switch electrical wire (B, **Figure 139**).

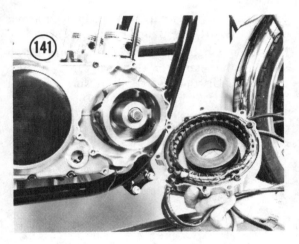

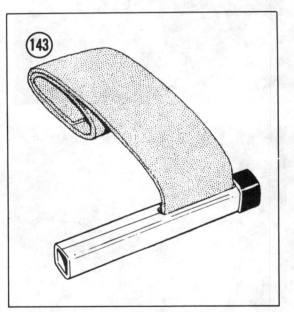

4. Disconnect the electrical connectors from the alternator to their related components.

5. Remove the 5 Allen bolts (**Figure 140**) securing the alternator cover/coil assembly and remove it (**Figure 141**).

6. Remove the bolt (**Figure 142**) securing the rotor.

> NOTE: *If necessary, use a strap wrench (Figure 143) to keep the rotor from turning while removing the bolt.*

7. Screw in flywheel puller (**Figure 144**) until it stops. Use a wrench on the puller (**Figure 145**) and tap on the end of it with your hand or plastic mallet until the rotor disengages. Remove the puller and the rotor (**Figure 146**).

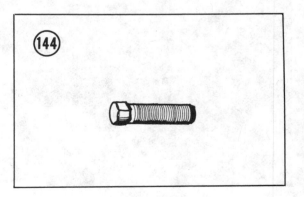

8. Install by reversing the removal steps. Secure the rotor bolt to 25 ft.-lb. (34 N•m) using a torque and strap wrench (**Figure 147**).

OIL PUMP

Removal/Installation

1. Remove the engine from the frame as described under *Engine Removal/Installation* in this chapter.

2. Turn the engine upside down on the workbench.

> CAUTION
> *If the cylinder and head have been removed, place the engine on blocks of wood to protect the cylinder studs.*

3. Remove the 13 Allen bolts (**Figure 148**) securing the pan and remove it.

4. Remove the 3 screws (**Figure 149**) securing the pick-up screen and remove it.

5. Remove the 2 Allen bolts (**Figure 150**) securing the pick-up screen base and remove it.

> *NOTE*
> *Early production models of XS750-D, prior to engine serial No. 1J7-010651, are equipped with a slightly modified oil strainer assembly other than the one shown in* ***Figure 150.***

6. Remove the 2 Allen bolts (**Figure 151**) securing the oil pump assembly and remove it.

> NOTE: *Do not lose the 2 locating dowels (Figure 152) nor the O-ring seal on the bottom of the oil pump assembly (Figure 153).*

7. Install by reversing the removal steps, noting the following.

8. Make sure the O-ring seal (**Figure 153**) is in good condition, replace if necessary.

9. Pour some new engine oil into the opening (**Figure 154**) of the oil pump to prime it, prior to installing the pick-up screen assembly.

10. Remove the 4 screws (**Figure 155**) securing the baffle plate in the oil pan and remove it. Thoroughly clean out the pan with solvent and dry with compressed air. Reinstall the baffle plate. Make sure there is no solvent residue left in the pan as it will contaminate the engine oil.

11. Clean the pick-up screen with solvent and dry with compressed air.

12. Remove all traces of old gasket material from the pan and lower crankcase.

13. Install a new pan gasket and install the pan.

> NOTE
> *Apply Loctite Lock N' Seal to the pan bolts prior to installation.*

Inspection

Refer to **Figure 156** for this procedure.

1. Inspect the outer housing for cracks.

2. Remove the nut and spring washer securing the drive gear and remove it.

3. Remove the 3 Allen bolts securing the pump cover and remove it.

4. Remove inner and outer rotor (**Figure 157**) and check for scratches or abrasion. Replace both parts if evidence of this is found.

5. Check the clearance between the housing and outer rotor (**Figure 158**) with a flat feeler gauge. The clearance should be between 0.0035-0.0059 in. (0.090-0.150 mm). If the clearance is greater, replace the worn part.

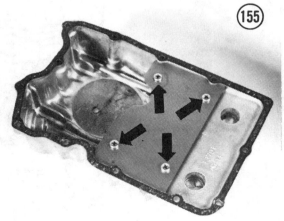

4

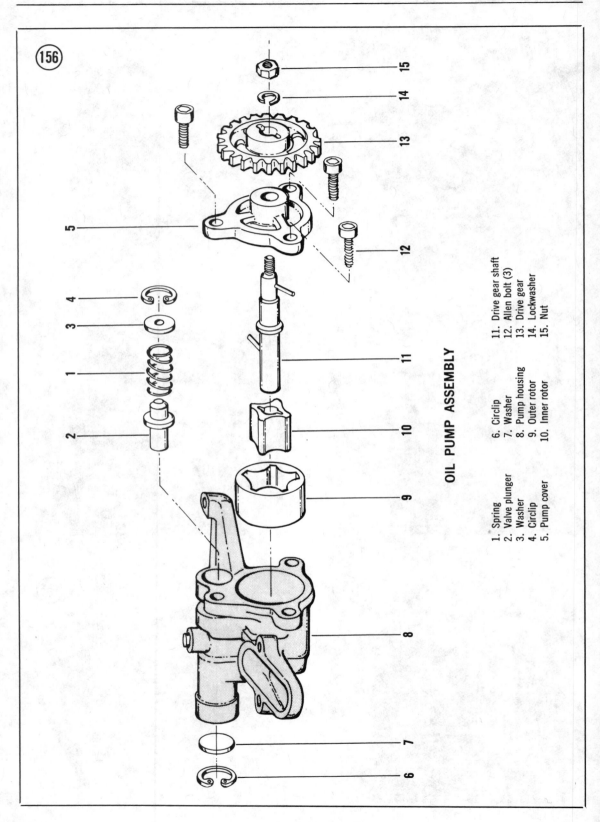

OIL PUMP ASSEMBLY

1. Spring
2. Valve plunger
3. Washer
4. Circlip
5. Pump cover
6. Circlip
7. Washer
8. Pump housing
9. Outer rotor
10. Inner rotor
11. Drive gear shaft
12. Allen bolt (3)
13. Drive gear
14. Lockwasher
15. Nut

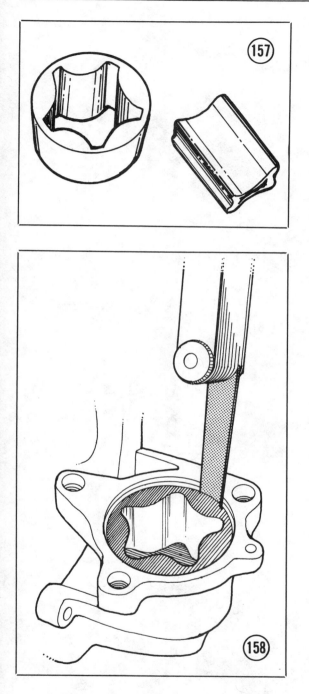

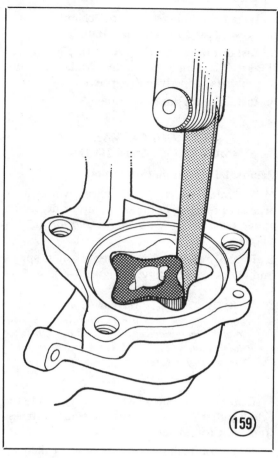

are positioned into the top of the inner rotor and the backside of the drive gear.

8. Make sure the O-ring seal **(Figure 153)** at the pump outlet is in good condition. Replace it if it has lost its resiliency or is deteriorating.

OIL PRESSURE RELIEF VALVE

Removal/Inspection/Installation

1. To gain access to the pressure relief valve, remove the oil pump as described under *Oil Pump Removal/Installation* in this chapter.

2. Remove the circlip, washer, spring, and valve plunger.

3. Inspect the valve plunger and the cylinder that it rides in for wear and scratches. Replace if found defective.

4. Make sure the spring is not broken or distorted; replace if necessary.

6. Check the clearance between the inner and outer rotor **(Figure 159)** with a flat feeler gauge. The clearance should be between 0.0011-0.0035 in. (0.03-0.09mm). If the clearance is greater, replace the worn part.

7. Reassemble the oil pump. Be sure the cross pins are inserted into the drive gear shaft and

5. Install the plunger with the chamfered side out toward the spring (**Figure 160**).

6. Install the spring (**Figure 161**), flat washer (**Figure 162**), and the circlip. Make sure the circlip seats properly in the groove.

7. Install the oil pump assembly.

OIL CHECK VALVE
(MODELS D AND 2D ONLY)

Removal/Inspection/Installation

1. To gain access to the check valve it is necessary to remove the oil pump as described under *Oil Pump Removal/Installation* in this chapter.

2. Remove the circlip, dished washer, spring and check valve plunger (**Figure 163**).

> NOTE: *This check valve is located opposite the oil pressure relief valve explained in the preceding procedure. On later models, this check valve is discontinued and the area is blocked off with a solid washer and circlip.*

3. Inspect the check valve body and the cylinder that it rides in for wear and scratches. Replace if found defective.

4. Make sure the spring is not broken or distorted; replace if necessary.

5. Install check valve plunger, spring, dished washer, and circlip in the order shown in **Figure 163**.

6. Make sure the circlip is seated correctly in the groove.

7. Install the oil pump assembly.

MIDDLE GEAR CASE

Removal/Installation

1. Remove the drive shaft, left-hand shock absorber and the rear wheel as described in Chapter Nine.

2. Remove the 7 Allen bolts securing the middle gear housing to the crankcase.

> NOTE: *Leave 2 bolts in place (on opposite sides of the case), remove the other 5. Remove the remaining 2 slowly to gradually release the spring pressure on the drive cam.*

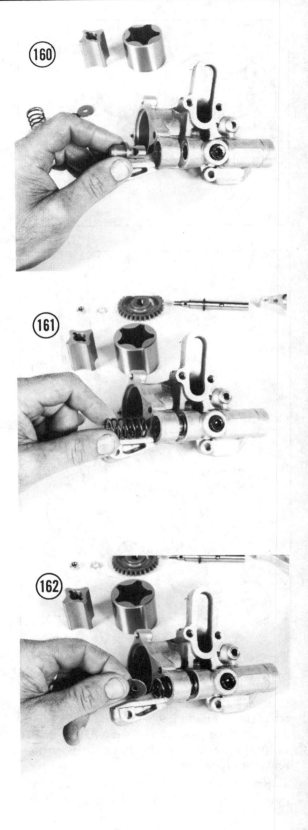

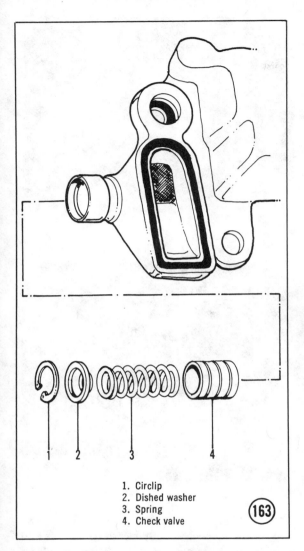

1. Circlip
2. Dished washer
3. Spring
4. Check valve

(163)

(164)

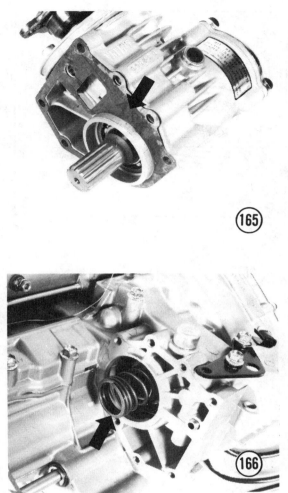

(165)

(166)

3. Remove the middle gear case, spring, and drive cam.

4. Do not lose the locating dowel (**Figure 164**).

5. Install by reversing these removal steps.

6. Be sure to use a new gasket (**Figure 165**).

7. On the early production run of XS750-D, engine No. 1J7-000101 - 1J7-006198, the cam spring (**Figure 166**) was wound in a normal configuration (not progressively wound). If your bike is equipped with the older type, the factory recommends that it be replaced with the new progressively wound type. **Figure 167** shows the difference between the two types. The new spring part No. is 90501-40467-00.

NOTE: *If your bike is equipped with this older type spring it is a good idea to take the middle gear case assembly to*

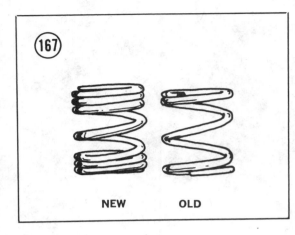

(167)

NEW   OLD

(169)

(168)

(170)

your Yamaha dealer and have them check it out. In accordance with Yamaha Technical Bulletin M6-039A dated 9/3/76, there are other parts that should be replaced as well (new cap, bolts, gaskets, and shims).

8. When installing the 7 Allen bolts, draw in the spring first with 2 bolts (on opposite sides of the case) until the case is snug up against the crankcase. Install the remaining 5 bolts and tighten all to 16 ft.-lb. (22 N•m).

9. Install the drive shaft, left-hand shock absorber and rear wheel as described in Chapter Nine.

10. If the oil was drained, refill with the recommended type and quantity. Refer to Chapter Three.

Inspection

Visually inspect the outer case for cracks and signs of oil leakage; check condition of splines and the output drive flange (**Figure 168**).

Although it may be practical for you to disassemble the case assembly for inspection, it requires special tools and equipment to replace the bearings and seals. If there is trouble with the middle gear unit, take it to your Yamaha dealer and let them overhaul it. They are also better equipped to check and adjust gear lash.

CRANKCASE

Service to the lower end requires that the crankcase assembly be removed from the motorcycle frame.

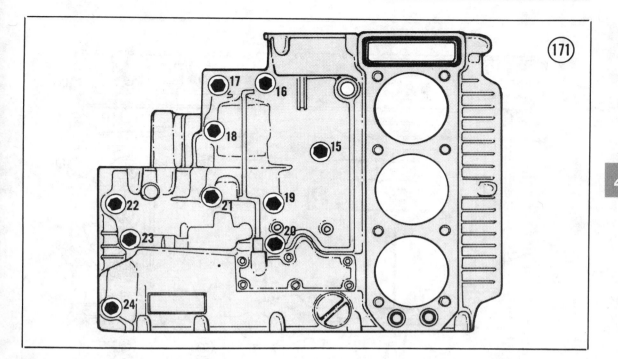

While the engine is still in the frame it is easier to remove the cylinder head, cylinder, pistons, electric starter, alternator, and clutch. In addition, the decrease of engine weight makes it easier to remove the crankcase from the frame.

Disassembly

1. Remove the engine as described under *Engine Removal* in this chapter. Remove all exterior assemblies from the crankcase. Set the engine on the workbench right side up.

2. Remove the 4 Allen bolts (**Figure 169**) securing the transmission countershaft bearing support housing and remove it.

3. Loosen the unnumbered bolt (**Figure 170**) located within the left-hand side of the crankcase.

4. Loosen by ½ turn all numbered bolts (24-15) in the upper crankcase half (**Figure 171**), starting with the highest number first. The numbers are cast into the case, adjacent to the bolt hole. After loosening all bolts, remove all of them (don't forget the unnumbered bolt shown in **Figure 170**).

> NOTE: *Don't forget bolt No. 20 (**Figure 172**) located just below crankcase the breather housing.*

5. Turn the crankcase over. Set it on wooden blocks to prevent damage to the cylinder studs.

6. Loosen by ½ turn all numbered bolts (14-1), starting with highest number first (**Figure 173**). After loosening all bolts, remove all of them.

7. Carefully turn crankcase over, right side up.

8. Carefully tap around the perimeter of the crankcase with a plastic mallet — do not use a metal hammer — to help separate the 2 case halves.

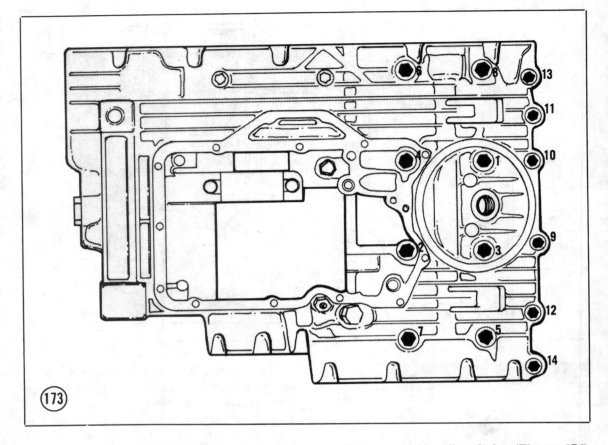

(173)

CAUTION
If it is necessary to pry the halves apart,
do it very carefully so that you do not
mar the gasket surfaces. If you do, the
cases will leak and must be replaced.
They cannot be repaired.

9. Lift up on the upper crankcase and separate it from the lower. The transmission and crankshaft assemblies should stay with the lower crankcase. After removal, check that the upper crankshaft bearings are still in place. If they are loose or have fallen out, reinstall them immediately in their original positions.

10. Don't lose the rubber O-ring (**Figure 174**) on the oil control orifice.

11. Remove the crankshaft assembly.

12. Remove transmission assemblies, shift forks, shift drum, and related items as described in Chapter Five.

13. Remove the 6 Allen bolts (**Figure 175**) securing the crankcase breather housing and remove it.

14. Remove the 3 Allen bolts (**Figure 176**) securing the kickstarter engagement assembly and remove it (**Figure 177**).

15. Remove the screws (**Figure 178**) securing the oil baffle plates in the lower crankcase and remove them.

16. Remove the 2 screws (**Figure 179**) securing starter clutch assembly bearing and remove it.

17. Remove the crankcase main bearing inserts from the upper and lower crankcase halves. Mark the backside of the inserts with No. 1, 2, 3, and 4, U (upper) and L (lower) starting from the left-hand side, so they will be installed into the same position.

NOTE: *The No. 3 bearing (**Figure 180**) in the upper crankcase is a special side thrust bearing.*

NOTE: *The left-hand side refers to the engine as it sits in the bike frame — not as it sits on your workbench.*

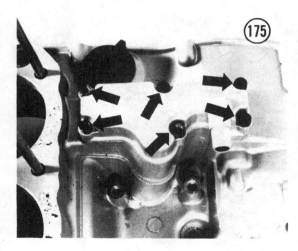

Inspection

Thoroughly clean the inside and outside of both crankcase halves with cleaning solvent. Dry with compressed air. Make sure there is no solvent residue left in the cases as it will contaminate the engine oil.

Make sure all oil passages are clean; be sure to blow them out with compressed air.

Check the crankcases for possible damage such as cracks or other damage. Inspect the mating surfaces of both halves. They must be free of gouges, burrs, or any damage that could cause an oil leak.

Make sure the cylinder studs are not bent and the threads are in good condition. Make sure they are screwed into the crankcase tightly.

Assembly

Prior to installation of all parts, coat surfaces with assembly oil or engine oil.

1. Install the main bearing inserts in both the upper and lower crankcase halves. If reusing the old bearings, make sure that they are installed in the same location. Refer to marks made in *Disassembly*, Step 17.

2. Install the 3 oil baffles in the lower crankcase.

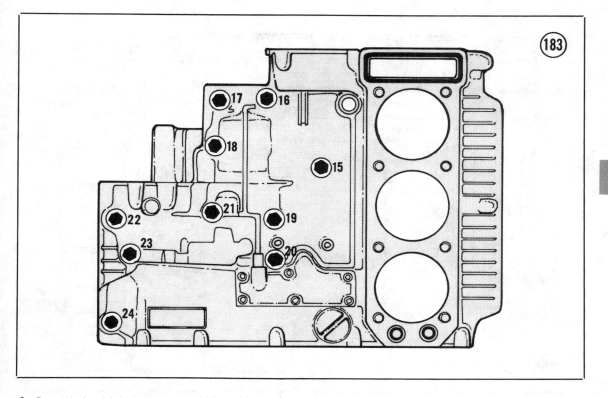

3. Install the kickstarter assembly and crankcase breather housing.

4. Install the transmission assemblies, shift drum and forks, and all related parts as described in Chapter Five.

5. Apply assembly oil to the main bearing inserts and install the crankshaft assembly.

6. Be sure the O-ring (A, **Figure 181**) on the oil control orifice is installed.

7. Install the locating dowel in the lower (B, **Figure 181**) and upper (**Figure 182**) crankcase.

8. Make sure case half sealing surfaces are perfectly clean and dry.

9. Apply a light coat of gasket sealer to the sealing surfaces of both halves. Cover only flat surfaces, not curved bearing surfaces. Make the coating as thin as possible or the case can shift and hammer out the bearings.

> NOTE: *Make sure the upper crankcase main bearing inserts are in place and correctly positioned.*

> NOTE: *Use Gasgacinch Gasket Sealer, Yamabond No. 4, or equivalent. When selecting an equivalent, avoid thick and hard setting materials.*

10. Join both halves and tap together lightly with a plastic mallet — do not use a metal hammer as it will damage the cases.

11. Apply oil to the threads of all bolts and install bolts No. 5, 6, 7, and 8 with copper washers under them. Install all remaining bolts and tighten in two stages as follows:

    a. First stage—8mm bolts to 7 ft.-lb. (9 N•m) and 10mm bolts to 13 ft.-lb. (19 N•m)

    b. Second stage—8mm bolts to 14 ft.-lb. (19 N•m) and 10mm bolts to 27 ft.-lb. (36 N•m)

Tighten bolts No. 1-14 (lower crankcase) first and then No. 15-25 (upper crankcase). Tighten the unnumbered bolt last. The torque pattern is indicated by the bolt number adjacent to the bolt hole. See **Figure 183** for the upper crankcase and **Figure 184** for the lower crankcase bolt numbers.

CAUTION
*Do not forget the hidden, unnumbered bolt (**Figure 185**) in the left-hand side of the crankcase.*

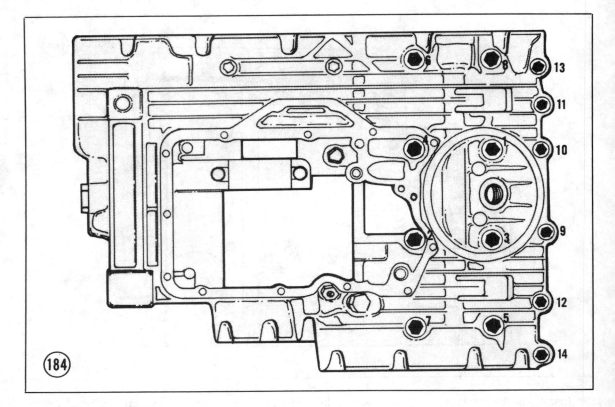

(184)

12. Install the transmission countershaft bearing support housing (**Figure 186**).

13. Install all engine assemblies that were removed.

14. Install the engine as described under *Engine Removal/Installation* in this chapter.

15. Fill the crankcase with the recommended type and quantity of engine oil. Refer to Chapter Three.

CRANKSHAFT

Removal/Installation

1. Split the crankcase as described under *Crankcase Disassembly* in this chapter.

2. Remove the crankshaft assembly and remove the connecting rods.

> NOTE: *Prior to disassembly, mark the rods and caps. Number them 1, 2, and 3 starting from the left-hand side. The left-hand side refers to the engine as it sits in the bike frame — not as it sits on your workbench.*

3. Install by reversing these removal steps, noting the following procedures.

4. Insert the bearing shells into each connecting rod and cap. Make sure they are locked in place correctly.

> CAUTION
> *If the old bearings are reused, be sure they are installed in their exact original positions.*

5. Lubricate the bearings and crankpins with assembly oil and install the rods. Apply molybdenum disulfide grease to the threads of the connecting rods. Install the caps and tighten the cap nuts evenly, in a couple of steps, to 27 ft.-lb. (36 N•m).

> CAUTION
> *On the final tightening sequence, if a torque of 24 ft.-lb. (33 N•m) is reached, **do not stop** until the final torque value is achieved. If the tightening is interrupted between 24-27 ft.-lb. (33-36 N•m), loosen the nut to less than 24 ft.-lb. (33 N•m), start again, and tighten to the final torque value.*

6. Rotate the crankshaft a couple of times to make sure the bearings are not too tight.

Crankshaft Inspection

1. Clean crankshaft thoroughly with solvent. Clean oil holes with rifle cleaning brushes; flush thoroughly and dry with compressed air. Lightly oil all journal surfaces immediately to prevent rust.

2. Carefully inspect each journal (**Figure 187**) for scratches, ridges, scoring, nicks, etc. Very small nicks and scratches may be removed with crocus cloth. More serious damage must be removed by grinding — a job for a machine shop.

3. If the surface on all journals is satisfactory, take the crankshaft to your dealer or local machine shop. They can check out-of-roundness, taper, and wear on the journals. They can also check crankshaft alignment and inspect for cracks. Check against measurements given in **Table 1** at the end of this chapter.

Main Bearing and Journal Inspection

1. Check the inside and outside surfaces of the bearing inserts for wear, bluish tint (burned), flaking, abrasion, and scoring. If the bearings are good, they may be reused. If any insert is questionable, replace the entire set.

2. Measure the main bearing oil clearance. Clean the bearing surfaces of the crankshaft and the main bearing inserts.

3. Set the upper crankcase upside down on the workbench. Set it on wood blocks to prevent damage to the cylinder studs.

4. Install the existing inserts into the upper crankcase.

5. Install the crankshaft into the upper crankcase.

6. Place a strip of Plastigage over each main bearing journal parallel to the crankshaft.

> NOTE: *Do not rotate the crankshaft while the Plastigage strips are in place.*

7. Install the existing bearing inserts into the lower crankcase.

8. Carefully turn the crankcase over and install it onto the upper crankcase.

9. Apply oil to the bolt threads and install bolts No. 1-10; be sure to place copper washers under No. 5, 6, 7, and 8.

10. Tighten to the specified torque values in two stages as follows:

   a. First stage—8mm bolts to 7 ft.-lb. (9 N•m) and 10mm bolts to 13 ft.-lb. (19 N•m)

   b. Second stage—8mm bolts to 14 ft.-lb. (19 N•m) and 10mm bolts to 27 ft.-lb. (36 N•m)

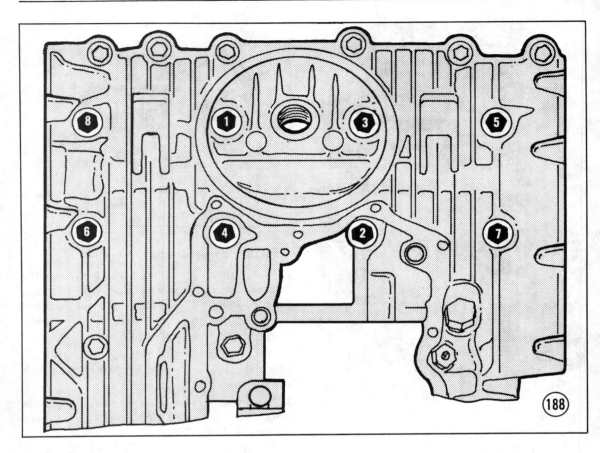

The torque pattern is indicated by the bolt number adjacent to the bolt hole (**Figure 188**).

11. Remove bolts No. 1-10 in the reverse order of installation.

12. Carefully remove the lower crankcase. Do not move the crankshaft.

13. Measure the width of the flattened Plastigage according to manufacturer's instructions. Measure both ends of Plastigage strip (**Figure 189**). A difference of 0.001 in. (0.025 mm) or more indicates a tapered journal. Confirm with a micrometer. Used bearing clearance must not exceed 0.003 in. (0.08 mm). New bearing clearance should be 0.0009-0.0017 in. (0.022-0.044 mm). Remove the Plastigage strips.

14. If the bearing clearance is greater than specified, use the following steps for new bearing selection.

15. The crankshaft is marked on the left-hand counterbalancer with the numbers 1, 2, or 3 (**Figure 190**). The group of four numbers relates

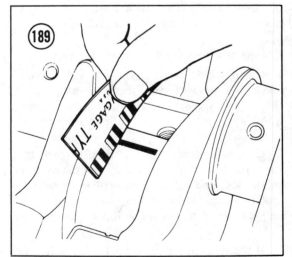

to the crankshaft main bearing journals (the group of 3 numbers relates to the crankshaft connecting rod journals — *do not* refer to these three numbers). Each crankcase bearing journal is marked with numbers 4, 5, or 6 (**Fig-**

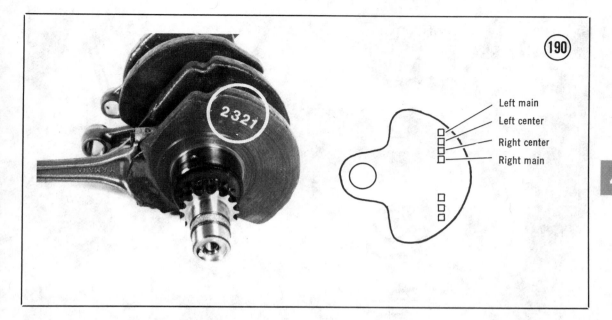

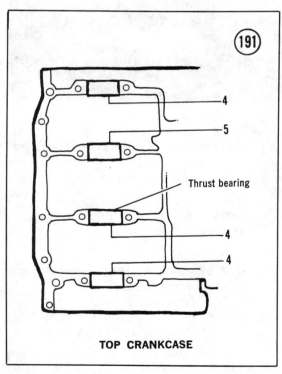

TOP CRANKCASE

Example:

Crankcase journal number	5
Crankshaft bearing journal number	− 2
New bearing insert number	3

Repeat for all four bearings.

NOTE: *Bearing selection for the special side thrust bearing (Figure 192) is the same as for the others. This bearing takes up side thrust of the crankshaft.*

ure 191). These numbers are stamped on the front mating surface of both halves.

16. To select the proper bearing insert number and color, subtract the crankshaft bearing journal number from the crankcase bearing journal number.

17. After new bearings have been installed, recheck the clearance to the specifications given in Step 13.

ELECTRIC STARTER GEARS

Removal/Installation

1. Drain the engine oil as described under *Changing Engine Oil and Filter* in Chapter Three.

2. Remove the ignition assembly as described under *Ignition Governor Assembly Removal/Installation* in this chapter.

3. Loosen the bolt securing the shift lever and remove the lever.

4. Remove the 11 Allen bolts (**Figure 193**) securing the left-hand crankcase cover and remove it.

5. Remove idler gear and shaft (**Figure 194**).

6. Remove the nut (**Figure 195**) securing the oil pump drive gear. To hold the gear while loosening the nut, place a rag between it and the starter gear assembly (**Figure 196**).

7. Remove the gear (**Figure 197**).

8. Remove the front thrust washer (**Figure 198**) and remove the starter gear assembly. Do not lose the rear thrust washer (**Figure 199**).

> NOTE: *The inner gear on the starter gear assembly drives the oil pump.*

9. Install by reversing these removal steps, noting the following items.

10. Apply Loctite Lock N' Seal to the threads (**Figure 195**) prior to installing the oil pump drive gear. Tighten nut to 73 ft.-lb. (99 N•m).

11. When installing the left-hand cover be sure to install the 2 washers (A, **Figure 193**) under the 2 indicated bolts. This will help prevent an oil leak. Be sure to install the 2 electrical wire clamps (**Figure 200**) as indicated.

12. Fill the crankcase with the recommended type and quantity of engine oil. Refer to Chapter Three.

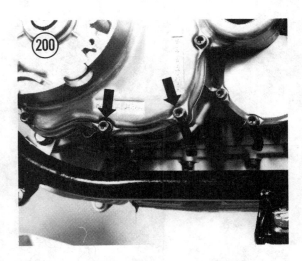

KICKSTARTER

Removal/Installation

Refer to **Figure 201** for this procedure.

1. Drain the oil as described under *Changing Oil and Filter* in Chapter Three.

2. Remove alternator as described under *Alternator Removal/Installation* in this chapter.

3. Remove the clutch assembly as described under *Clutch Removal/Installation* in Chapter Five.

4. Remove the large circlip (**Figure 202**) securing the kickstarter idle gear.

5. Remove the large shim washer (**Figure 203**).

6. Remove the kickstarter idle gear (**Figure 204**).

7. Remove the roller bearing (**Figure 205**) and shim washer (A, **Figure 206**).

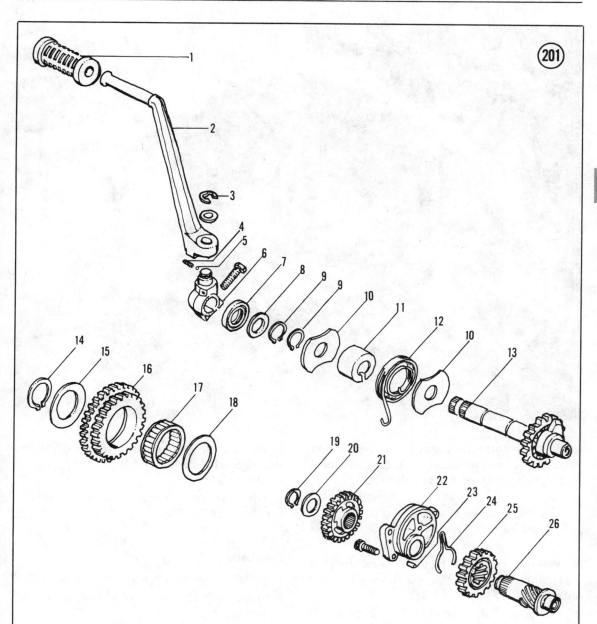

KICKSTARTER MECHANISM

1. Rubber cover
2. Kickstarter arm
3. Circlip
4. Spring
5. Ball
6. Holder
7. Oil seal
8. Washer
9. Circlip

10. Spring cover
11. Spacer
12. Return spring
13. Kickstarter assembly shaft
14. Large circlip
15. Large shim washer
16. Idle gear assembly
17. Roller bearing
18. Shim washer

19. Circlip
20. Washer
21. Kickstarter gear
22. Assembly holder
23. Pin
24. Retaining clip
25. Engagement gear
26. Engagement gear shaft

8. Unhook the return spring (B, **Figure 206**) from the lug on the crankcase housing. Remove the kickstarter assembly **(Figure 207)**.

> NOTE: *Do not lose the flat washer (C, Figure 206).*

9. Remove the circlip **(Figure 208)** securing the kickstarter gear. Remove the flat washer and the gear.

10. Remove the 3 Allen bolts (A, **Figure 209**) securing the kickstarter engagement assembly. Install a bolt into the threaded hole (B, **Figure 209**) and screw it in until the assembly holder is pushed free from the crankcase. Remove it and the engagement gear assembly.

Inspection

1. Check for broken, chipped, or missing teeth on all gears. Replace any if necessary.

2. Make sure the engagement gear operates smoothly on its shaft **(Figure 210)**.

3. Be sure the retaining clip rides snug in the groove in the shaft. If it is loose, tighten by bending it a little.

4. Check all parts for uneven wear; replace any that are questionable.

Installation

1. Install by reversing the removal steps.

2. Apply assembly oil to all sliding surfaces of all parts.

3. Install kickstarter assembly. Temporarily install the kickstarter arm onto the shaft. Hook the spring onto the lug on the crankcase; rotate the assembly *counterclockwise* until the flat on the inner washer is in line with the idle gear. Then push the assembly in all the way until it bottoms out. This enables the lug on the backside of the kickstarter gear (A, **Figure 211**) to be positioned correctly in the depression (B, **Figure 211**) in the crankcase housing. Check the operation of the assembly; remove the kickstarter lever.

4

4. Place the idle gear into position and then slip the roller bearing into it. Don't forget to first install the flat washer.

NOTE: *Apply assembly oil to the roller bearing prior to installation.*

BREAK-IN

Following cylinder servicing (boring, honing, new rings, etc.) and major lower end work, the engine should be broken in just as if it were new. The performance and service life of the engine depend greatly on a careful and sensible break-in.

For the first 500 miles, no more than one-third throttle should be used and speed should be varied as much as possible within the one-third throttle limit. Prolonged, steady running at one speed, no matter how moderate, is to be avoided, as is hard acceleration.

Following the 500-mile service, increasingly more throttle can be used but full throttle should not be used until the motorcycle has covered at least 1,000 miles and then it should be limited to short bursts until 1,500 miles have been logged.

The mono-grade oils recommended for break-in and normal use provide a more superior bedding pattern for rings and cylinders than do multi-grade oils. As a result, piston ring and cylinder bore life are greatly increased. During this period, oil consumption will be higher than normal. It is therefore important to frequently check and correct the oil level. At no time, during break-in or later, should the oil level be allowed to drop below the bottom line on the dipstick; if the oil level is low, the oil will become overheated resulting in insufficient lubrication and increased wear.

500-Mile Service

It is essential that oil and filter be changed after the first 500 miles. In addition, it is a good idea to change the oil and filter at the completion of break-in (about 1,500 miles) to ensure that all of the particles produced during break-in are removed from the lubrication system. The small added expense may be considered a smart investment that will pay off in increased engine life.

Table 1 ENGINE SPECIFICATIONS

Item	Specifications	Wear Limit
General		
Number of cylinders	3	—
Bore x stroke	2.677 x 2.701 in. (68 x 68.6mm)	—
Displacement	45.58 cu. in. (747 cc)	—
Compression ratio		
Model D, 2D	8.5 to 1	—
Models E, F, SE and SF	9.2 to 1	—
Compression pressure		
Warm at sea level	142 ± 14 psi (10 ± 1 kg/cm²)	—
Cylinders		
Bore	2.677 - 2.678 in. (68.00 - 68.02mm)	2.681 in. (68.10mm)
Out-of-round	—	0.002 in. (0.05mm)
Cylinder/piston clearance	0.0020-0.0022 in. (0.050-0.055mm)	0.004 in. (0.1mm)
Pistons		
Diameter	2.6755-2.6759 in. (67.96-67.97mm)	—
Clearance in bore	0.0020-0.0022 in. (0.050-0.055mm)	0.004 in. (0.1mm)
Piston Rings		
Number per piston		
Compression	2	—
Oil control	1	—
Ring end gap		
Top	0.008-0.016 in. (0.2-0.4mm)	0.024 in. (0.60mm)
Second	0.008-0.016 in. (0.2-0.4mm)	0.024 in. (0.60mm)
Oil control	0.008-0.035 in. (0.2-0.9mm)	0.043 in. (1.10mm)
Ring side clearance		
Top	0.0015-0.0031 in. (0.04-0.08mm)	—
Second and oil control	0.001-0.003 in. (0.03-0.07mm)	—
Crankshaft		
Main bearing oil clearance	0.0009-0.0017 in. (0.022-0.044mm)	—
Connecting rod oil clearance	0.0013-0.0021 in. (0.032-0.054mm)	—
Main bearing runout	—	0.0012 in. (0.03mm)
Camshaft		
Valve timing - intake		
Model D	Opens 36°BTDC, closes 60°ABDC	—
Model 2D	Opens 40°BTDC, closes 64°ABDC	—
Models E, F, SE and SF	Opens 38°BTDC, closes 66°ABDC	—
Valve timing - exhaust		
Model D	Opens 60°BBDC, closes 36°ATDC	—
Model 2D	Opens 64°BBDC, closes 40°ATDC	—
Models E, F, SE and SF	Opens 64°BBDC, closes 40°ATDC	—

(continued)

4

Table 1   ENGINE SPECIFICATIONS (continued)

Item	Specifications	Wear Limit
Cam lobe height		
Intake	1.4489 ± 0.0019 in. (36.803 ± 0.05mm)	1.4468 in. (36.75mm)
Exhaust	1.4292 ± 0.0019 in. (36.303 ± 0.05mm)	1.4232 in. (36.15mm)
Camshaft to cap clearance	0.0008-0.002 in. (0.020-0.054mm)	0.006 in. (0.160mm)
Runout limit	—	0.004 in. (0.1mm)
Valves		
Valve stem clearance		
Intake	0.0008-0.0016 in. (0.020-0.041mm)	0.0004 in. (0.010 mm)
Exhaust	0.0014-0.0023 in. (0.035-0.059mm)	0.005 in. (0.12mm)
Valve guide inner diameter - intake and exhaust	0.276-0.277 in. (7.01-7.02mm)	0.280 in. (7.10mm)
Valve seat width	0.050 in. (1.3mm)	0.080 in. (2.0mm)
Valve Springs		
Free length (inner)		
Intake and exhaust	1.402 in. (35.6mm)	1.322 in. (33.6mm)
Free length (outer)		
Intake and exhaust	1.571 in. (39.9mm)	1.491 in. (37.9mm)
Allowable tilt from vertical		
Intake	—	0.063 in. (1.6mm)
Exhaust	—	0.069 in. (1.75mm)

NOTE: If you own a 1980 or later model, first check the Supplement at the back of the book for any new service information.

CHAPTER FIVE

CLUTCH AND TRANSMISSION

CLUTCH

The clutch on the Yamaha XS750 is a wet multi-plate type which operates immersed in the engine oil.

All clutch parts can be removed with the engine in the frame. Refer to **Figure 1** for all clutch components.

Removal

1. Place the bike on the centerstand and remove the rear brake lever and front footpeg.

2. Drain the engine oil as described under *Changing Oil and Filter* in Chapter Three.

3. Remove the exhaust system as described under *Exhaust System Removal/Installation* in Chapter Six.

4. Slacken the clutch cable at the hand lever **(Figure 2)** and remove the cable.

5. Lift up the rubber protective flap and lift up on the clutch cable retaining clip **(Figure 3)**. Remove the cable from the actuating mechanism link arm **(Figure 4)**.

6. Remove the alternator as described under *Alternator Removal/Installation* in Chapter Seven.

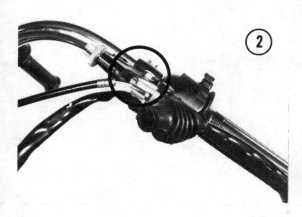

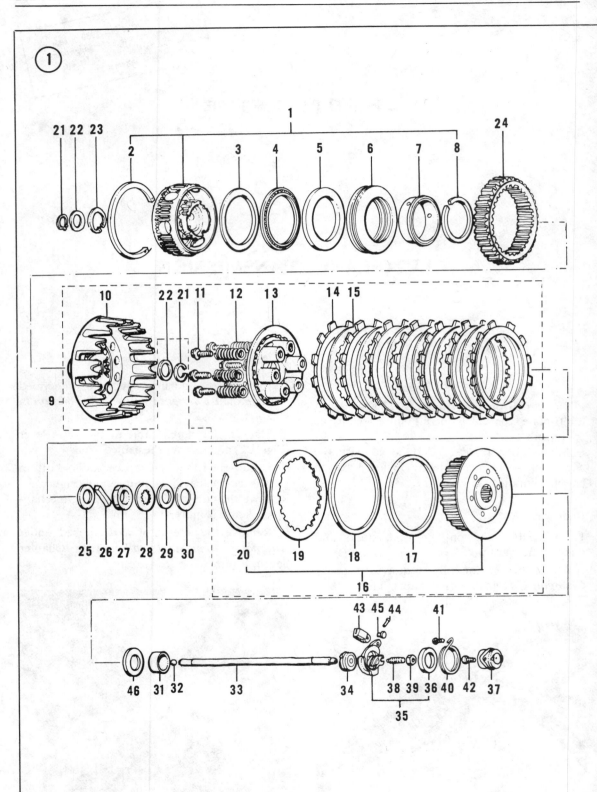

CLUTCH ASSEMBLY

1. Damper assembly
2. Circlip (Models D, 2D only)
3. Plate washer
4. Bearing
5. Plate washer
6. Spring damper
7. Collar
8. Circlip
9. Clutch assembly
10. Outer clutch housing
11. Clutch bolts (6)
12. Clutch springs (6)
13. Pressure plate
14. Friction plate
15. Clutch plate
16. Clutch boss assembly
17. Plate seat
18. Spring
19. Plate
20. Circlip
21. Circlip
22. Plate washer
23. Circlip
24. Primary driven gear
25. Washer
26. Rectangular push bar
27. Clutch nut
28. Lockwasher
29. Conical washer
30. Washer
31. Collar
32. Ball
33. Clutch pushrod
34. Oil seal
35. Clutch lifting mechanism
36. Washer
37. Lifting mechanism (outer)
38. Adjustment screw
39. Locknut
40. Return spring
41. Screw—spring anchor
42. Lifting mechanism screw (2)
43. Link arm
44. Cotter pin
45. Clevis pin
46. Washer

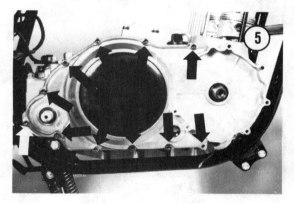

7. Remove the 11 Allen bolts (**Figure 5**) securing the right-hand side cover and remove it.

> NOTE: *Figures 5 thru 23 are shown with the engine partially disassembled. It is not necessary to do so for clutch removal.*

8. Remove the thrust washer (**Figure 6**) on the kickstarter shaft.

9. Remove the 4 Allen bolts (**Figure 7**) securing the bearing housing bracket and remove it.

10. Remove the outer small circlip, flat washer, and shim (**Figure 8**).

11. Remove the inner large circlip (**Figure 9**).

12. Remove the clutch damper assembly (**Figure 10**).

13. Remove the primary driven gear and the Hy-Vo chain (**Figure 11**).

14. Remove the clutch outer housing (A, **Figure 12**) and large thin shim (B, **Figure 12**).

15. Remove the washer and circlip (**Figure 13**) in front of the clutch pressure plate.

16. Remove the 6 clutch bolts and springs (**Figure 14**) and remove the pressure plate and clutch discs and plates (**Figure 15**).

17. Remove the washer, rectangular push bar, and ball bearing (**Figure 16**).

> NOTE: *The ball bearing is located behind the push bar and is easily lost. Tape it to the push bar for safe keeping.*

18. Remove the clutch nut, lockwasher, and conical washer (**Figure 17**) securing the clutch boss assembly. Nut removal requires the use of a very deep socket — Yamaha special tool No. 90890-01221-00 and a clutch holding tool — Yamaha special tool No. 90890-01228-00 or the combination of the following tools.

> NOTE: *The nut can be removed with a 1$\frac{9}{32}$ in. plumber's faucet socket (Figure 18) available at most large hard-*

ware stores for about $5 for a set. The clutch can be held with a special tool called the "Grabbit". This tool is available from Precision Mfg. and Sales Co. Box 149, Clearwater, FL 33517.

19. Secure the clutch boss assembly with the "Grabbit" tool **(Figure 19)**. Place the 1⅞₂ in.

plumber's socket onto the nut and insert the next size larger socket from the set onto it **(Figure 20)**. Use a drift as a pry bar and remove the nut. Remove the clutch boss assembly.

20. Remove flat washer and spacer **(Figure 21)**.

21. Remove the ignition assembly as described under *Ignition Governor Assembly Removal/ Installation* in Chapter Four.

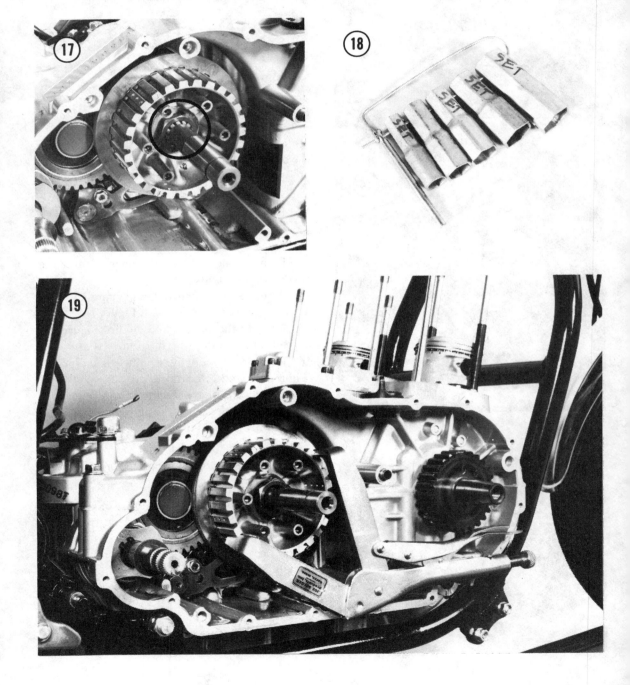

22. Loosen the bolt securing the shift lever and remove the lever.

23. Remove the left-hand front footpeg.

24. Remove the 11 Allen bolts **(Figure 22)** securing the left-hand crankcase cover and remove it.

25. Remove the clutch pushrod and oil seal **(Figure 23)**.

Inspection

1. Clean all clutch parts in petroleum-based solvent such as kerosene and thoroughly dry with compressed air.

2. Measure the free length of each clutch spring as shown in **Figure 24**. Replace the springs that are 1.63 in. (41.5 mm) or less.

3. Measure the thickness of each friction disc at several places around the disc as shown in **Figure 25**. The standard thickness is 0.12 in. (3.0mm). Replace any disc that is 0.11 in. (2.8mm) or less.

4. Check the metal clutch plates for warpage as shown in **Figure 26**. Replace any plate that is warped 0.002 in. (0.05mm) or greater.

5. Inspect all mating surfaces (**Figure 27**) of the clutch damper for signs of wear, galling, or burred teeth.

> **CAUTION**
> *Due to the internal spring pressure, this unit requires the use of a press for disassembly and work should be performed by a Yamaha dealer. Disassembly is only required in the case of severe clutch chatter.*

6. Inspect the clutch outer housing and clutch boss assembly for cracks or galling in the grooves where the clutch friction discs slide. They must be smooth for chatter-free clutch operation.

7. Check the pushrod ends for any signs of indentation. The ends should be flat; if worn, it makes clutch adjustment difficult. Replace the rod if either end is worn.

8. Inspect the condition of the clutch rod oil seal; replace it if cracked or deteriorated.

9. Check the condition of the return spring (**Figure 28**) within the clutch actuating mechanism located in the left-hand crankcase cover. Replace if it is not operating smoothly or is not retracting lifting mechanism completely.

10. Check condition of the bearing (**Figure 29**) in the bearing housing bracket. Make sure it rotates smoothly with no signs of wear or damage. Replace if necessary.

Installation

1. Install spacer and flat washer (**Figure 21**).

2. Install the clutch boss assembly.

3. Install the conical washer *with the convex side out*, lockwasher, and nut. Secure the nut with same tool setup used in *Removal* Step 18 (**Figure 20**). Tighten the nut to 88 ft.-lb. (119 N•m).

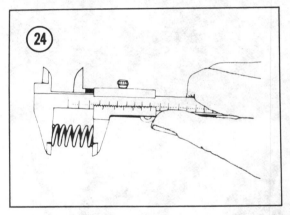

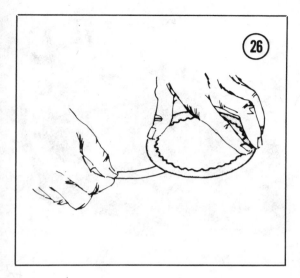

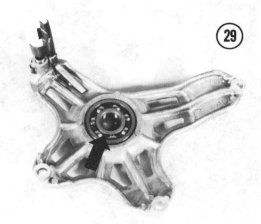

NOTE: *Be sure to bend up a tab on the lockwasher against one side of the nut (Figure 30).*

4. Install a friction disc, then a clutch plate and alternate in this order until all plates and discs are installed.

5. Install the clutch pushrod and oil seal **(Figure 23)** from the left-hand side.

6. Install the left-hand side cover. Make sure the locating dowel (A, **Figure 28**) is in place.

7. Install the ball bearing, rectangular push bar, and washer.

NOTE: *Make sure the ball bearing does not fall out while installing the remaining parts.*

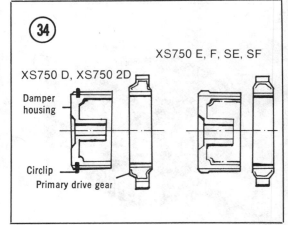

XS750 E, F, SE, SF

XS750 D, XS750 2D

Damper housing

Circlip

Primary drive gear

8. Install the pressure plate, align the tabs on the friction plates, and install only 2 springs and bolts. Tighten the bolts only finger-tight at this time.

> NOTE: *Make sure the back of the pressure plate seats correctly into the push bar.*

9. Slip on the clutch outer housing (**Figure 31**) for final alignment of all tabs, then remove it.

10. Install the remaining 4 springs and bolts and tighten to 6 ft.-lb. (8 N•m).

> NOTE: *Before final tightening of the bolts, slip on the clutch outer housing for a final alignment check, then remove it.*

11. Install the washer and circlip (**Figure 13**).

12. Install clutch outer housing (A, **Figure 32**).

13. Install the Hy-Vo chain and primary drive gear of the clutch damper assembly (**Figure 33**).

14. Slide the inner clutch damper assembly onto the shaft and mesh it into the outer gear.

> NOTE: *On Models D and 2D, install the large circlip onto the clutch damper assembly (Figure 34).*

15. Install the large inner circlip (**Figure 9**).

16. Install the shim, flat washer, and small outer circlip (**Figure 8**).

17. Install bearing housing bracket (**Figure 7**). Tighten the bolts to 15 ft.-lb. (20 N•m).

18. Install the ignition governor assembly as described under *Ignition Governor Assembly Removal/Installation* in Chapter Four.

19. Install the shift lever and left-hand front footpeg.

20. Continue installation by reversing *Removal* Steps 1 thru 8.

21. Adjust the clutch and mechanism as described under *Clutch Adjustment* in Chapter Three.

22. Refill the crankcase with the recommended type and quantity engine oil; refer to Chapter Three.

SHIFT MECHANISM

NOTE
Yamaha has recalled all 1977 and 1978 XS750 models because the lockwasher on the bolt that positions the shift cam may allow the bolt to work loose, allowing the bolt to fall into the crankcase. If this happens, it could result in the transmission locking into two gears simultaneously. This will cause the rear wheel to immediately lock up.

Correct by installing a lockwasher with an improved lock tab. For more information, contact your local dealer as soon as possible.

Removal

1. Remove the clutch as described under *Clutch Removal/Installation* in this chapter.

2. Remove the kickstarter gears as described under *Kickstarter Gear Removal/Installation* in Chapter Four.

3. Remove the E-clip and washer (**Figure 35**) on the left-hand end of the shift arm shaft.

NOTE: *Figure 35 is shown with the engine and middle gear case removed for clarity only.*

4. Withdraw the shift arm shaft and shift lever (**Figure 36**) from the right-hand side.

5. Remove the E-clip (**Figure 37**) securing the forward shift lever.

6. Flip the shift pawl (A, **Figure 38**) out of the shift drum.

7. Remove the forward shift lever arm, spring, and pawl (B, **Figure 38**).

8. Remove the 2 screws **(Figure 39)** securing the shift lever shaft and remove it.

Installation

1. Install the shift lever shaft **(Figure 39)**.

2. Install the shift arm shaft and shift lever. Install the washer and E-clip **(Figure 35)**.

3. Install the forward shaft lever and insert the E-clip. Align the 2 dots **(A, Figure 40)** of each lever.

> NOTE: *This alignment is necessary for proper gear shifting.*

4. Shift the transmission into second gear. Make sure the line on the shift lever aligns with the line on the shift drum **(Figure 41)**. If alignment is incorrect, adjust by looseninng the locknut and turning the eccentric screw (B, **Figure 40)** on the rear shift lever. After alignment is correct, tighten the locknut.

5. Complete installation by installing the kickstarter gears and clutch assembly.

6. Refill the crankcase with the recommended type and quantity of engine oil, refer to Chapter Three.

CLUTCH CABLE

Replacement

In time, the cable will stretch to the point where it is no longer useful and will have to be replaced.

1. Hinge up the seat and remove the rear bolt securing the fuel tank.

2. Turn both fuel shutoff valves to the ON or RES position. Lift up on the rear of the fuel tank and remove the fuel lines to the carburetors and the vacuum lines to the intake manifolds **(Figure 42)**.

3. Pull the tank to the rear and remove it.

4. Loosen the adjustment nut **(Figure 43)** and remove the cable from the hand lever.

5. Push back the rubber protective flap and lift up on the clutch cable retaining clip **(Figure 44)**.

6. Remove the cable from the actuating mechanism link arm (A, **Figure 45)**. Pull the cable out from the sleeve leading into the actuating mechanism (B, **Figure 45)**.

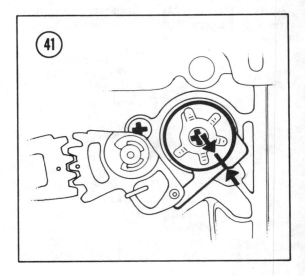

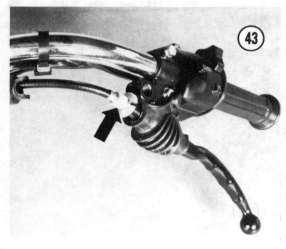

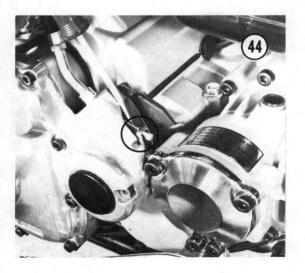

7. Slip the cable out from the retaining clip on the left-hand carburetor.

> NOTE: *Prior to removing the cable, make a drawing of the cable routing through the frame. It is very easy to forget how it was, once it has been removed. Replace it exactly as it was, avoiding any sharp turns.*

8. Remove the cable from the frame and replace with a new one.

9. Adjust the cable free play as described under *Clutch Adjustment* in Chapter Three.

10. Reinstall the fuel tank; connect fuel and vacuum lines.

TRANSMISSION

The crankcase must be disassembled to gain access to the transmission components.

Disassembly

1. Perform Steps 1-11 in *Crankcase Disassembly* in Chapter Four.

2. Remove middle gear assembly (**Figure 46**).

3. Remove the E-clip on the left-hand end of the shift fork shaft. Slide out shaft (**Figure 47**) and remove it and the shift fork.

4. Remove main shaft assembly (**Figure 48**).

> NOTE: *Do not lose oil seal (Figure 49) on right-hand end of the shaft.*

5. Turn the crankcase over. Remove the E-clip (**Figure 50**) on the shift fork shaft. Slide the shaft out, do not lose the washer (A, **Figure 51**), and remove the shift forks (B, **Figure 51**) and the shaft.

6. Remove the nuts and washers on the countershaft bearing cap and remove the cap (**Figure 52**).

7. Remove the Allen bolt, spring washer, and washer (**Figure 53**) securing the middle drive gear to the countershaft.

8. Turn the crankcase over. Pivot the counter-shaft assembly up (**Figure 54**) and carefully remove it.

Assembly

Prior to assembly, coat all bearings and bearing surfaces with assembly oil.

1. Install countershaft assembly (**Figure 55**).

2. Install the countershaft bearing cap. Make sure the 1/2 circlip (**Figure 56**) is installed in the cap. Tighten the nuts to 14 ft.-lb. (19 N•m).

> *NOTE*
> *Apply Loctite Lock N' Seal to the threads prior to installation.*

5

NOTE: *Make sure the pin followers are installed into each shift fork prior to installation.*

NOTE: *Be sure to install the cap with the shift fork shaft clearance hole (Figure 57) toward the front of the engine.*

3. Install the washer, spring washer, and Allen bolt (**Figure 53**) securing the middle gear to the countershaft.

4. Turn the lower crankcase over. Partially insert the shift fork shaft and washer (**Figure 52**). Position both shift forks onto the countershaft assembly and shift drum (**Figure 58**). Slide the shaft the rest of the way in and install the E-clip (**Figure 50**).

5. Turn the lower crankcase over. Install the main shaft assembly and shift drum and install the shift fork shaft (**Figure 59**). Secure it with the E-clip.

NOTE: *Be sure to install the shift fork as shown in Figure 59.*

7. Install the middle gear assembly (**Figure 46**). Models D and 2D are equipped with only one circlip on each of the bearings. On later models there are two circlips on the ball bearing (**Figure 60**) and ½ circlip on the roller bearing.

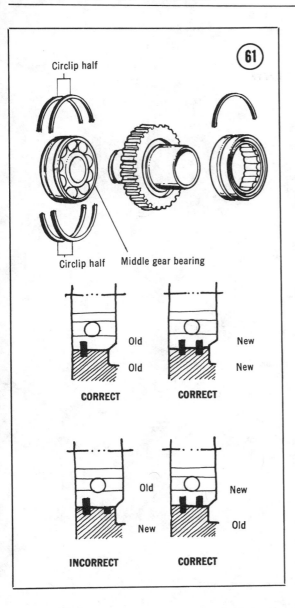

Circlip half

Middle gear bearing

Circlip half

CORRECT | CORRECT

INCORRECT | CORRECT

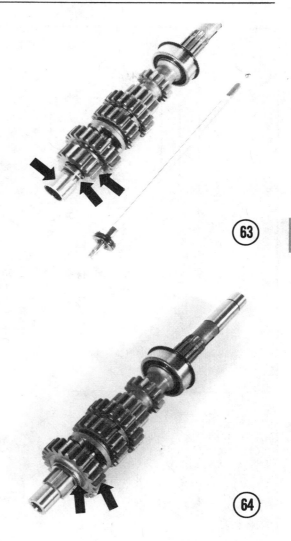

Make sure the circlips seat properly into the crankcase. Install the ½ circlip into the lower crankcase side.

CAUTION
Do not install a ball bearing designed for only one circlip into a crankcase that has grooves for two circlips. Refer to **Figure 61** *for the correct and incorrect factory recommended combinations.*

NOTE: *When a new seal is installed, apply grease to the lips prior to installation.*

8. Perform Steps 5-15, *Crankcase Assembly* in Chapter Four.

Main Shaft Disassembly/Assembly

Refer to **Figure 62** for this procedure.

1. Slide off the roller bearing, washer, and 2nd gear (**Figure 63**).

2. Remove the circlip, washer, and 5th gear (**Figure 64**).

3. Remove washer and circlip; slide off 3rd gear (**Figure 65**).

4. Remove circlip and washer; slide off 4th gear (**Figure 66**).

5. If necessary, remove the ball bearing (**Figure 67**) from the shaft.

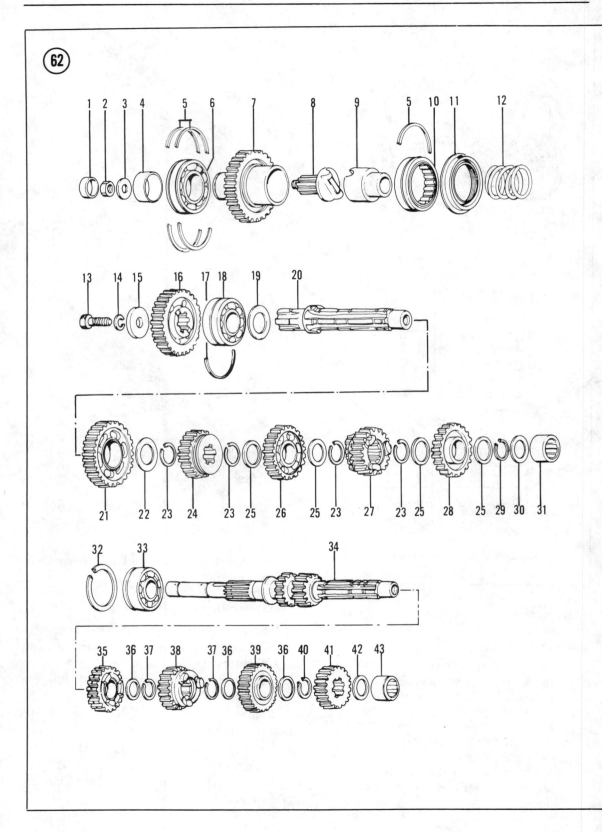

TRANSMISSION ASSEMBLY

1. Plug
2. Nut
3. Washer
4. Collar
5. Circlip
6. Middle gear bearing
7. Middle driven gear
8. Driven cam
9. Drive cam
10. Roller bearing
11. Oil seal
12. Spring
13. Allen bolt
14. Lockwasher
15. Washer
16. Middle drive gear
17. Circlip
18. Countershaft bearing
19. Washer
20. Countershaft
21. Countershaft first gear
22. Washer
23. Circlip
24. Countershaft fourth gear
25. Washer
26. Countershaft third gear
27. Countershaft fifth gear
28. Countershaft second gear
29. Circlip
30. Shim
31. Needle bearing
32. Circlip
33. Main shaft bearing
34. Main shaft
35. Main shaft fourth gear
36. Washer
37. Circlip
38. Main shaft third gear
39. Main shaft fifth gear
40. Circlip
41. Main shaft second gear
42. Washer
43. Roller bearing

65

5

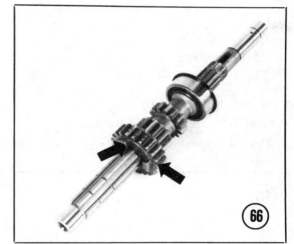

66

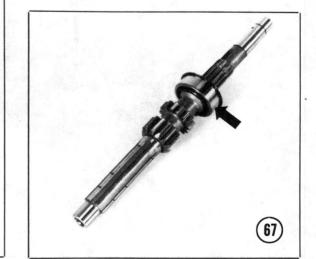

67

6. Clean all parts in cleaning solvent and thoroughly dry.

7. Check each gear for excessive wear, burrs, pitting, or chipped or missing teeth. Make sure the lugs on ends of gears are in good condition.

> NOTE: *Defective gears should be replaced, and it is a good idea to replace the mating gear on the countershaft even though it may not show as much wear or damage.*

8. Make sure that all gears slide smoothly on the main shaft splines.

9. Check the condition of the bearing. Make sure it rotates smoothly (**Figure 68**) with no signs of wear or damage. Replace if necessary.

10. Assemble by reversing these removal steps. Refer to **Figure 69** for correct placement of the gears. Make sure that all circlips are seated correctly in the main shaft grooves.

11. Make sure each gear engages properly to the adjoining gear where applicable.

Countershaft Disassembly/Assembly

Refer to **Figure 62** for this procedure.

1. Slide off middle drive gear (**Figure 70**).

2. Slide off the bearing (**Figure 71**).

3. Slide off washer and 1st gear (**Figure 72**).

4. Slide off the washer (**Figure 73**).

5. Slide off the needle bearing and shim.

6. Remove the circlip, washer, and 2nd gear (**Figure 74**).

7. Remove the washer, circlip, and 5th gear (**Figure 75**).

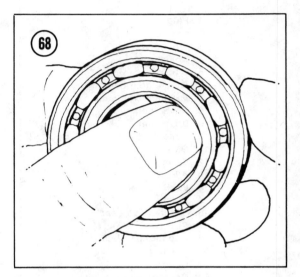

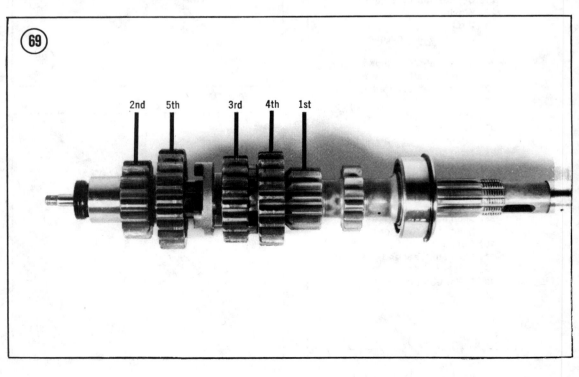

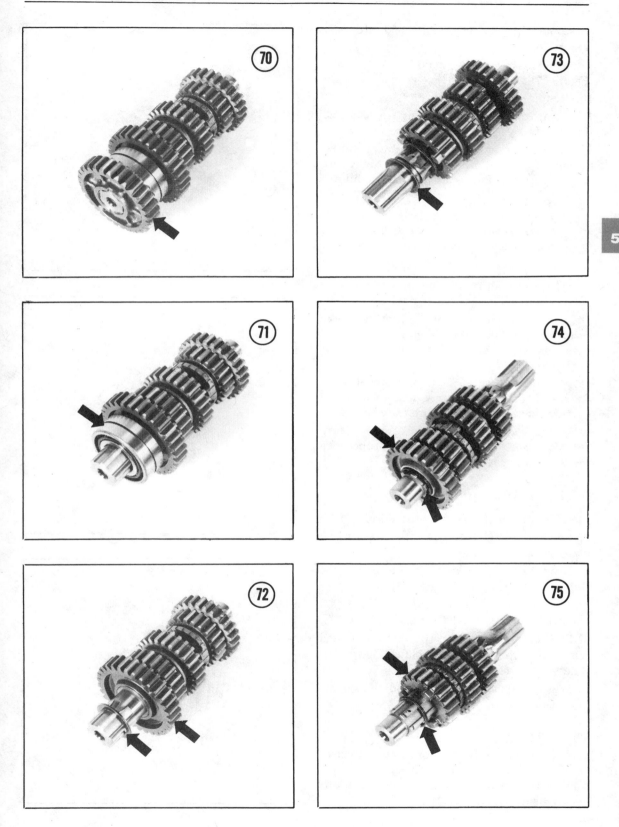

8. Remove the circlip, shim, and 3rd gear (**Figure 76**).

9. Remove the shim, circlip, and 4th gear (**Figure 77**).

10. Remove the circlip (**Figure 78**).

11. Clean all parts in cleaning solvent and thoroughly dry.

12. Check each gear for excessive wear, burrs, pitting, or chipped or missing teeth. Make sure the lugs on ends of gears are in good condition.

> NOTE: *Defective gears should be replaced, and it is a good idea to replace the mating gear on the main shaft even though it may not show signs of wear or damage.*

13. Make sure all gears slide smoothly on the countershaft splines.

14. Check the condition of the bearing. Make sure it rotates smoothly (**Figure 68**) with no signs of wear or damage. Replace it if necessary.

15. Assemble by reversing these removal steps. Refer to **Figure 79** for correct placement of the gears. Make sure all circlips are seated correctly in the countershaft grooves.

16. Make sure each gear engages properly to the adjoining gear where applicable.

GEARSHIFT DRUM AND FORKS

Refer to **Figure 80** for this procedure.

1. Perform Steps 1 thru 8 of *Transmission Disassembly* in this chapter.

2. Bend down the locking tab and remove the shift drum locating bolt (**Figure 81**).

3. Remove the shift drum detent (A, **Figure 82**) and neutral safety switch (B, **Figure 82**).

4. Slide the shift drum partially out and remove circlip and stopper plate (**Figure 83**). Remove the shift drum.

5. Wash all parts in solvent and thoroughly dry them.

Inspection

1. Inspect each shift fork for signs of wear or cracking. Make sure the forks slide smoothly on their respective shafts. Make sure the shafts are not bent.

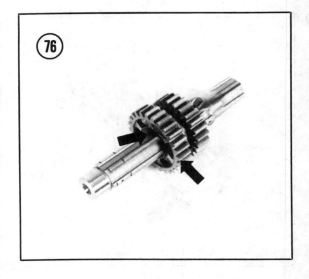

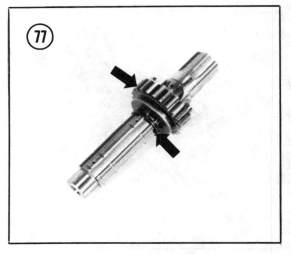

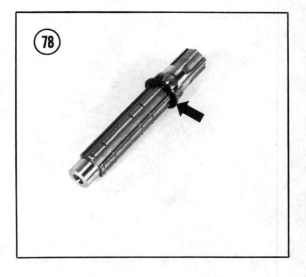

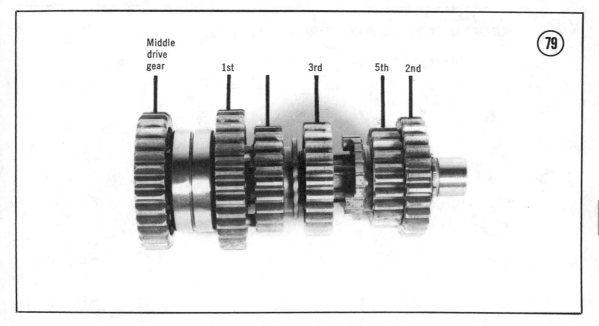

Figure 79

NOTE: *Check for any arc shaped wear marks on the shift forks. If this is apparent, the shift fork has come in contact with the gear, indicating the fingers are worn beyond use and the fork must be replaced.*

2. Check the grooves in the shift drum (A, **Figure 84**) for wear or roughness.

3. Check the shift drum bearing (B, **Figure 84**). Make sure it operates smoothly with no signs of wear or damage.

80 GEARSHIFT DRUM AND FORKS

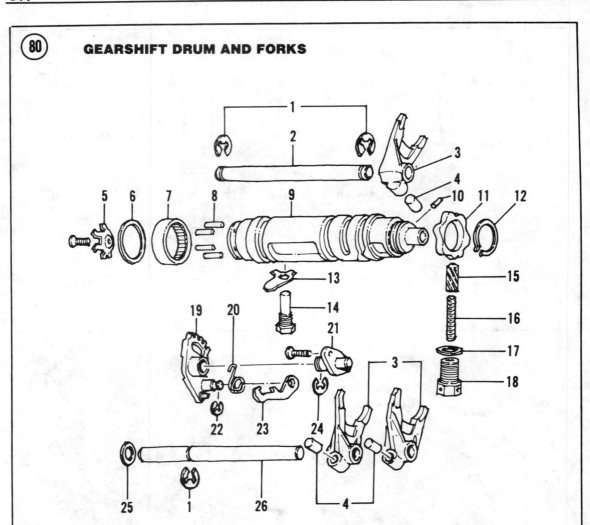

1. E-clip
2. Shift fork shaft
3. Shift fork
4. Guide pin
5. Side plate
6. Circlip
7. Roller bearing
8. Pins
9. Shift drum
10. Dowel pin
11. Stopper plate
12. Circlip
13. Locking tab
14. Shift drum locating bolt
15. Shift drum detent
16. Spring
17. Washer
18. Shift drum detent bolt
19. Shift lever
20. Spring
21. Shift lever shaft
22. E-clip
23. Shift pawl
24. E-clip
25. Washer
26. Shift fork shaft

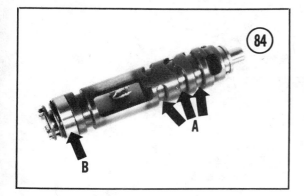

4. Check the cam pin followers in each shift fork. It should fit snug but not too tight. Check the end that rides in the shift drum for wear or burrs. Replace as necessary.

5. Check the stopper plate for wear; replace if necessary.

Assembly

1. Coat all of the bearing surfaces with assembly oil.

2. Install the shift drum from the right-hand side (**Figure 85**) and install the stopper plate and circlip (**Figure 83**).

3. Install the shift drum detent (A, **Figure 86**) and tighten to 31 ft.-lb. (41 N•m).

4. Install the neutral safety switch (B, **Figure 86**).

5. Install shift drum locating bolt (**Figure 81**) and tighten to 13 ft.-lb. (18 N•m).

CAUTION
Be sure to bend up the locking tab onto the side of the bolt.

6. Perform Steps 1-8, *Transmission Assembly* in this chapter.

NOTE: If you own a 1980 or later model, first check the Supplement at the back of the book for any new service information.

CHAPTER SIX

FUEL AND EXHAUST SYSTEMS

The fuel system consists of the fuel tank, two shutoff valves with fuel filters, three Mikuni constant velocity carburetors, and an air cleaner.

The exhaust system consists of three exhaust pipes, a crossover pipe, and two mufflers.

This chapter includes service procedures for all parts of the fuel and exhaust system.

AIR CLEANER

The air cleaner must be cleaned every 1,000 miles (1,600km) or more frequently in dusty areas.

Service the air cleaner element as described under *Air Cleaner* in Chapter Three.

CARBURETORS

Basic Principles

An understanding of the function of each of the carburetor components and their relationship to one another is a valuable aid for pinpointing a source of carburetor trouble.

The carburetor's purpose is to supply and atomize fuel and mix it in correct proportions with air that is drawn in through the air intake. At the primary throttle opening — at idle — a small amount of fuel is siphoned through the pilot jet by the incoming air. As the throttle is opened further, the air stream begins to siphon fuel through the main jet and needle jet. The tapered needle increases the effective flow capacity of the needle jet, as it is lifted with the air slide, in that it occupies decreasingly less of the area of the jet. In addition, the amount of cutaway in the leading edge of the throttle slide aids in controlling the fuel/air mixture during partial throttle openings.

At full throttle, the carburetor venturi is fully open and the needle is lifted far enough to permit the main jet to flow at full capacity.

Service

The carburetor service recommended at 10,000-mile intervals involves routine removal, disassembly, cleaning, and inspection. Alterations in jet size, throttle slide cutaway, changes in needle position, etc., should be attempted only if you are experienced in this type of "tuning" work; a bad guess could result in costly engine damage or, at the very least, poor performance. If after servicing the carburetors and making the adjustments described in Chapter Three, the motorcycle does not perform correctly (and assuming that other factors affecting performance are correct, such as ignition

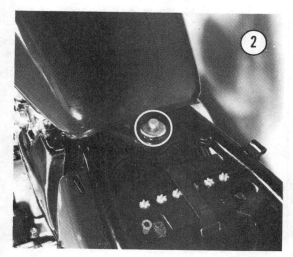

timing and condition, valve adjustment, etc.) the motorcycle should be checked by a Yamaha dealer or a qualified performance tuning specialist.

Removal/Installation

1. Place the bike on the centerstand; remove the right- and left-hand side covers.

2. Hinge up the seat and disconnect the battery negative lead (**Figure 1**).

3. Loosen the inboard hinge nuts. Pivot the hinge pin retainers up and remove the hinge pins. Remove the seat.

4. Remove the rear bolt (**Figure 2**) securing the fuel tank.

5. Turn both fuel shutoff valves to the ON or RES position, lift up on the rear of the tank and remove the fuel lines to the carburetors and vacuum lines to the intake manifolds (**Figure 3**).

6. Pull the tank to the rear and remove it.

7. Remove the clutch cable from the holding bracket on the left-hand carburetor.

8. Loosen the clamping screws on the front rubber intake manifolds (A, **Figure 4**) and slide the clamps away from the carburetors.

9. Loosen the clamping screws on the rear rubber boots (B, **Figure 4**).

10. Remove the chrome trim panels on the air box. Remove the 4 bolts (**Figure 5**) securing the air cleaner box to the frame and push it to the rear.

11. Pull the carburetor assembly back to the rear to disengage it from the intake manifolds.

12. Pull the carburetor assembly to the left (**Figure 6**).

13. Remove the throttle cable (**Figure 7**) and remove the carburetor assembly.

14. Install by reversing these removal steps.

Disassembly/Assembly

Refer to **Figure 8** for this procedure.

It is recommended that only one carburetor

CARBURETOR ASSEMBLY

1. Spacer—choke shaft
2. Spring
3. Choke shaft
4. Clip
5. Jet needle
6. O-ring
7. Valve seat assembly
8. Washer
9. Filter
10. Float
11. Float pin
12. Gasket
13. Float bowl
14. Pilot jet
15. Screw
16. Lockwasher
17. Main jet
18. Washer
19. Plug
20. Diaphragm assembly
21. Needle jet
22. Clip—needle jet
23. Plate—needle fttting
24. Diaphragm spring
25. Diaphragm cover
26. Screw
27. Lockwasher
28. Gasket
29. Starter body
30. Starter plunger
31. Plunger spring
32. Washer
33. Plunger cap
34. Plunger cover
35. Bushing
36. Circlip
37. Ring
38. Washer
39. Choke lever
40. Washer
41. Spring
42. Washer
43. Screw
44. Spring
45. Pilot screw
46. Pilot screw cap
47. Nut
48. Washer
49. Spring collar
50. Throttle lever

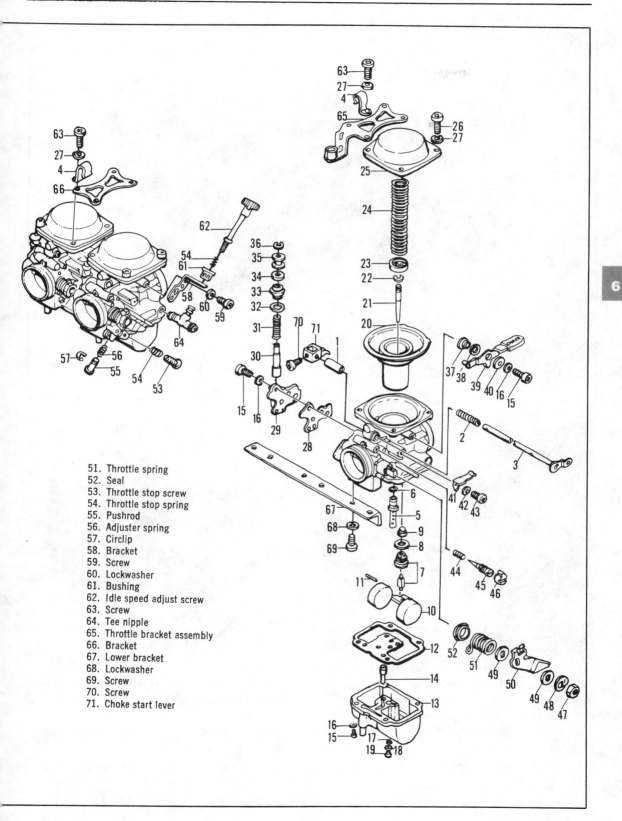

51. Throttle spring
52. Seal
53. Throttle stop screw
54. Throttle stop spring
55. Pushrod
56. Adjuster spring
57. Circlip
58. Bracket
59. Screw
60. Lockwasher
61. Bushing
62. Idle speed adjust screw
63. Screw
64. Tee nipple
65. Throttle bracket assembly
66. Bracket
67. Lower bracket
68. Lockwasher
69. Screw
70. Screw
71. Choke start lever

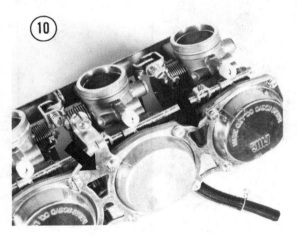

be disassembled and cleaned at one time. This will prevent the intermix of parts.

1. Loosen the 3 setscrews (**Figure 9**) on the choke start shaft and remove the shaft from all three carburetors.

> NOTE: *Do not lose the 2 small steel positioning balls on the 2 outer carburetors when the shaft is removed.*

2. Remove the upper (**Figure 10**) and lower (**Figure 11**) assembly brackets and separate the carburetors.

3. Remove the plug (A, **Figure 12**) and washer. Remove the main jet.

4. Remove the 4 screws (B, **Figure 12**) securing the float bowl to the main body and remove it.

5. Remove the starter jet (**Figure 13**).

(12)

(15)

6

(13)

(16)

(14)

6. Remove the float pin (A, **Figure 14**).

> NOTE: *On some later models, the pin is wedged in place. Do not remove it unless the float has to be removed.*

8. Remove the 4 screws (**Figure 15**) securing the diaphragm cover and remove it and any brackets.

7. Lift out the float assembly. Do not lose the float valve needle located under the float adjustment tang (B, **Figure 14**).

9. Remove the diaphragm spring (**Figure 16**) and the needle jet (A, **Figure 17**).

10. Carefully remove diaphragm (**Figure 18**).

> NOTE: *The idle mixture (**Figure 19**) is pre-set at the factory with the use of special equipment. **It must not be reset.** If it has been tampered with, the setting is approximately 2¼ turns out from a lightly seated position. After resetting, the carburetors should be checked by a Yamaha dealer so they will be within the required emission standards.*

11. Clean all parts, except rubber or plastic parts, in a good grade of carburetor cleaner. Follow the manufacturer's instructions for correct soaking time (usually about ½ hour).

> NOTE: *It is recommended that one carburetor be cleaned at a time to avoid the interchange of parts.*

12. Remove all parts from the cleaner and blow dry with compressed air. Blow out the jets with compressed air. *Do not* use a piece of wire to clean them as minor gouges in a jet can alter the flow rate and upset the fuel/air mixture.

13. Repeat Steps 3-11 for the other two carburetors. Do not intermix the parts — keep them separated.

14. Prior to assembly, check the float height as described under *Float Height Adjustment* in this chapter.

15. Assemble by reversing these disassembly steps. Be sure to position the tab on the diaphragm (B, **Figure 17**) correctly into the recess in the carburetor body.

16. Make sure the 3 setscrews (**Figure 9**) seat properly into the detents in the choke start shaft.

Float Adjustment

The carburetor assembly has to be removed and partially disassembled for this adjustment.

1. Remove carburetor assembly as described under *Carburetor Removal/Installation* in this chapter.

2. Remove lower bracket assembly (**Figure 11**) only. It is not necessary to remove the upper ones.

3. Remove the float bowl (**Figure 12**) from the main body.

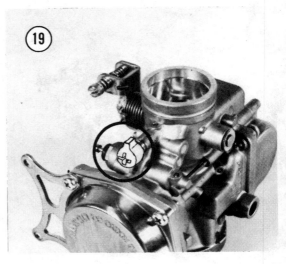

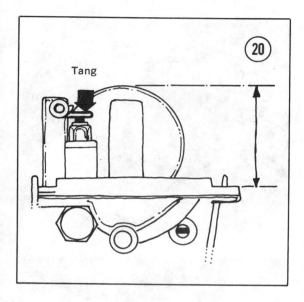

Tang

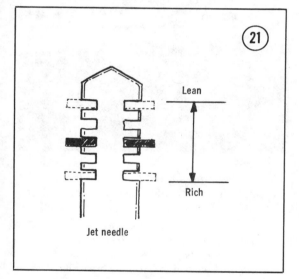

Lean

Rich

Jet needle

4. Turn the carburetor assembly upside down.

5. Measure the distance from the bottom of the float to the float bowl gasket surface (without a gasket in place). See **Figure 20**. The correct height is as follows:
   a. Model D, 2D — 1.047 ± 0.04 in. (26.6 ± 1.0mm)
   b. Model E, F, SE, SF—1.012 +/-0.04 in. (25.7+/-1.0mm)

6. Adjust by carefully bending the tang on the float arm (**Figure 20**).

> NOTE: *Both floats within the same carburetor must be at the same height.*

> CAUTION
> *The floats in all 3 carburetors must be adjusted to exactly the same height to maintain the same fuel/air mixture to all 3 cylinders.*

7. If the float level is set too high, the result will be a rich fuel/air mixture. If it is set too low, the mixture will be too lean.

8. Reassemble and install the carburetors by reversing these steps.

Needle Jet Adjustment

Needle position can be adjusted to affect the fuel/air mixture for medium throttle openings.

The carburetor assembly will have to be removed and partially disassembled for this adjustment.

1. Remove the carburetors as described under *Carburetor Removal/Installation* in this chapter.

2. Remove the upper brackets (**Figure 10**) and remove the diaphragm covers (**Figure 15**).

3. Remove the diaphragm spring (**Figure 16**) and the needle jet (**Figure 17**).

4. Note the original position of the needle clip (**Figure 21**). The standard setting is in the middle. Raising the needle (lowering the clip) will enrich the mixture during mid-throttle opening, while lowering it (raising the needle clip) will lean the mixture.

> CAUTION
> *Needle jet setting must be the same for all 3 carburetors.*

5. Reassemble and install the carburetors by reversing these steps.

FUEL SHUTOFF VALVE

Removal/Installation

Refer to *Fuel Shutoff Valve/Filter Removal/Installation* in Chapter Three.

FUEL TANK

Removal/Installation

1. Place the bike on the centerstand.

2. Hinge up the seat and disconnect the battery negative lead (**Figure 22**).

3. Remove the rear bolt **(Figure 23)** securing the fuel tank.

4. Turn both fuel shutoff valves to the ON or RES position. Lift up on the rear of the tank and remove the fuel lines to the carburetors and vacuum lines to intake manifolds **(Figure 24)**.

5. Pull the tank to the rear and remove it.

6. Install by reversing these removal steps.

Sealing (Pin Hole Size)

A small pin hole size leak can be sealed with the use of a product called Thextonite Gas Tank Sealer Stick or equivalent. Follow the manufacturer's instructions.

Sealing (Small Hole Size)

This procedure requires the use of a non-petroleum based solvent.

If you feel unqualified to accomplish it, take the tank to your dealer and let him seal the tank.

WARNING
Before attempting any service on the fuel tank, be sure to have a fire extinguisher rated for gasoline or chemical fires within reach. Do not smoke or work where there are any open flames. The work area must be well-ventilated.

1. Remove the tank as described under *Fuel Tank Removal/Installation* in this chapter.

2. Mark the spot on the tank where the leak is visible with a grease pencil.

3. Turn both fuel shutoff valves to the PRIME position and completely drain the tank. Blow the interior of the tank completely dry with compressed air.

4. Turn both fuel shutoff valves to the RESERVE position and pour about one quart (one liter) of non-petroleum based solvent into

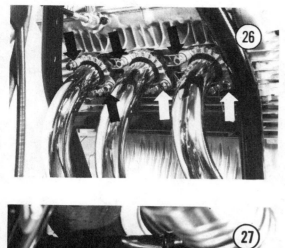

the tank, install the fuel fill cap and shake the tank vigorously one or two minutes. This is used to remove all fuel residue.

5. Drain the solution into a safe storable container. This solution may be reused.

6. Remove both fuel shutoff valves by unscrewing the fittings from the tank. If necessary, plug the tank with corks or tape it closed with duct tape.

7. Again blow the tank interior completely dry with compressed air.

8. Position the tank so that the point of the leak is located at the lowest part of the tank. This will allow the sealant to accumulate at the point of the leak.

9. Pour the sealant into the tank (a silicone rubber base sealer like Pro-Tech Fuel Tank Sealer, or equivalent, may be used). This is available at most motorcycle supply stores.

10. Let the tank set in this position for at least 48 hours.

11. After the sealant has dried, install the fuel shutoff valves, turn them to the RESERVE or ON position and refill the tank with fuel.

12. After the tank has been filled, let it sit for at least 2 hours and recheck the leak area.

13. Install the tank on the motorcycle.

EXHAUST SYSTEM

The exhaust system consists of three exhaust pipes, a crossover pipe, and two mufflers.

Removal/Installation

1. Place the bike on the centerstand.

2. Loosen the Allen bolt **(Figure 25)** securing the clamp on the crossover pipe.

3. Remove the 6 Allen bolts **(Figure 26)** securing the exhaust pipe flanges to the cylinder head.

4. Remove the 2 bolts **(Figure 27)** securing each muffler to the frame.

5. Separate the exhaust pipes at the crossover joint. Pull the exhaust pipes forward to clear them from the cylinder head studs and remove.

6. Install by reversing these removal steps. Make sure all gaskets are in place and are in good condition.

6

NOTE: If you own a 1980 or later model, first check the Supplement at the back of the book for any new service information.

CHAPTER SEVEN

ELECTRICAL SYSTEM

The electrical system includes the following systems (each is described in detail in this chapter):

a. Charging system
b. Ignition system
c. Lighting system
d. Directional signals
e. Horn

WIRING DIAGRAMS

Full color wiring diagrams are located at the end of this book.

CHARGING SYSTEM

The charging system consists of the battery, alternator and voltage regulator/rectifier. **Figure 1** is for Model D only, as it uses a mechanical contact point type voltage regulator. **Figure 2** (Models 2D, E, F, SE and SF) shows the solid state type non-adjustable voltage regulator.

The alternator generates an alternating current (AC) which the rectifier converts to direct current (DC). The regulator maintains the voltage to the battery and load (lights, ignition, etc.) at a constant voltage regardless of variations in engine speed and load.

Testing Charging System

Whenever a charging system trouble is suspected, make sure the battery is good before going any further. Clean and test the battery as described under *Battery Testing* in Chapter Three.

To test the charging system, disconnect the voltage regulator/rectifier black electrical wire, connect a 0-15 DC voltmeter and a 0-10 DC ammeter as shown in **Figure 3**. Connect the ammeter in series to the positive battery terminal. Connect the positive voltmeter terminal to the positive battery terminal and negative voltmeter terminal to ground.

> CAUTION
> *Since the ammeter is connected between the positive battery terminal and the starter cable, the ammeter will burn out if the electric starter is used. Use the kickstarter only.*

Start the engine with the kickstarter and run at 2,000 rpm. Minimum charging current should be 5 amperes. Voltmeter should read 14.5 volts.

All of the measurements are made with lights on high beam. If charging current is considerably lower than specified, check the alternator and voltage regulator/rectifier. It is less

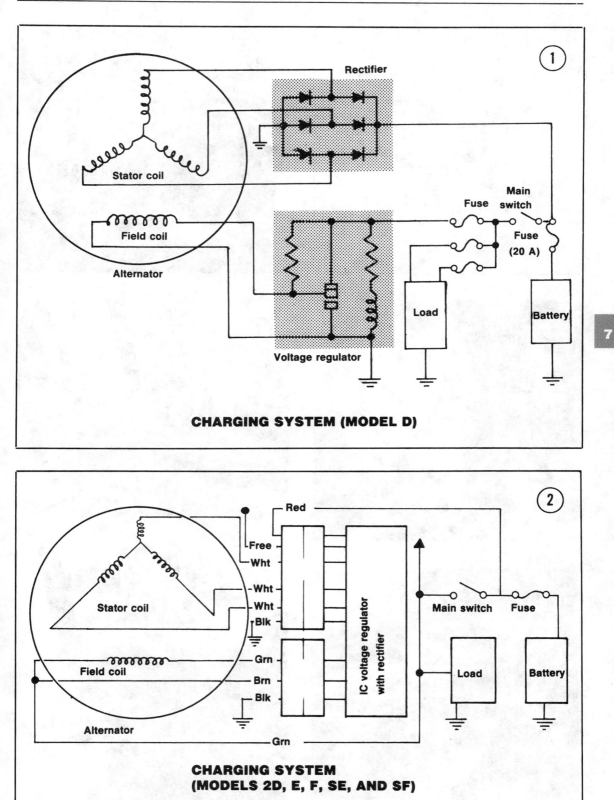

CHARGING SYSTEM (MODEL D)

**CHARGING SYSTEM
(MODELS 2D, E, F, SE, AND SF)**

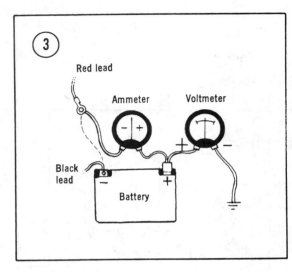

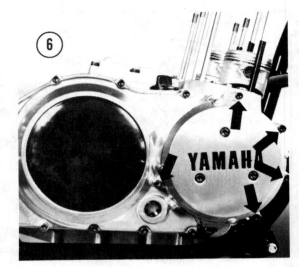

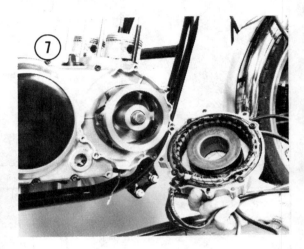

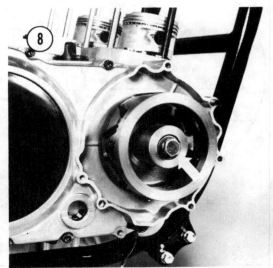

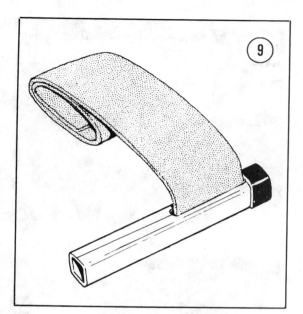

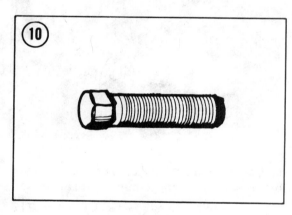

likely that the charging current is too high; in that case, the regulator is probably at fault.

Test the separate charging system components as described under the appropriate heading in the following sections.

Battery Care, Inspection, and Testing

For complete battery information refer to *Battery* in Chapter Three.

ALTERNATOR

An alternator is a form of electrical generator in which a magnetized field called a rotor revolves within a set of stationary coils called a stator. As the rotor revolves, alternating current is induced in the stator. The current is then rectified and used to operate the electrical accessories on the motorcycle and for charging the battery.

Removal/Installation

This procedure is shown with the cylinder and cylinder head removed. It is not necessary to remove them.

1. Remove the exhaust system as described under *Exhaust System Removal/Installation* in Chapter Six.

2. Loosen the bolt securing the kickstarter arm (**Figure 4**) to the shaft and remove the arm.

3. Loosen the 3 bolts and straps (A, **Figure 5**) securing the alternator electrical cable to the crankcase. Disconnect the oil pressure sending switch electrical wire (B, **Figure 5**).

4. Disconnect the electrical connectors from the alternator to their related components.

5. Remove the 5 Allen bolts (**Figure 6**) securing the alternator cover/coil assembly and remove it (**Figure 7**).

6. Remove the bolt (**Figure 8**) securing the rotor.

> NOTE: *If necessary, use a strap wrench (Figure 9) to keep the rotor from turning while removing the bolt.*

7. Screw in a flywheel puller (**Figure 10**) until it stops. Use a wrench on the puller (**Figure 11**)

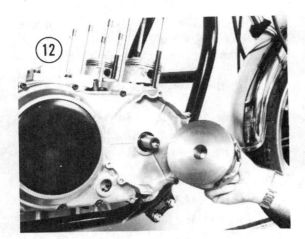

and tap on the end of it with your hand or a plastic mallet until the rotor disengages. Remove the puller and the rotor (**Figure 12**).

8. Install by reversing the removal steps. Secure the rotor bolt to 25 ft.-lb. (34 N•m) using a torque and strap wrench (**Figure 13**).

Stator and Rotor Testing

1. Remove the left-hand side cover (**Figure 14**).

2. Disconnect the stator electrical leads (**Figure 15**). The field coil connector contains 2 wires — 1 green and 1 black (A, **Figure 16**). The stator connector contains 3 wires — all 3 are white (B, **Figure 16**).

3. Remove the alternator as described under *Alternator Removal/Installation* in this chapter.

4. Visually inspect the stator (**Figure 17**) for signs of damage to the coils and electrical wires leading to it.

5. Use an ohmmeter and measure the resistance between the following terminals. See **Figure 18**.

   a. Field coil terminals — black to green. The value should be 4.04 ohms ± 10% at 70°F (21°C).

   b. Stator coil terminals — W1-W2, W2-W3, and W3-W1. The value should be 0.48 ohms ± 10% at 70°F (21°C).

6. If the values are not within the specified range, check the electrical wires to and within the terminal connectors. If they are OK, then there is an open or short in the coils and the stator or rotor must be replaced.

VOLTAGE REGULATOR (MODEL D)

Testing

Varying engine speeds and electrical system loads affect alternator output. The voltage regulator controls alternator output by varying

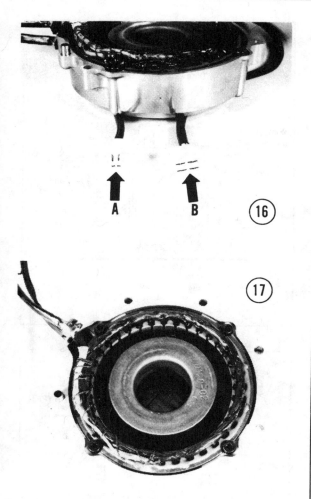

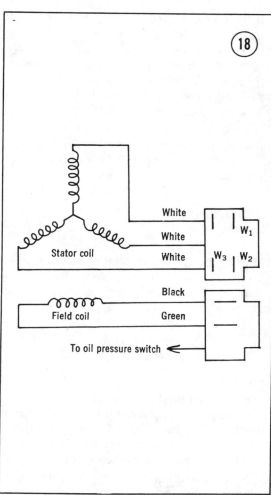

its field current. Before making any voltage regulator test, be sure that the battery is in good condition, and is at or near full charge.

1. Remove the left-hand side cover (**Figure 14**).

2. Disconnect electrical connector (**Figure 15**) containing 5 wires — 3 white, 1 red, and 1 black. Remove the red wire from the connector and connect the positive (+) lead of the 20V DC voltmeter to this red wire from the rectifier. Connect the negative (−) lead of the voltmeter to a good ground.

3. Start the engine — the reading should be 14.5-15V (DC). If the voltage fluctuates by more than 0.5V, the regulator needs adjustment.

CAUTION
Do not short the red wire as it will damage the rectifier.

Adjustment

1. Disconnect the negative battery lead from the battery.

2. Remove the left-hand side cover (**Figure 14**).

3. Disconnect electrical connector (**Figure 15**) containing 5 wires—3 white, 1 red and 1 black.

4. Remove the voltage regulator from the bike and remove the cover from it.

5. Check the condition of the breaker points. If rough, smooth them with a few strokes of a clean point file or Flexstone (available at most auto parts stores). Do not use emery cloth or sandpaper, as particles remain on the points and cause arcing and burning. If a few strokes of the file do not smooth the points completely, replace the regulator.

If the points are still serviceable after filing, remove all residue with a commercially available contact point cleaner or lacquer thinner. Close the points on a piece of clean white paper such as a business card. Continue to pull the card through the closed points until no particles or discoloration are transferred to the card.

6. Check the points and core gap (**Figure 19**) and adjust if necessary. The correct setting is — point gap 0.012-0.016 in. (0.3-0.4mm) and core gap 0.024-0.40 in. (0.6-1.0mm).

NOTE: *The yoke gap does not require adjustment.*

7. Install the voltage regulator, electrical connections, and battery cable. Repeat the test procedure. If voltage is still incorrect, replace the regulator.

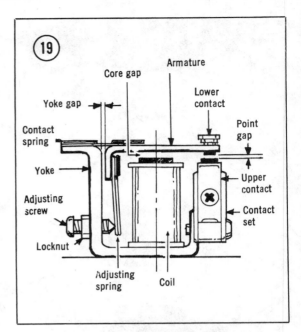

RECTIFIER
(MODEL D)

Testing

The rectifier (**Figure 20**) converts three-phase alternating current produced by the alternator into direct current, which is used to operate electrical accessories and to charge the battery.

To test the rectifier, proceed as follows:

1. Disconnect the negative battery cable from the battery.

2. Remove the right-hand side cover.

3. Disconnect the rectifier terminal connector (**Figure 16**).

4. Measure resistance between each of the following pairs of terminals with an ohmmeter. Record each of the measurements.

   a. B and U
   b. B and V
   c. B and W
   d. U and E
   e. V and E
   f. W and E

5. Reverse ohmmeter leads, the repeat Step 4. Each set of measurements must be high with the ohmmeter connected one way, and low with the ohmmeter leads reversed. It is not possible to specify exact meter indications, but each set of

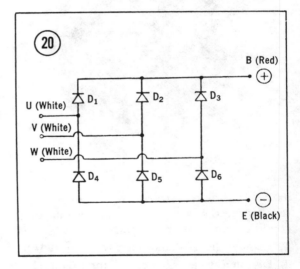

measurements should differ by a factor of not less than 10.

VOLTAGE REGULATOR/RECTIFIER
(MODELS 2D, E, F, SE AND SF)

Voltage Regulator Testing

Refer to **Figure 21** for this test procedure.

1. Remove the left-hand side cover.

2. Tests are made on the electrical connector (**Figure 22**) containing 3 wires — 1 green, 1 black, and 1 brown.

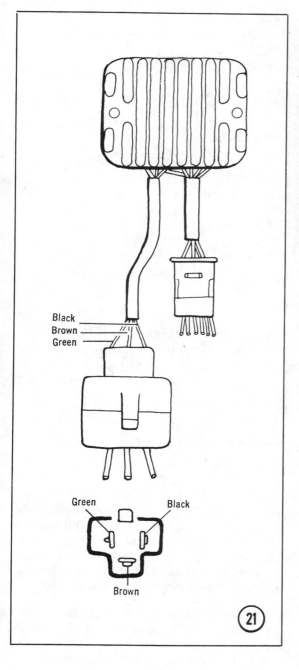

Black
Brown
Green

Green   Black

Brown

㉑

CAUTION

Do not short-circuit the voltage regulator when connecting the test leads or it will be damaged.

3. Turn the ignition switch to the ON position. Connect a 20V DC voltmeter — negative (−) lead to black and the positive (+) lead to green. The voltage should be less than 1.8 volts.

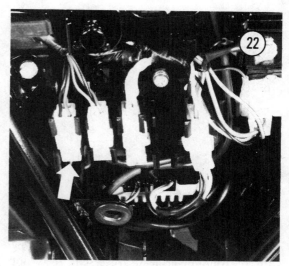

NOTE: *Do not turn on the headlight or turn signals.*

4. Start the engine and recheck. This reading should gradually increase up to 9-11 volts when the engine is started and as rpm increases.

5. Connect the voltmeter — negative (−) lead to black and positive (+) to brown. The voltage should be 14.2-14.8 volts with the engine running and should remain there as engine rpm is increased.

6. If the voltage specified in Steps 3 and 4 are not met in these tests, the voltage regulator/rectifier must be replaced. It cannot be serviced.

Rectifier Testing

Refer to **Figure 23** for this test procedure.

1. Disconnect the battery negative cable from the battery.

2. Remove the right-hand cover.

3. Disconnect the voltage regulator/rectifier terminal connectors (**Figure 22**). One connector contains 5 wires — 3 white, 1 black, and 1 red. The other connector contains 3 wires — 1 brown, 1 green, and 1 black.

CAUTION

If the rectifier is subjected to overcharging it can be damaged. Be careful not to short-circuit it or incorrectly connect the battery positive and negative leads. Never directly connect the rectifier to the battery for a continuity check.

4. Measure the resistance between each of the following terminals with an ohmmeter. Record each of the measurements.

   a. B_1 and U

   b. B_1 and V

   c. B_1 and W

   d. B_1 and B_2

   e. U and G_1

   f. V and G_1

   g. W and G_1

   h. B and G_1

5. Reverse the ohmmeter leads, then repeat Step 4. Each set of measurements must be high with the ohmmeter connected one way, and low with the ohmmeter leads reversed. It is not possible to specify exact ohmmeter readings, but each set of measurements should differ by a factor of not less than 10.

6. Even if only one of the elements is defective, the entire unit must be replaced; it cannot be serviced.

Voltage Regulator Performance Test

Connect a voltmeter to the battery terminals. Start the engine and let it idle; increase engine speed until the voltage going to the battery reaches 14.0-15.0 volts. At this point, the voltage regulator must prevent further voltage increase. If this does not happen, the voltage regulator/rectifier must be replaced.

IGNITION SYSTEM (CONTACT BREAKER POINT TYPE)

Figure 24 is a diagram of the ignition circuit on Models D and 2D.

When the breaker points are closed, current flows from the battery through the primary winding of the ignition coil, thereby building a magnetic field around the coil. The breaker cam rotates and is so adjusted that the breaker points open as the piston reaches the firing position.

As the points open, the magnetic field collapses. When this occurs, a very high voltage is induced (up to approximately 15,000 volts) in the secondary winding of the ignition coil. This high voltage is sufficient to jump the gap at the spark plug causing the plug to fire.

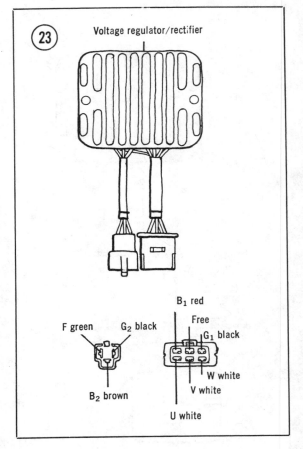

Voltage regulator/rectifier

B_1 red

Free

F green G_2 black G_1 black

W white

V white

B_2 brown

U white

Condenser

The condenser assists the coil in developing high voltage, and also serves to protect the points. Inductance of the ignition coil primary winding tends to keep a surge of current flowing through the circuit even after the points have started to open. The condenser stores this surge and thus prevents arcing at the points.

The condenser is a sealed unit that requires no maintenance. Be sure that all connections are clean and tight.

Two tests can be made on the condenser. Measure condenser capacity with a condenser tester. Capacity should be about 0.24 microfarad. The other test is insulation resistance, which should not be less than 5 megohms, measured between the condenser pigtail and case.

In the event that no test equipment is available, a quick test of the condenser may be

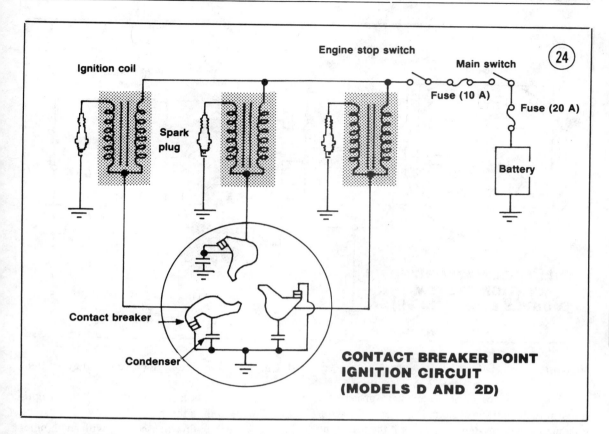

Engine stop switch

Main switch

(24)

Ignition coil

Fuse (10 A)

Fuse (20 A)

Spark plug

Battery

Contact breaker →

Condenser

CONTACT BREAKER POINT IGNITION CIRCUIT (MODELS D AND 2D)

7

made by connecting the condenser case to the negative terminal of a 12-volt battery, and the positive lead to the positive battery terminal. Allow the condenser to charge for a few seconds, then quickly disconnect the battery and touch the condenser pigtail to the condenser case. If you observe a spark as the pigtail touches the case, you may assume that the condenser is good.

Service

Two major service items are required on breaker point ignition models: breaker point service and ignition timing. Both are vitally important to proper engine operation and reliability. Refer to Chapter Three for breaker point service and ignition timing procedures.

IGNITION SYSTEM (FULLY TRANSISTORIZED)

Models E, SE, and SF are equipped with a fully transistorized ignition system. This solid state system does not use breaker points. This system provides a longer life for components and delivers a more efficient spark throughout speed range of the engine. Ignition timing is maintained for a long time without periodic adjustment.

Figure 25 is a diagram of the ignition circuit.

When the raised portion on the crankshaft driven rotor passes one of the cylinder pick-up coils, a pulse is generated within the pick-up coil. This pulse (electrical current) flows to the switching and distributing circuits in the ignitor unit. The magnetic field that has built up in the coil, from the battery, is now interrupted by this pulse and causes the field to collapse. When this happens, a very high voltage is induced (up to 15,000 volts) into the secondary windings of that cylinder's ignition coil. This voltage is sufficient to jump the gap at the spark plug of that cylinder, causing the plug to fire. The same sequence of events happens to the other two cylinders and is controlled by the rotation of the driven rotor.

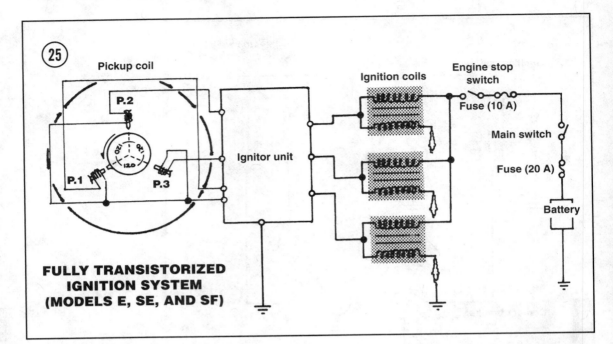

(25)

**FULLY TRANSISTORIZED
IGNITION SYSTEM
(MODELS E, SE, AND SF)**

Precautions

Certain measures must be taken to protect the transistorized ignition system. Damage to the semiconductors in the system may occur if the following precautions are not observed.

1. Never connect the battery backwards. If the battery polarity is wrong, damage will occur to the voltage regulator/rectifier, alternator, and ignitor unit.
2. Do not disconnect the battery when the engine is running. A voltage surge will occur which will damage the voltage regulator/rectifier and possibly burn out the lights.
3. Keep all connections between the various units clean and tight. Be sure that the wiring connectors are pushed together firmly.
4. Do not substitute another type of ignition coil(s) or battery.
5. Each unit is mounted with a rubber vibration isolator. Always be sure that the isolators are in place when replacing any units.

Troubleshooting

Problems with the transistorized ignition system are usually production of a weak spark or no spark at all.

1. Check all connections to make sure they are tight and free of corrosion.
2. Check the ignition coils as described under *Ignition Coil Testing* in this chapter.
3. Check the pick-up coil assembly with an ohmmeter. The coil resistance should be 560 ohms ± 20% at 70°F (21°C).
4. If the ignition coil and pick-up coil check out OK, the ignitor unit is at fault and must be replaced. It cannot be serviced.

Ignitor Unit Replacement

1. Hinge up the seat and disconnect the negative battery lead from the battery.
2. Remove the right-hand side panel.
3. Disconnect the 2 electrical connectors (A, **Figure 26**).
4. Remove attachment screws (B, **Figure 26**) and remove the unit.
5. Install by reversing these removal steps.

Ignitor Unit Testing

Tests may be performed on the unit but a good one may be damaged by someone unfamiliar with test equipment. To play it safe, have the tests performed by your Yamaha

dealer or substitute a unit suspected to be bad with one that is known to be good.

IGNITION COIL

Removal/Installation

Each cylinder has its individual coil.

1. Hinge up the seat and disconnect the battery negative lead from the battery.

2. Remove the rear bolt (**Figure 27**) securing the fuel tank.

3. Turn both fuel shutoff valves to the ON or RES position, lift up on the rear of the tank and remove the fuel lines to the carburetors and vacuum lines to intake manifolds (**Figure 28**).

4. Pull the tank to the rear and remove it.

5. Disconnect the spark plug lead and the primary electrical wires (A, **Figure 29**) from each coil.

6. Remove the 2 nuts and lockwashers (B, **Figure 29**) securing each coil to the frame and remove them.

7. Install by reversing these removal steps. Make sure to correctly connect the primary electrical wires to the correct coils and the spark plug leads to the correct spark plug. Refer to the elctrical schematics at the end of this book.

Testing

The ignition coil is a form of transformer which develops the high voltage required to

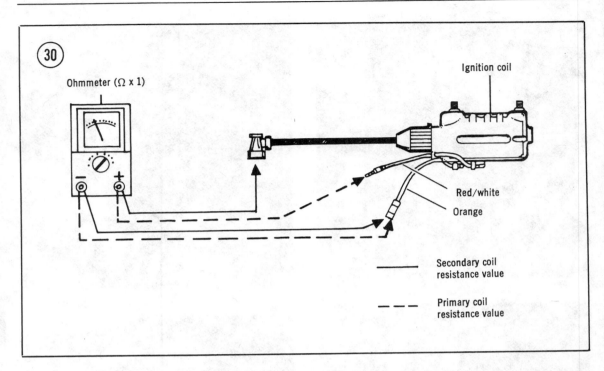

(30)

Ohmmeter (Ω x 1)

Ignition coil

Red/white

Orange

———— Secondary coil resistance value

– – – – Primary coil resistance value

jump the spark plug gap. The only maintenance required is that of keeping the electrical connections clean and tight, and occasionally checking to see that the coil is mounted securely.

If coil condition is doubtful, there are several checks which may be made. Disconnect coil wires before testing.

1. Measure coil primary resistance, using an ohmmeter, between both coil primary terminals (**Figure 30**). Resistance should measure approximately: Models D and 2D — 4.0 ohms ± 10% at 70°F (21°C) and Models E, SE, and SF — 2.75 ohms ± 10% at 70°F (21°C).

2. Measure the coil secondary resistance between either primary lead and the high voltage cable. The secondary resistance should be approximately: Models D and 2D—11.0 K ohms ± 10% at 70° F (21° C) and Models E, SE, and SF—7.9 K ohms ±10% at 70° F (21° C).

3. Replace any coil if the spark plug lead exhibits visible damage and/or if they do not test within these specified measurements.

IGNITION ADVANCE MECHANISM

Both ignition systems use the same type of ignition advance mechanism. It must be inspected periodically to make certain it operates freely.

1. Remove the ignition governor assembly as described under *Ignition Governor Assembly Removal/Installation* in Chapter Four.

2. Inspect the pivot points (A, **Figure 31**) of each weight. It must pivot freely to maintain proper ignition advance. Apply lightweight grease to the pivot pins.

3. Inspect the pivot cam (B, **Figure 31**) operation on the shaft. It must rotate smoothly.

4. Inspect surface of both cams (C, **Figure 31**). If worn, scratched, or pitted, the assembly must be replaced.

SPARK PLUGS

The spark plugs recommended by the factory are usually the most suitable for your machine. If riding conditions are mild, it may be advisable to go to spark plugs one step hotter than normal. Unusually severe riding conditions may require slightly colder plugs. See Chapter Three for details.

STARTING SYSTEM

The starting system consists of the starting motor, starter solenoid, and the starter button.

The layout of the starting system is shown in **Figure 32**. When the starter button is pressed, it

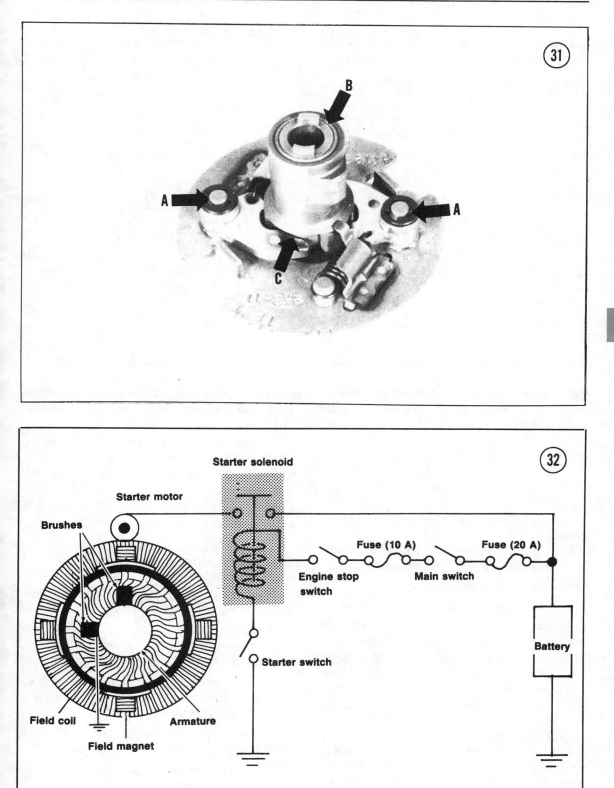

31

32

Starter solenoid

Starter motor

Brushes

Fuse (10 A)   Fuse (20 A)

Engine stop
switch   Main switch

Battery

Starter switch

Field coil   Armature

Field magnet

Table 1   STARTER TROUBLESHOOTING

Symptom	Probable Cause	Remedy
Starter does not work	Low battery Worn brushes Defective relay Defective switch Defective wiring or connection Internal short circuit	Recharge battery Replace brushes Repair or replace Repair or replace Repair wire or clean connection Repair or replace defective component
Starter action is weak	Low battery Pitted relay contacts Worn brushes Defective connection Short circuit in commutator	Recharge battery Clean or replace Replace brushes Clean and tighten Replace armature
Starter runs continuously	Stuck relay	Replace relay
Starter turns: does not turn engine	Defective starter clutch	Replace starter clutch

engages the solenoid switch that closes the circuit. The electricity flows from battery to the starting motor.

CAUTION
Do not operate the starter for more than five seconds at a time. Let it rest for approximately ten seconds, then use it again.

The starter gears and kickstarter are covered in Chapter Four.

Table 1 lists possible starter problems, probable causes, and the most common remedies.

Starter Removal/Installation

1. Turn the ignition switch to the OFF position.

2. Hinge up the seat and disconnect the negative battery lead from battery (**Figure 33**).

3. Remove the lower end of the clutch cable. Loosen the adjustment nut at the clutch lever and remove the cable from it.

4. Pull back the rubber protective flap on the lower end of the clutch cable and lift up on the clutch cable retaining clip (**Figure 34**).

5. Remove the cable from the actuating mechanism link arm (A, **Figure 35**). Pull the cable out from the sleeve leading into the activating mechanism (B, **Figure 35**).

6. Remove carburetor assembly as described under *Carburetor Removal/Installation* in Chapter Six.

7. Remove the 2 Allen bolts (**Figure 36**) securing the motor cover and remove it.

8. Remove the electrical wire (A, **Figure 37**) from the motor.

9. Remove the 2 Allen bolts (B, **Figure 37**) securing the starting motor.

NOTE: *Figures 36 and 37 are shown with the engine partially disassembled for clarity only.*

10. Pull the motor to the right and carefully disengage the gears and remove it.

11. Install by reversing these removal steps. Adjust the clutch (Chapter Three).

Starter Disassembly/Assembly

The overhaul of a starter motor is best left to an expert. This section shows how to determine if the unit is defective.

1. Remove the starter motor case screws and separate the case.

NOTE: *Write down how many thrust washers are used and install the same number when reassembling the starter.*

2. Clean all grease, dirt, and carbon dust from the armature, case, and end covers.

CAUTION

Do not immerse brushes or the wire windings in solvent or the insulation might be damaged. Wipe the windings with a cloth lightly moistened with solvent and dry thoroughly.

3. Remove the brushes and use a vernier caliper (**Figure 38**) to measure the length of the brush. If it is worn to less than 0.21 in. (5.5 mm). it should be replaced.

4. Inspect the condition of the commutator (**Figure 39**). The mica in the normal commutator is cut below the copper. A worn

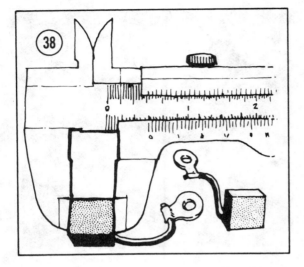

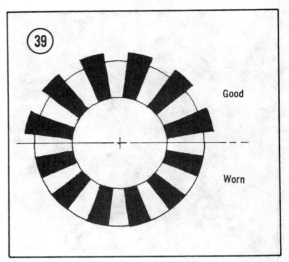

Good

Worn

commutator is also shown: the copper is worn to the level of the mica. A worn commutator can be undercut, but it requires a specialist. Take the job to your Yamaha dealer or motorcycle electrical repair shop.

5. Inspect the commutator bars for discoloration. If a pair of bars are discolored, that indicates grounded armature coils.

6. Check the electrical continuity between pairs of armature bars and between the commutator bars and the shaft mounting. If there is a short, the armature should be replaced.

7. Inspect the field coil by checking continuity from the cable terminal to the motor case. Also check from the cable terminal to the brush wire. If there is a short or open, the case should be replaced.

8. Assemble the case together; make sure that the punch marks on the case and covers align (**Figure 40**).

9. Inspect condition of the gears (**Figure 41**). If they are chipped or worn, remove the circlip and replace the gear.

10. Inspect the front and rear cover bearings for damage. Replace the starter if they are worn or damaged.

Starter Solenoid
Removal/Installation

1. Turn the ignition switch to the OFF position.

2. Remove the right-hand side cover.

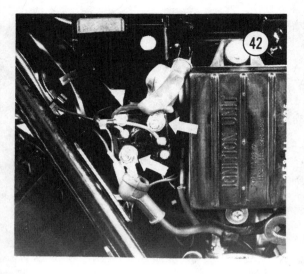

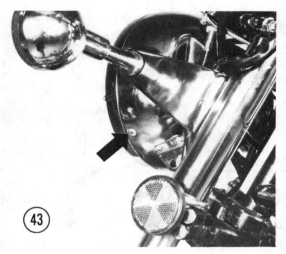

Table 2   REPLACEMENT BULBS

Item	Wattage	Candlepower
Headlight		
Models D, 2D, E, F		
and SE	40/50	—
Model SF	55/60	—
Tail/brakelight	8/27	3/32
Directional lights	27	32
Instrument lights	3.4	2
Meter light	3.4	2

3. Slide off the rubber protective boots and disconnect the 2 electrical wires from the large terminals (**Figure 42**).

4. Remove the solenoid from the frame along with the 2 smaller electrical wires that are attached to it.

5. Install by reversing these removal steps.

LIGHTING SYSTEM

The lighting system consists of the headlight, taillight/brakelight combination, directional signals, warning lights, and speedometer and tachometer illumination lights. **Table 2** lists replacement bulbs for these components.

The headlight circuit is equipped with a reserve lighting system that automatically switches the current from the burned out headlight filament to the reserve filament. It also notifies the rider that one filament is burned out by an indicator light on the instrument cluster.

Headlight Replacement

1. Remove the 2 mounting screws (**Figure 43**) on each side of the headlight housing.

2. Pull the trim bezel and headlight unit out and disconnect the electrical connector from the backside.

3. Remove the 2 screws (**Figure 44**) securing the inner ring and remove it. Remove the sealed beam unit.

4. Install by reversing these removal steps.

5. Adjust the headlight as described under *Headlight Adjustment* in this chapter.

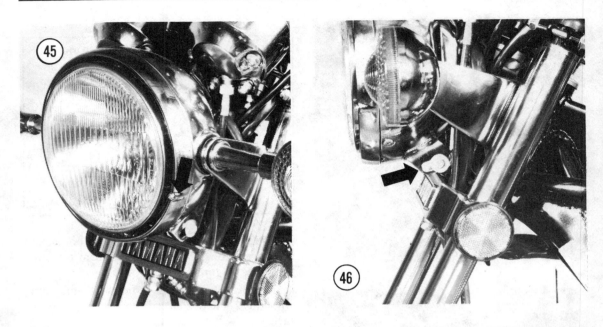

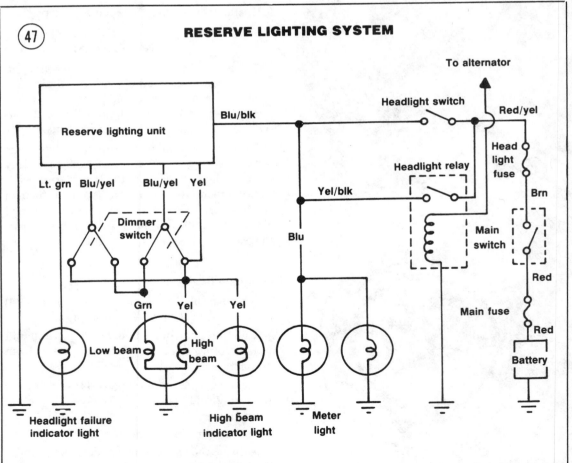

RESERVE LIGHTING SYSTEM

To alternator

Reserve lighting unit

Blu/blk

Headlight switch

Red/yel

Head light fuse

Headlight relay

Yel/blk

Brn

Main switch

Lt. grn   Blu/yel   Blu/yel   Yel

Red

Dimmer switch

Main fuse

Red

Blu

Grn   Yel   Yel

Low beam   High beam

Battery

Headlight failure indicator light

High beam indicator light

Meter light

NOTE: *This system relates to the headlight only, not to any of the other lights on the bike.*

1. Hinge up the seat and disconnect the battery negative lead from the battery.

2. Remove the rear bolt securing the fuel tank.

3. Turn the fuel shutoff valves to the ON or RES position. Lift up on the rear of the tank and remove the fuel lines to the carburetors and vacuum lines to intake manifolds (**Figure 48**).

4. Pull the tank to the rear and remove it.

5. Disconnect the electrical connectors to the reserve lighting unit (**Figure 49**) and remove it from the frame.

6. Install by reversing these removal steps. Make sure all electrical connections are tight.

Taillight Replacement

Remove the screws securing the lens and remove it. Wash out the inside and outside of the lens with a mild detergent and wipe dry. Wipe off the reflective base surrounding the bulb with a soft cloth. Replace the bulbs and install the lens; do not overtighten screws or the lens may crack.

Directional Signal Light Replacement

Remove the two screws securing the lens and remove it. Wash out the inside and outside of it with a mild detergent. Replace the bulb. Install the lens; do not overtighten the screws as that will crack the lens.

Speedometer and Tachometer Illumination Light Replacement

1. Disconnect the drive cable(s) from the chrome housing(s). See A, **Figure 50**.

2. Remove the acorn nuts and washers (B, **Figure 50**), 2 per unit, securing the speedometer or tachometer units into the chrome housings.

3. Pull the unit(s) and rubber ring(s) up and out of the housing(s) and remove it.

4. Replace the defective bulb(s).

Neutral Indicator and High Beam Indicator Light Replacement

Follow procedure for replacement of speedometer and tachometer illumination lights.

Headlight Adjustment

Adjust the headlight horizontally and vertically according to Department of Motor Vehicle regulations in your area.

To adjust headlight horizontally, turn the screw (**Figure 45**). Screwing it in turns the light to the right, and loosening it will turn the light to the left. For vertical adjustment, loosen the bolt (**Figure 46**) under the headlight and move the headlight assembly up or down. After adjustment is correct, be sure to tighten the bolt.

Headlight Reserve Lighting System Removal/Installation

If the reserve lighting unit becomes defective, it must be replaced as it cannot be serviced. **Figure 47** is a diagram of the system.

7

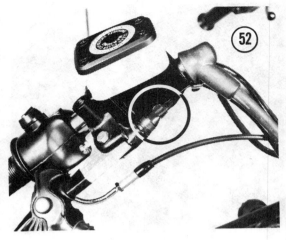

Turn, Oil Pressure, Headlight Failure Indicator Light Replacement

Remove the four screws (**Figure 51**) securing the indicator housing to the mounting bracket and remove it. Replace the defective bulb(s).

Front Brake Light Switch Replacement

Pull back the rubber protective boot on the hand lever. Pull small rubber boot (**Figure 52**) away from the switch and remove the switch. Disconnect the electrical wires and replace the switch.

Rear Brake Light Switch Replacement

1. Unhook spring from brake arm (**Figure 53**).
2. Unscrew the switch housing and locknut from bracket.

3. Pull up the rubber boot and remove the electrical wires.

4. Replace the switch; reinstall and adjust as described under *Rear Brake Light Switch Adjustment* in this chapter.

Rear Brake Light Switch Adjustment

1. Turn the ignition switch to the ON position.
2. Depress the brake pedal. Light should come on just as the brake begins to work.
3. To make the light come on earlier, hold the switch body and turn adjusting locknut *clockwise* as viewed from the top. Turn *counterclockwise* to delay the light.

> NOTE: *Some riders prefer the light to come on a little early. This way, they can tap the pedal without braking to warn drivers who follow too closely.*

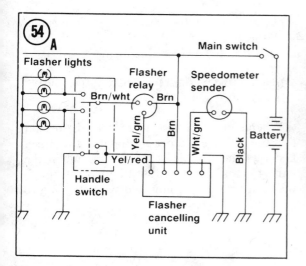

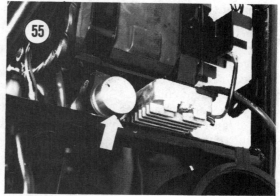

7

on, zero ohms. If this is not the indication, the handlebar switch circuit or wiring is faulty.
5. If the system is still inoperative after the above tests, replace the flasher cancelling unit.
6. If the signal flashes only when the handlebar switch is turned to "left" or "right" and it turns off immediately after the switch lever returns to OFF, replace the flasher cancelling unit.

Flasher Cancelling Unit Replacement

Remove the left-hand side cover and pull out the old unit (**Figure 54B**). Disconnect the electrical wires and transfer them to the new unit. Install the new unit.

Flasher Relay Replacement

The flasher unit is located just behind the engine next to the voltage regulator/rectifier. Pull the old flasher relay (**Figure 55**) out of the rubber mount. Transfer wires to new relay and install the relay in the rubber mount.

NOTE
Figure 55 *is shown with the engine removed for clarity only.*

Horn Removal/Installation

1. Disconnect horn connector from electrical harness.
2. Remove the bolt securing horn to bracket.
3. Installation is the reverse of these steps.

Horn Testing

1. Disconnect horn wires from harness.
2. Connect horn wires to 12-volt battery. If it is good, it will sound.

Self-cancelling Flasher System Testing

Refer to **Figure 54A**. The self-cancelling system switches off the turn signals after either 10 seconds or 142 yards (130 meters), whichever is greater, have elapsed. Test as follows.
1. Remove the left-hand side cover and disconnect the connector from the flasher cancelling unit (**Figure 54B**).
2. Turn on either turn signal. If it operates normally, the flasher unit bulb(s), wiring and switch are okay.
3. Connect an ohmmeter between the white-green and black wires. Rotate the speedometer shaft. If the ohmmeter's needle swings back and forth between zero and infinity, the speedometer's sensor circuit is okay. If not, the sender or wire is faulty.
4. Connect the ohmmeter between the yellow-red wire and ground. With the switch off, resistance should indicate infinity; switch

Instrument Cluster
Removal/Installation

1. Hinge up the seat and disconnect the negative battery lead from the battery.
2. Disconnect all electrical terminals leading to the instrument cluster.
3. Remove the tachometer and speedometer cables (**Figure 56**) from the instrument cluster.
4. Remove the 2 bolts (**Figure 57**) securing the instrument cluster to brackets and remove it.
5. Install by reversing these removal steps.

> *CAUTION*
> *Install the instrument cluster with the attachment bracket below the top fork bridge (**Figure 58**). If it is mounted above, the speedometer and tachometer drive cables will be stretched and damaged when the steering is turned to its limits.*

FUSES

There are four fuses used on the XS750. All are located in the fuse panel located under the seat (**Figure 59**).

The main fuse (20A) is at the top of the panel with the headlight (10A), turn signals (10A) and ignition (10A) fuses below it.

Inside the cover are two spare fuses; always carry spares.

Whenever a fuse blows, find out the reason for the failure before replacing the fuse. Usually, the trouble is a short circuit in the wiring. This may be caused be worn-through insulation or a disconnected wire shorting to ground.

> *CAUTION*
> *Never substitute tinfoil or wire for a fuse. Never use a higher amperage fuse than specified. An overload could result in fire and complete loss of the bike.*

NOTE: If you own a 1980 or later model, first check the Supplement at the back of the book for any new service information.

CHAPTER EIGHT

FRONT SUSPENSION AND STEERING

This chapter describes repair and maintenance of the front wheel, forks, and steering components.

FRONT WHEEL

Refer to **Figure 1** for this procedure.

Removal

1. Place a wooden block under the crankcase to lift the front of the motorcycle off the ground.

2. Remove the setscrew securing the speedometer cable (**Figure 2**) and pull the cable out.

3. Remove the axle nut cotter pin and nut (**Figure 3**). Discard the cotter pin.

NOTE: *Never reuse a cotter pin.*

4. *On Models D, 2D, E and F* remove the 2 nuts securing the front axle holder (**Figure 4**) and remove it.

5. *On Models SE and SF* remove the plastic protective cap and remove the caliper mounting bolt assembly (**Figure 5**) on the left-hand caliper. Remove the caliper from the disc — *do not* remove the brake hose. Tie the caliper up with wire to the lower fork bridge to keep tension off the brake hose.

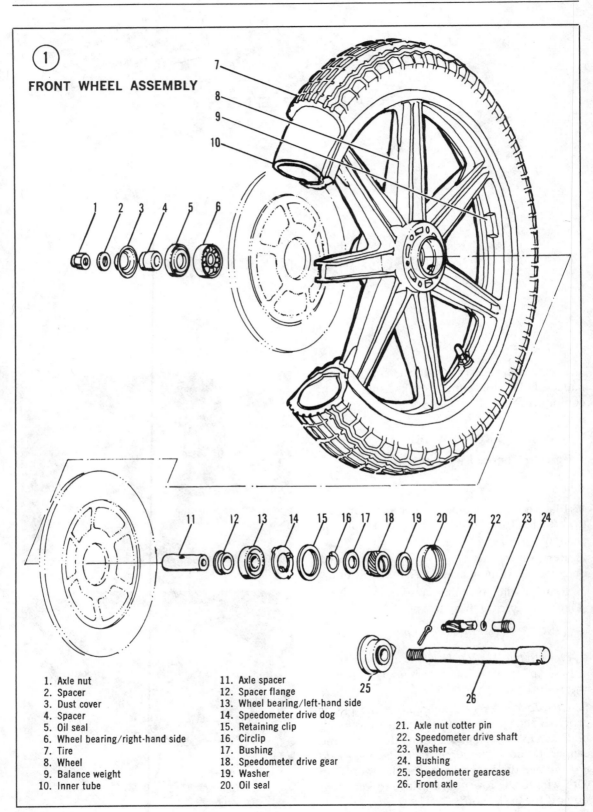

1

FRONT WHEEL ASSEMBLY

1. Axle nut
2. Spacer
3. Dust cover
4. Spacer
5. Oil seal
6. Wheel bearing/right-hand side
7. Tire
8. Wheel
9. Balance weight
10. Inner tube

11. Axle spacer
12. Spacer flange
13. Wheel bearing/left-hand side
14. Speedometer drive dog
15. Retaining clip
16. Circlip
17. Bushing
18. Speedometer drive gear
19. Washer
20. Oil seal

21. Axle nut cotter pin
22. Speedometer drive shaft
23. Washer
24. Bushing
25. Speedometer gearcase
26. Front axle

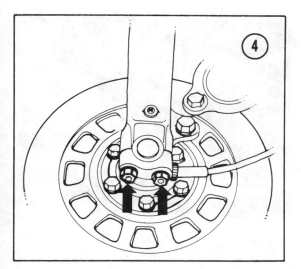

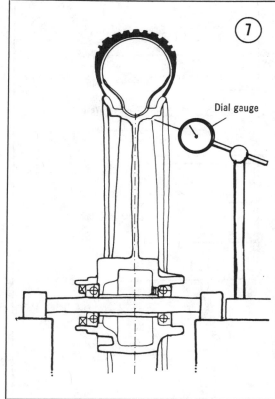

6. *On Models SE and SF* loosen the axle pinch bolt **(Figure 6)**.

7. Push the axle out with a drift or screwdriver and remove it.

8. Remove the wheel; pull the wheel forward to disengage the disc from the right-hand caliper.

> NOTE: *Insert a piece of wood in both calipers in place of the discs. That way, if the brake lever is inadvertently squeezed, the piston will not be forced out of the cylinder. If this does happen, the caliper might have to be disassembled to reseat the piston and the system will have to be bled. By using the wood, bleeding the brake is not necessary when installing the wheel.*

Inspection

Measure the lateral and vertical runout of the wheel rim with a dial indicator as shown in **Figure 7**. The maximum lateral runout is 0.04 in. (1mm) and the maximum vertical runout is 0.08 in. (2mm). If the runout exceeds these

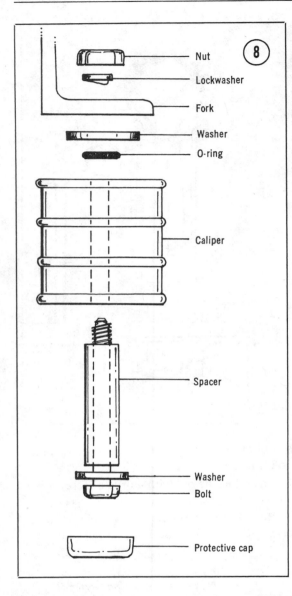

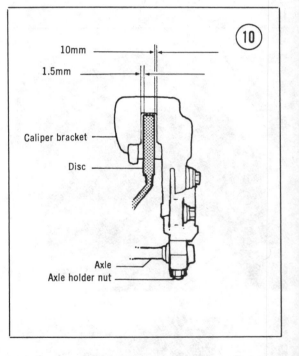

dimensions, check the wheel bearing condition and/or replace the wheel. The stock Yamaha aluminum wheel cannot be serviced, but must be replaced.

Installation

1. *Carefully* insert the disc between the pads when installing the wheel.

2. Make sure the locating slot in the speedometer gear case is aligned with the boss on the fork tube.

3. Insert the axle and install the axle nut, but do not tighten it at this time.

4. *On Models SE and SF* install the left-hand brake caliper assembly.

> NOTE: *Install the caliper mounting bolt assembly in the order shown in* **Figure 8**. *Install the plastic protective cap. Torque the bolt to 25 ft.-lb. (34 N•m).*

> NOTE: *Make sure the locating lug on the front fork (***Figure 9***) is positioned correctly into the caliper.*

5. *On Models D, 2D, E and F.* Install the axle holder, washers, and self-locking nuts; do not tighten the nuts at this time. Tighten the axle

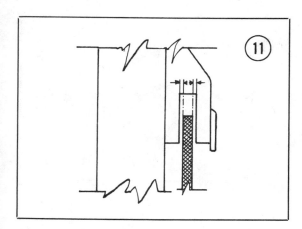

nut on Model D to 61 ft.-lb. (82 N•m and on Models 2D and E to 76 ft.-lb. (103 N•m). Install a new cotter pin. Move the left-hand fork leg in and out sideways until the correct clearance between the disc and caliper bracket are obtained. See **Figure 10** for details. Tighten the axle holder nuts to 16 ft.-lb. (22 N•m).

NOTE: *Tighten the front nut first then the back one.*

NOTE: *Never reuse a cotter pin on the axle nut; always install a new one.*

6. *On Models SE and SF:* Tighten the axle nut to 76 ft.-lb. (103 N•m) and install a new cotter pin. Move the front forks up and down several times. Move the right-hand fork sideways until the left-hand disc is centered within the caliper assembly **(Figure 11)**. Tighten the axle pinch bolt to 16 ft.-lb. (20 N•m).

NOTE: *Never reuse a cotter pin on the axle nut; always install a new one.*

7. Insert the speedometer cable and install the setscrew.

NOTE: *Rotate the wheel slowly when inserting the cable so that it will engage properly.*

8. After the wheel is installed, completely rotate it and apply the brake several times to make sure it rotates freely.

FRONT HUB

Disassembly

1. Remove the front wheel as described under *Front Wheel Removal/Installation* in this chapter.

2. Remove the dust seal **(Figure 12)** and oil seal **(Figure 13)** on the right-hand side.

3. Remove the oil seal (A, **Figure 14)** and speedometer drive dog (B, **Figure 14)** on the left-hand side.

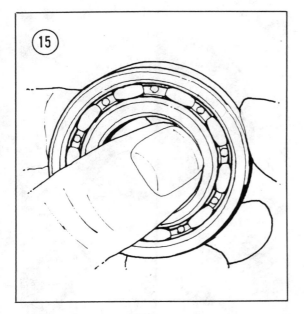

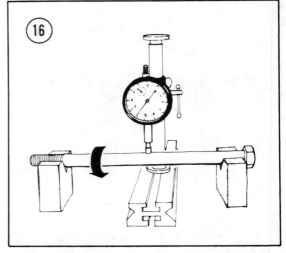

4. Remove the wheel bearings and spacer. Tap the bearings out with a soft aluminum or brass drift.

CAUTION
Tap only on the outer bearing race. The bearing will be damaged if struck on the inner race.

Inspection

1. Clean bearings thoroughly in solvent and dry with compressed air. Do not let the bearing spin while drying.

2. Clean the inside and outside of the hub with solvent. Dry with compressed air.

3. Turn each bearing by hand (**Figure 15**). Make sure bearings turn smoothiy. Check balls for evidence of wear, pitting or excessive heat (bluish tint). Replace bearings if necessary; always replace as a complete set.

4. Check the axle for wear and straightness. Use "V" blocks and a dial indicator as shown in **Figure 16**. If the runout is 0.008 in. (0.2mm) or greater, the axle must be replaced.

Assembly

1. Pack the bearings thoroughly with multipurpose grease. Work the grease in between the balls thoroughly.

2. Pack the wheel hub and axle spacer with multipurpose grease.

3. Install the right-hand wheel bearing.

4. Press in the bearing spacer.

5. Install the left-hand wheel bearing.

NOTE: *Install the wheel bearings with the sealed side facing outward.*

CAUTION
Tap the bearings squarely into place and tap on the outer race only. Use a socket that matches the outer race diameter. Do not tap on the inner race or the bearing might be damaged. Be sure that the bearings are completely seated.

6. Lubricate the dust seal with grease.

7. Install the dust seal and the oil seal in the right-hand side.

8. Install the speedometer drive dog and oil seal in the hub on the left-hand side.

9. Lubricate the oil seals.

10. Disassemble the speedometer gear box and lubricate the gears and sliding faces with a lightweight lithium soap base grease. Reassemble it.

11. Install the speedometer gear into the hub. Align the tangs of the gear with the notches in the wheel retainer.

12. Install the front wheel as described under *Front Wheel Removal/Installation* in this chapter.

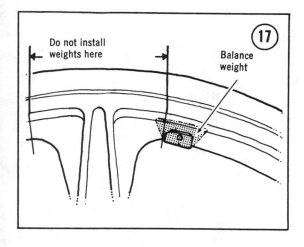

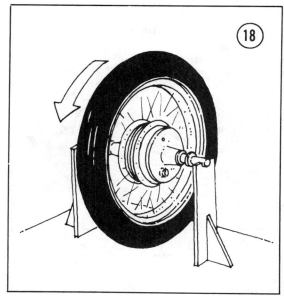

WHEEL BALANCING

An unbalanced wheel results in unsafe riding conditions. Depending on the degree of unbalance and the speed of the motorcycle, the rider may experience anything from a mild vibration to a violent shimmy which may even result in loss of control.

On the stock aluminum wheel, weights are attached to the rim. A kit of Tape-A-Weight, or equivalent, may be purchased from most motorcycle supply stores. This kit contains test weights and strips of adhesive-backed weights that can be cut to desired weight and attached directly to the rim.

Weights should not be placed near the spokes as shown in **Figure 17**.

NOTE: *Be sure to balance the wheel with the brake discs in place as they also affect the balance.*

Before you attempt to balance the wheel, check to be sure that the wheel bearings are in good condition and properly lubricated. The wheel *must rotate freely*.

1. Remove the wheel as described under *Front Wheel Removal* in this chapter.

2. Mount the wheel on a fixture such as the one in **Figure 18** so it can rotate freely.

3. Give the wheel a spin and let it coast to a stop. Mark the tire at the lowest point.

4. Spin the wheel several more times. If the wheel keeps coming to rest at the same point, it is out of balance.

5. Tape a test weight to the upper (or light) side of the wheel.

6. Experiment with different weights until the wheel, when spun, comes to rest at a different position each time.

7. Remove the test weight and install the correct size adhesive-backed weight.

TIRE CHANGING

The stock Yamaha wheel is aluminum and the exterior appearance can easily be damaged. Special care must be taken with tire irons when changing a tire to avoid scratches and gouges to the outer rim surface.

Removal

1. Remove the valve core to deflate the tire.

2. Press the entire bead on both sides of the tire into the center of the rim.

3. Lubricate the beads with soapy water.

4. Insert the tire iron under the bead next to the valve (**Figure 19**). Force the bead on the opposite side of the tire into the center of the rim and pry the bead over the rim with the tire iron.

5. Insert a second tire iron next to the first to hold the bead over the rim. Then work around the tire with the first tire iron, prying the bead over the rim (**Figure 20**). Be careful not to pinch the inner tube with the tire irons.

8

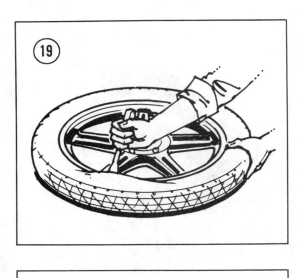

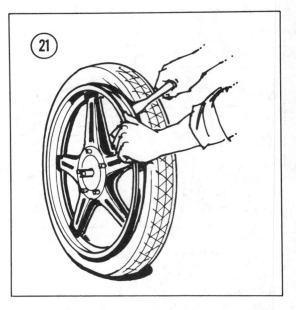

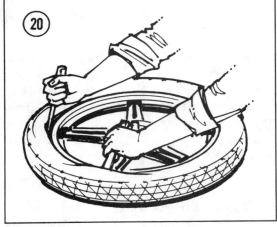

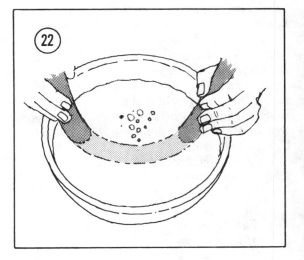

6. Remove the valve from the hole in the rim and remove the tube from the tire.

> NOTE: *Step 7 is required only if it is necessary to completely remove the tire from the rim, such as for tire replacement.*

7. Stand the tire upright. Insert the tire iron between the second bead and the side of the rim that the first bead was pried over **(Figure 21)**. Force the bead on the opposite side from the tire iron into the center of the rim. Pry the second bead off the rim, working around as with the first.

Tube Inspection

1. Install the valve core into the valve stem and inflate the tube slightly. Do not overinflate.

2. Immerse the tube in water a section at a time. See **Figure 22**. Look carefully for bubbles indicating a hole. Mark each hole and continue checking until you are certain that all holes are discovered and marked. Also make sure that the valve core is not leaking; tighten it if necessary.

> NOTE: *If you do not have enough water to immerse sections of the tube, try running your hand over the tube slowly and very close to the surface. If your hand is damp, it works even better. If you suspect a hole anywhere, apply some saliva to the area to verify it (Figure 23).*

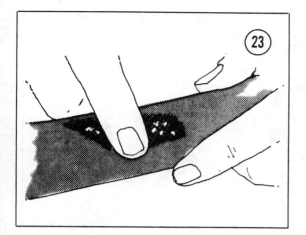

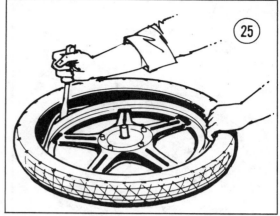

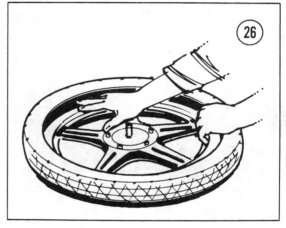

8

3. Apply a patch using either the hot or cold patch techniques described under *Tire Repairs* in this chapter.

4. Dust the patch area with talcum powder to prevent it from sticking to the tire.

5. Carefully check inside the tire casing for glass particles, nails or other objects which may have damaged the tube. If inside of tire is split, apply a patch to the area to prevent it from pinching and damaging the tube again.

6. Deflate tube prior to installation in the tire.

Installation

1. Carefully inspect the tire for any damage, especially inside.

2. A new tire may have balancing rubbers inside. These are not patches and should not be disturbed. A colored spot near the bead indicates a lighter point on the tire. This spot should be placed next to the valve stem.

3. Inflate the tube just enough to round it out. Too much air will make installation difficult.

4. Place the tube inside the tire.

5. Lubricate both beads of the tire with soapy water.

6. Place the backside of the tire into the center of the rim and insert the valve stem through the stem hole in the wheel. The lower bead should go into the center of the rim and the upper bead outside. Work around the tire in both directions (**Figure 24**). Use a tire iron for the last few inches of bead (**Figure 25**).

7. Press the upper bead into the rim opposite the valve (**Figure 26**). Pry the bead into the rim

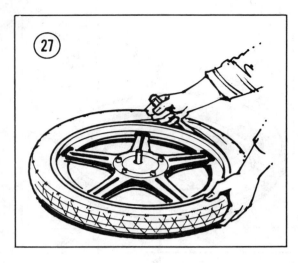

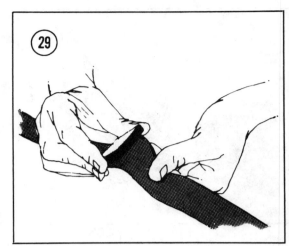

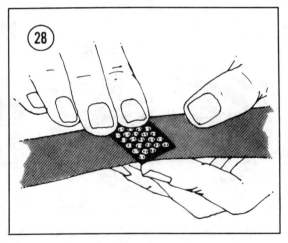

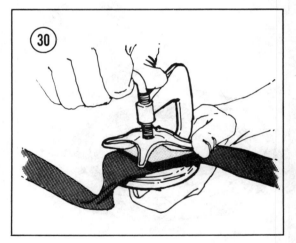

on both sides of the initial point with a tire iron, working around the rim to valve **(Figure 27)**.

8. Wiggle the valve to be sure the tube is not under the bead. Set the valve squarely in its hole before screwing in the valve nut to hold it against the rim.

9. Check the bead on both sides of the tire for even fit around the rim. Inflate the tire slowly to seat the beads in the rim. It may be necessary to bounce the tire to complete the seating. Inflate to the required pressure. Balance the wheel as described previously.

TIRE REPAIRS

Tire/tube damage will eventually strike even the most careful rider. Repair is fairly simple on all tires.

Tire Repair Kits

Tire repair kits can be purchased from motorcycle dealers and some auto supply stores. When buying, specify that the kit you want is for motorcycle tires.

There are two types of tire repair kits for motorcycles:

a. Hot patch
b. Cold patch

Hot patches are strongest because they actually vulcanize to the tube, becoming part of it. The repair kit for hot patching is bulkier and heavier than cold patch kits, therefore, hot patch kits are more suited for home repairs.

Cold patches are not vulcanized to the tube; they are simply glued to it. Though not as strong as hot patches, cold patches are still very

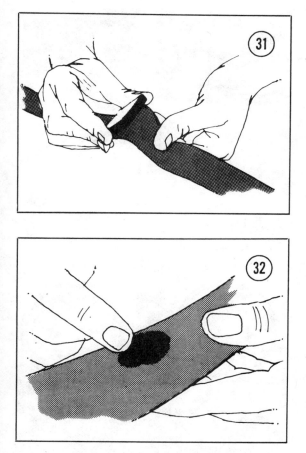

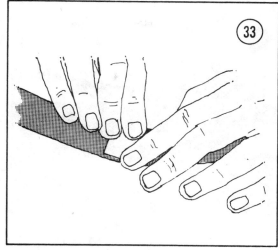

durable. Cold patch kits are less bulky than hot and more easily applied under adverse conditions. Cold patch kits are best for emergency repairs on the road.

Hot patch repair

1. Remove the tube from tire as described under *Tire Removal* in this chapter.

2. Roughen area around hole slightly larger than the patch (**Figure 28**). Use a pocket knife or similar tool to scrape the tube; be careful that you don't cause further damage.

3. Remove the backing from patch.

CAUTION
Do not touch newly exposed rubber with your fingers. This will prevent a good seal.

4. Center the patch over hole (**Figure 29**).

5. Install clamp around tube so that it holds the fuel container over the patch (**Figure 30**).

6. Pry up a corner of the fuel and light it. Let all of the fuel burn away.

CAUTION
The clamp gets hot, so don't touch it until it cools.

7. Remove the clamp and peel the tube off the fuel container (**Figure 31**).

Cold patch repair

1. Remove the tube from tire as described under *Tire Removal* in this chapter.

2. Roughen area around hole slightly larger than the patch; use the cap from the tire repair kit or a pocket knife. Do not scrape too vigorously or you may cause additional damage.

3. Apply a small quantity of special cement to the puncture and spread it evenly with a finger (**Figure 32**).

4. Allow cement to dry until tacky — usually thirty seconds or so is sufficient.

5. Remove the backing from the patch.

CAUTION
Do not touch the newly exposed rubber with your fingers or the patch will not stick firmly.

6. Center patch over hole. Hold patch firmly in place for about 30 seconds to allow the cement to set (**Figure 33**).

7. Dust the patched area with talcum powder to prevent sticking.

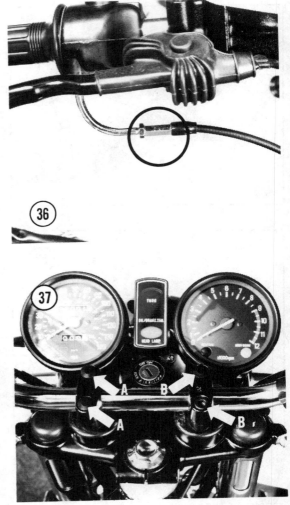

HANDLEBAR

Removal/Installation

1. Remove the 2 bolts **(Figure 34)** securing the master cylinder and lay it on the fuel tank. It is not necessary to remove the hydraulic brake line.

> CAUTION
>
> *Cover the fuel tank with a heavy cloth or plastic tarp to protect it from accidental spilling of brake fluid. Wash any brake fluid off of any painted or plated surface immediately, as it will destroy the finish. Use soapy water and rinse thoroughly.*

2. Slacken the clutch cable **(Figure 35)** and disconnect it from the hand lever.

3. Separate the 2 halves of the start switch assembly. Disconnect the throttle cable from the twist grip **(Figure 36)**.

4. Remove the rear view mirrors and clamps securing electrical cables to the handlebar.

5. Remove the 4 rubber plugs (A, **Figure 37**) and 4 Allen bolts (B, **Figure 37**) securing the handlebar holder and remove it.

6. Lift off the handlebars.

7. Install by reversing these steps. Align the punch marks on the handlebar with the line that separates the upper and lower handlebar holder.

8. Tighten the 4 Allen screws of the handlebar holder. Tighten to a torque of 13 ft.-lb. (18 N•m). Install the rubber plugs.

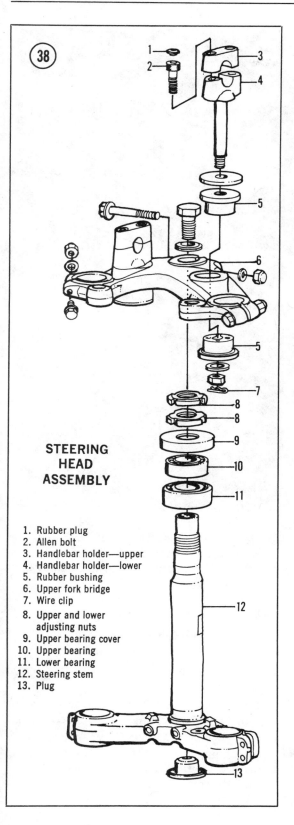

STEERING HEAD ASSEMBLY

1. Rubber plug
2. Allen bolt
3. Handlebar holder—upper
4. Handlebar holder—lower
5. Rubber bushing
6. Upper fork bridge
7. Wire clip
8. Upper and lower adjusting nuts
9. Upper bearing cover
10. Upper bearing
11. Lower bearing
12. Steering stem
13. Plug

8

STEERING HEAD

Disassembly

Refer to **Figure 38** for this procedure.

1. Remove the front wheel as described under *Front Wheel Removal/Installation*, this chapter.

2. Remove both front caliper assemblies as described under *Caliper Removal/Installation* in Chapter Ten.

3. Remove the union bolt (**Figure 39**) securing the hose from the master cylinder to the fitting. Remove the union bolt (**Figure 40**) securing the caliper hoses to the fitting and remove them.

4. Remove the handlebar as described under *Handlebar Removal/Installation*, this chapter.

5. Remove the tachometer and speedometer cables (**Figure 41**) from the instrument pod.

6. Remove the 2 bolts (**Figure 42**) securing the instrument pod and lay it over the fuel tank.

7. Remove the headlight and front turn indicators.

8. Loosen the pinch bolts (A, **Figure 43**) on the upper fork bridge.

9. Loosen lower fork bridge bolts (**Figure 44**).

10. Slide entire fork and fender assembly out.

11. Loosen crown pinch bolt (B, **Figure 43**).

12. Loosen steering stem bolt (C, **Figure 43**) and remove the upper fork bridge.

13. Remove the upper and lower adjusting nuts with the pin spanner, provided in the XS750 tool kit, or use an easily improvised unit (**Figure 45**).

14. Remove the upper bearing cover.

15. Pull the steering stem out of the frame. The upper and lower bearings are assembled roller bearings — don't worry about catching any loose ball bearings.

Inspection

1. Clean the bearing races in the steering head and both roller bearings with solvent.

2. Check for broken welds on the frame around the steering head.

3. Check the bearings for pitting, scratches, or discoloration, indicating wear or corrosion. Replace them *in sets* if any are bad.

4. Check upper and lower races in the steering head. See *Bearing Race Replacement* if races are pitted, scratched, or badly worn.

5. Check steering stem for cracks.

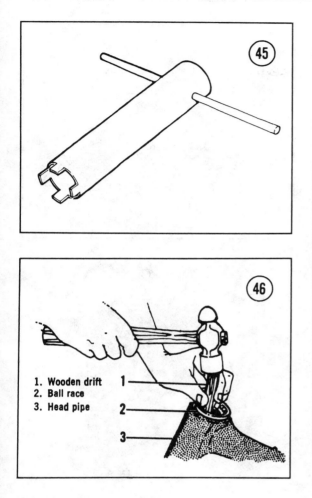

1. Wooden drift
2. Ball race
3. Head pipe

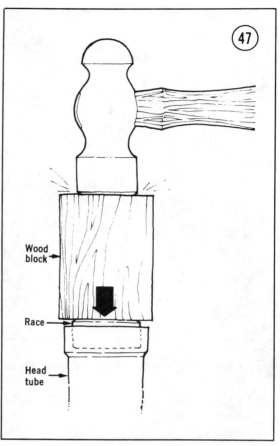

Wood block

Race

Head tube

8

Bearing Race Replacement

The headset and steering stem bearing races are pressed into place. Because they are easily bent, do not remove them unless they are worn and require replacement. Take old races to the dealer to ensure exact replacement.

To remove a headset race, insert a hardwood stick into the head tube and carefully tap the race out from the inside (**Figure 46**). Tap all around the race so that neither the race nor the head tube are bent. To install a race, fit it into the end of the head tube. Tap it slowly and squarely with a block of wood (**Figure 47**).

Assembly

Refer to **Figure 38** for this procedure.

1. Make sure the steering head bearing races are properly seated. Coat them with wheel bearing grease.

2. Thoroughly pack the bearings with wheel bearing grease.

3. Install the lower bearing onto the steering stem.

4. Insert the steering stem into the head tube. Hold it firmly in place.

5. Install the upper bearing and upper bearing cover.

6. Install the lower adjusting nut and tighten it (**Figure 48**) to approximately 7-9 ft.-lb. (9-12 N•m). *Do not* overtighten it. Install the upper adjusting nut tight up against the lower nut.

> NOTE: *The adjusting nuts should be just tight enough to remove play, both horizontal and vertical (**Figure 49**), yet loose enough so that the assembly will turn to both lock positions under its own weight after an initial assist.*

7. Continue assembling by reversing *Removal* Steps 12-1. Torque the bolts as follows:

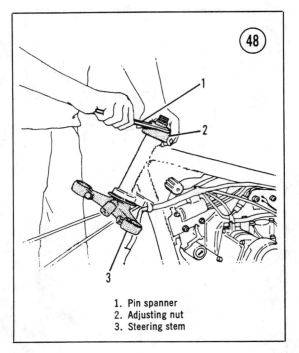

1. Pin spanner
2. Adjusting nut
3. Steering stem

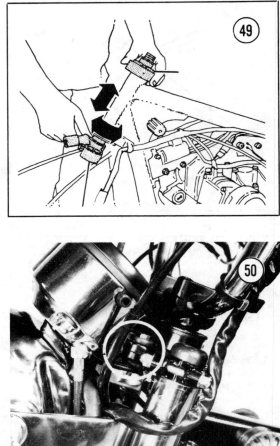

a. Upper fork pinch bolts (A, **Figure 43**) to 11 ft.-lb. (15 N•m).

b. Crown pinch bolt (B, **Figure 43**) to 11 ft.-lb. (15 N•m).

c. Steering stem bolt (C, **Figure 43**) to 39 ft.-lb. (53 N•m).

d. Lower fork bridge bolts (**Figure 44**) to 15 ft.-lb. (20 N•m).

8. After the total assembly is completed, check the stem for looseness or binding — readjust if necessary.

9. Install the instrument pod with the attachment bracket *below* top fork bridge (**Figure 50**). If it is mounted above, the tachometer and speedometer cables will be stretched and damaged when the steering is turned to its limits.

Steering Stem Adjustment

If play develops in the steering system, it may only require adjustment. However, don't take a chance on it. Disassemble the stem as explained in *Steering Head Disassembly* in this chapter.

FRONT FORK

The Yamaha front suspension consists of a spring-controlled, hydraulically dampened telescopic fork. Before suspecting major trouble, drain the fork oil and refill with the proper type and quantity; refer to Chapter Three. If you still have trouble, such as poor dampening, tendency to bottom out or top out, or leakage around rubber seals, then follow the service procedures in this section.

To simplify fork service and to prevent the mixing of parts, the legs should be removed, serviced and reinstalled individually.

Removal/Installation

1. Remove the front wheel as described under *Front Wheel Removal* in this chapter.

2. Remove the bolts (**Figure 51**) securing the front fender and remove it.

3. Remove the remaining caliper(s). Tie them up with wire to the frame to keep tension off the brake hoses.

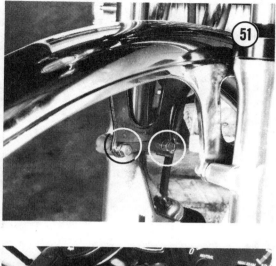

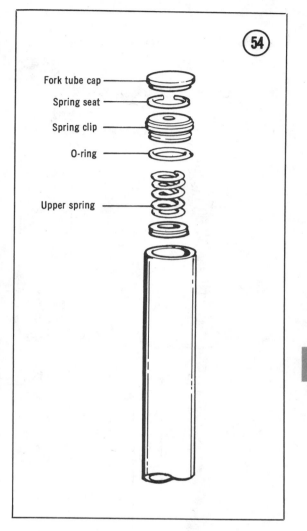

NOTE: *Insert a piece of wood in the calipers in place of the discs. That way, if the brake lever is inadvertently squeezed, the piston will not be forced out of the cylinder. If it does happen, the caliper might have to be disassembled to reseat the piston, and the system will have to be bled. By using the wood, bleeding the brake is not necessary when installing the wheel.*

4. Remove the top rubber cap (A, **Figure 52**).

5. Loosen the pinch bolts (B, **Figure 52**) on the upper fork bridge.

6. Loosen lower fork bridge bolts (**Figure 44**).

7. Install by reversing these removal steps. Torque the bolts as follows:

   a. Upper fork pinch bolts (B, **Figure 52**) to 11 ft.-lb. (15 N•m).

   b. Lower fork bolts (**Figure 44**) to 15 ft.-lb. (20 N•m).

Disassembly

Refer to **Figure 53** for this procedure.

1. *On Models D and 2D:* Hold the upper fork tube in a vise with soft jaws. Remove the fork tube cap, spring clip, spring seat with O-ring, and upper spring (**Figure 54**).

> NOTE: *It is necessary to depress the spring seat and upper spring to remove the spring clip. Use a small bladed screwdriver for spring clip removal.*

2. *On Models E, F, SE and SF:* Hold the upper fork tube in a vise with soft jaws. Remove

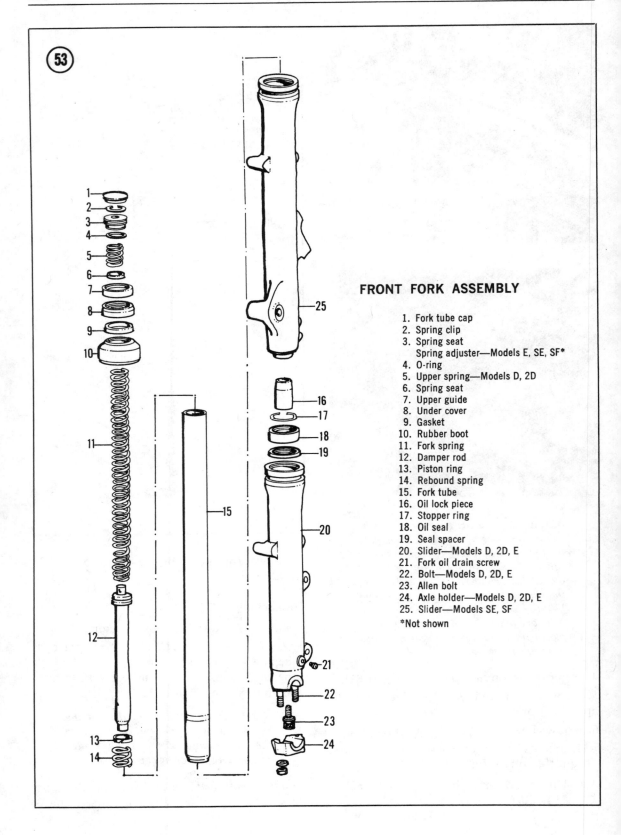

53

FRONT FORK ASSEMBLY

1. Fork tube cap
2. Spring clip
3. Spring seat
   Spring adjuster—Models E, SE, SF*
4. O-ring
5. Upper spring—Models D, 2D
6. Spring seat
7. Upper guide
8. Under cover
9. Gasket
10. Rubber boot
11. Fork spring
12. Damper rod
13. Piston ring
14. Rebound spring
15. Fork tube
16. Oil lock piece
17. Stopper ring
18. Oil seal
19. Seal spacer
20. Slider—Models D, 2D, E
21. Fork oil drain screw
22. Bolt—Models D, 2D, E
23. Allen bolt
24. Axle holder—Models D, 2D, E
25. Slider—Models SE, SF

*Not shown

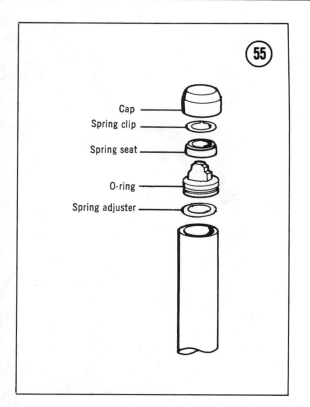

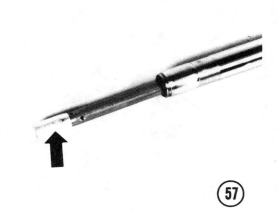

3. Remove the fork spring.

4. Remove the fork from vise and pour the oil out and discard it. Pump the fork several times by hand to expel most of the remaining oil.

5. Remove the rubber boot out of the notch in the slider and slide it off of the fork tube.

6. Clamp the slider in a vise with soft jaws.

7. Remove the Allen bolt (**Figure 56**) at the bottom of the slider and pull the fork tube out of the slider.

8. Remove the oil lock piece (**Figure 57**), the damper rod, and rebound spring.

9. Remove snap ring and oil seal (**Figure 58**).

> CAUTION
> *Use a dull screwdriver blade to remove oil seal. Do not damage the outer or inner surface of the slider.*

Inspection

1. Thoroughly clean all parts in solvent and dry. Check the fork tube for signs of wear or galling.

2. Check the damper rod for straightness. **Figure 59** shows one method. The rod should be replaced if the runout is 0.008 in. (0.2mm) or greater.

3. Carefully check the damper valve and the piston ring (**Figure 60**) for wear or damage.

4. Inspect the oil seals for scoring and nicks and loss of resiliency. Replace if its condition is questionable.

spring clip, spring seat, spring adjuster, and O-ring (**Figure 55**).

> NOTE: *This step requires the aid of an assistant. Depress the spring seat and adjuster with a broad-bladed screwdriver while your assistant removes the spring clip with a small screwdriver.*

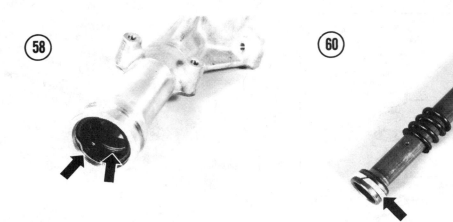

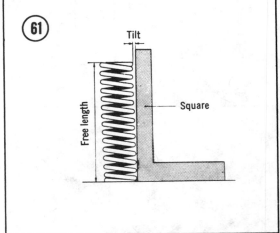

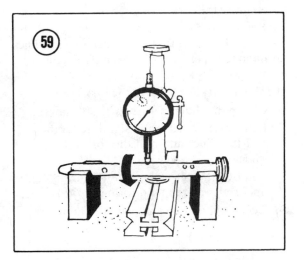

5. Check the upper fork tube exterior for scratches and straightness. If bent or scratched, it should be replaced.

6. Check the lower slider for dents or exterior damage that may cause the upper fork tube to hang up during riding conditions. Replace if necessary.

7. Measure uncompressed length of spring(s) with a square as shown in **Figure 61**. Models D and 2D are equipped with 2 springs, with a short one at the top. Replace spring(s) if they are shorter than the following dimensions:

    a. Models D and 2D
          upper spring—2.2 in. (55.8mm)
          lower spring—17.65 in. (448.3mm)

    b. Models E and F
          19.81 in. (503.2mm)

    c. Models SE and SF
          23.89 in. (606.8mm)

8. Check the O-ring on the top spring seat; replace if necessary.

9. Any parts that are worn or damaged should be replaced. Simply cleaning and reinstalling unserviceable components will not improve performance of the front suspension.

Assembly

1. Install the oil seal and snap ring (**Figure 58**).

    NOTE: *Make sure the seal seats square-ly and fully in the bores of the slider.*

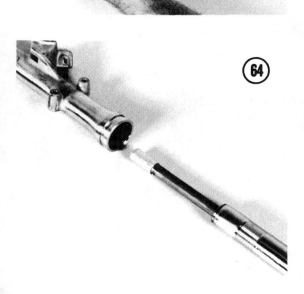

2. Insert the damper rod into the fork tube **(Figure 62)** and install oil lock piece **(Figure 63)**.

3. Apply a light coat of oil to the outside of the fork tube and install it into slider **(Figure 64)**. Apply Loctite Lock N' Seal to the threads of the Allen bolt and install it **(Figure 65)**.

4. Slide rubber boot into place on the slider.

5. Fill fork tube with fresh fork oil **(Figure 66)**. Capacity per each fork tube is as follows:

    a. Model D   5.9 oz. (175cc)
    b. Model 2D   6.8 oz. (200cc)
    c. Models E and F   6.4 oz. (190cc)
    d. Models SE and SF 7.91 oz. (234cc)

NOTE: *In order to measure the correct amount of fluid, use a plastic baby bottle. These have measurements in fluid* ounces (oz.) and cubic centimeters (cc) on the side (**Figure 67**). Many fork oil containers have a semi-transparent strip on the side of the bottle (A, **Figure 66**) to aid in the measuring.

6. Insert the spring with the tapered end down toward the axle.

7. *On Models D and 2D:* Install upper spring, spring seat, new spring clip, and fork tube cap.

8. *On Models E, F, SE and SF:* Install the spring adjuster, spring seat and new spring clip.

NOTE: *Always install a new spring clip.*

9. Install the fork as described under *Front Fork Removal/Installation* in this chapter.

Adjustment (Models E, F and SF)

Refer to **Figure 68** for this procedure.

1. Remove the fork's rubber cap.

2. Insert a large flat screwdriver and push down against the spring tension.

3. Turn in either direction. Make sure both forks are adjusted to the same position.

4. Reinstall the rubber cap and test ride. Continue to adjust until the ride is satisfactory.

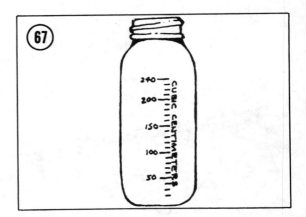

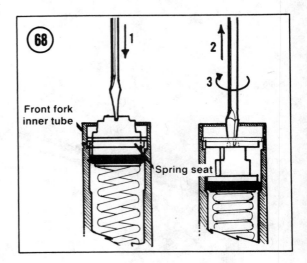

NOTE: If you own a 1980 or later model, first check the Supplement at the back of the book for any new service information.

CHAPTER NINE

REAR SUSPENSION AND FINAL DRIVE

This chapter includes repair and replacement procedures for the rear wheel, final drive unit, and rear suspension components.

REAR WHEELS

Refer to **Figure 1** for this procedure.

Removal/Installation

1. Place the bike on the centerstand or block up the engine so that the rear wheel clears the ground.

2. Raise seat and remove the 2 bolts (**Figure 2**) securing the rear fender. Raise the fender and reinstall the bolts to hold fender in the raised position.

3. *On Models D and 2D:* Loosen the clamps (**Figure 3**) securing the mufflers to the exhaust pipes. Remove the bolts (**Figure 4** securing the mufflers to the frame; remove bo... mufflers.

4. Remove cotter pin and axle nut (**Figure 5**). Discard the cotter pin.

5. Loosen rear axle pinch bolt (A, **Figure 6**).

6. Hold onto the caliper assembly and withdraw the rear axle (B, **Figure 6**). Do not lose the axle spacer (C, **Figure 6**).

7. Pivot the caliper assembly up (**Figure 7**) and place it on the hook on the frame.

9

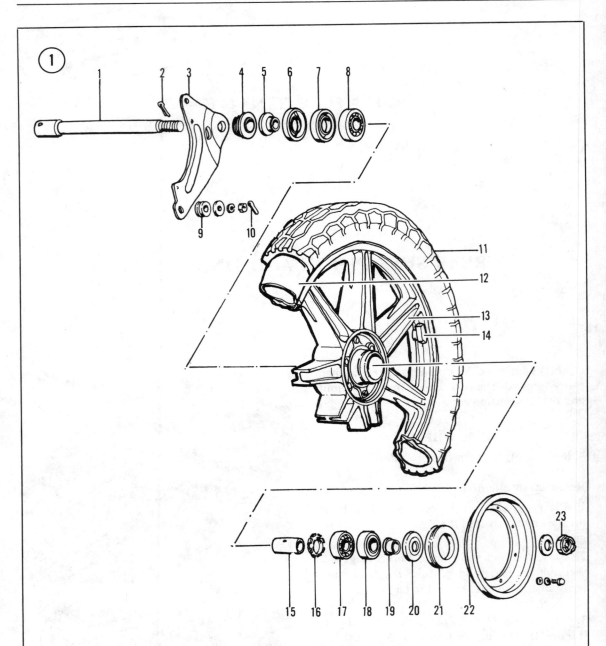

REAR WHEEL ASSEMBLY

1. Rear axle
2. Axle nut cotter pin
3. Torque plate
4. Collar
5. Shaft collar
6. Dust cover
7. Oil seal
8. Wheel bearing/right-hand side

9. Spacer
10. Cotter pin
11. Tire
12. Inner tube
13. Wheel
14. Balance weight
15. Axle spacer
16. Flange spacer

17. Wheel bearing/left-hand side
18. Bearing
19. Collar
20. Oil seal
21. Dust seal
22. Dust cover
23. Axle nut

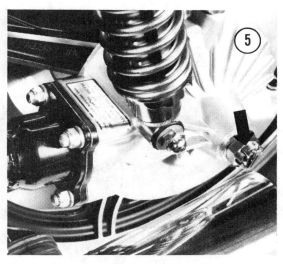

NOTE: *Insert a piece of wood in the caliper in place of the disc. This way, if brake lever is inadvertently depressed, the piston will not be forced out of the cylinder. If this does happen the caliper might have to be disassembled to reseat the piston, and the system will have to be bled. By using the wood, bleeding the brake is not necessary when installing the wheel.*

8. Slide the wheel to the right to disengage it from the hub drive splines and remove the wheel.

9. Install by reversing these removal steps. Apply molybdenum disulfide grease to the final drive flange splines on the wheel and the ring gear. Lightly grease the grease seals on each side of the wheel.

10. Make sure that the wheel hub splines engage with the final drive.

11. Torque the axle nut to 108 ft.-lb. (147 N•m) and the axle pinch bolt to 4 ft.-lb. (5 N•m).

NOTE: *Never reuse a cotter pin. Always install a new one.*

Inspection

Measure the lateral and vertical runout of the wheel rim with a dial indicator as shown in **Figure 8**. The maximum lateral runout is 0.04 in. (1mm) and the maximum vertical runout is 0.08 in. (2mm). If the runout exceeds these dimensions, check the wheel bearings' condition and/or replace the wheel. The stock Yamaha aluminum wheel cannot be serviced; it must be replaced.

REAR HUB

Disassembly

1. Remove the rear wheel as described under *Rear Wheel Removal/Installation* in this chapter.

2. Remove the dust seal (**Figure 9**) and oil seal (**Figure 10**) on the right-hand side.

3. Remove the oil seal and spacer (**Figure 11**) on the left-hand side.

4. Remove the wheel bearings and spacer. Tap the bearings out with a soft aluminum or brass drift.

> #### CAUTION
> *Tap only on the outer bearing race. The bearing will be damaged if struck on the inner race.*

Inspection

1. Clean bearings thoroughly in solvent and dry with compressed air. Do not let the bearing spin while drying.

2. Clean the inside and outside of the hub with solvent. Dry with compressed air.

3. Turn each bearing by hand (**Figure 12**). Make sure bearings turn smoothly. Check the balls for evidence of wear, pitting, or excessive heat (bluish tint). Replace if necessary; always replace as a complete set.

4. Check the axle for wear and straightness. Use "V" blocks and a dial indicator as shown in **Figure 13**. If the runout is 0.008 in. (0.2mm) or greater, the axle must be replaced.

Assembly

1. Pack the bearings thoroughly with multipurpose grease. Work grease in between the balls completely.

2. Install the left-hand wheel bearing.

3. Press in the bearing spacer.

4. Install the right-hand wheel bearing.

> NOTE: *Install bearings with the sealed side facing outward.*

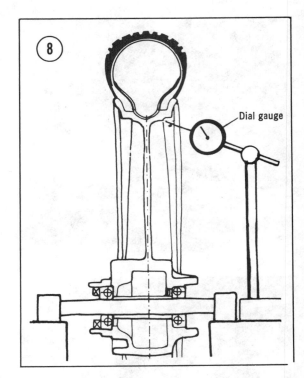

Dial gauge

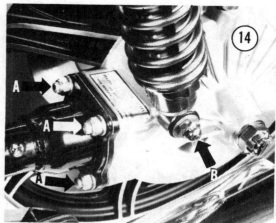

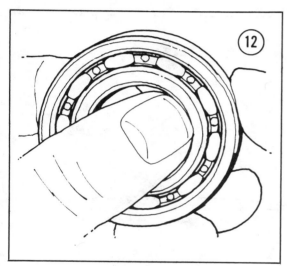

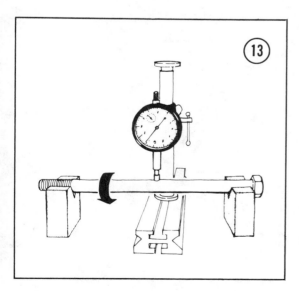

CAUTION
Tap the bearings squarely into place and tap on the outer race only. Do not tap on the inner race or the bearings might be damaged. Be sure that the bearings are completely seated.

5. Lubricate the oil and dust seals with grease.

6. Install the spacer and the oil and dust seal on the left-hand side.

7. Install the oil and dust seal on the right-hand side.

8. Install the rear wheel as described under *Rear Wheel Removal/Installation*, this chapter.

WHEEL BALANCING

For complete information refer to *Wheel Balancing* in Chapter Eight.

TIRE CHANGING

Refer to *Tire Changing* in Chapter Eight.

FINAL DRIVE

Removal/Installation

1. Remove the rear wheel as described under *Rear Wheel Removal/Installation*, this chapter.

2. Remove 4 nuts and washers (A, **Figure 14**) securing the final drive unit to the swing arm.

3. Remove the left-hand lower shock absorber acorn nut (B, **Figure 14**).

4. Pull the final drive unit straight back until it is free.

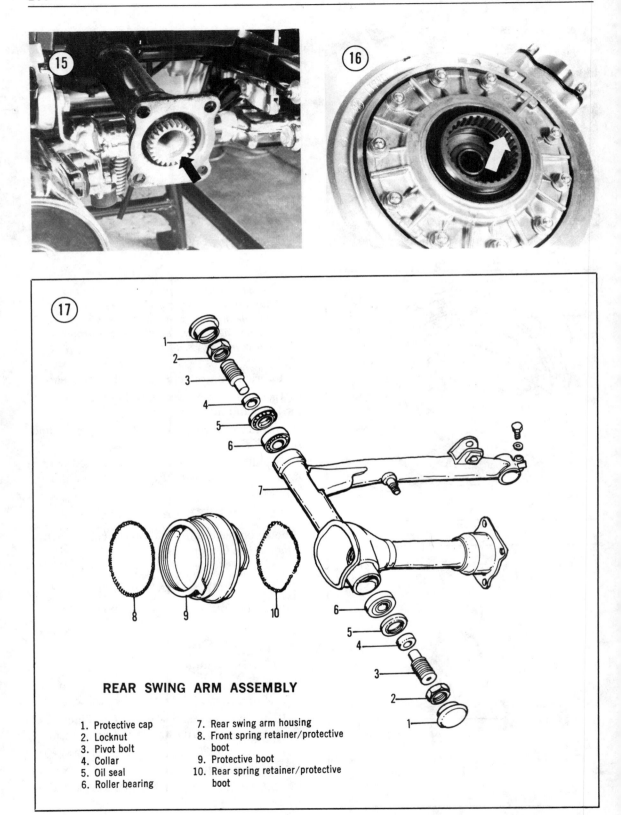

REAR SWING ARM ASSEMBLY

1. Protective cap
2. Locknut
3. Pivot bolt
4. Collar
5. Oil seal
6. Roller bearing
7. Rear swing arm housing
8. Front spring retainer/protective boot
9. Protective boot
10. Rear spring retainer/protective boot

5. Wipe the grease from the splines on the end of the drive shaft (**Figure 15**) and final drive unit (**Figure 16**).

6. Check the splines of both units carefully for signs of wear.

7. Pack the splines with multipurpose molybdenum disulfide grease.

8. Install the final drive unit onto the swing arm. Make sure that the splines of the drive shaft engage properly with the final drive unit.

9. Install 4 nuts and washers and tighten to 29 ft.-lb. (39 N•m) and the shock absorber acorn nut to 28 ft.-lb. (38 N•m).

10. Install the rear wheel as described under *Rear Wheel Removal/Installation*, this chapter.

Disassembly and Inspection

Although it may be practical for you to disassemble the final drive for inspection, you cannot replace the bearings or seals (which require bearing removal) without special tools. If there is trouble in the final drive unit, it may be best to remove the unit, and take it to your Yamaha dealer and let them overhaul it. They are also better equipped to check and adjust gear lash.

Inspect the exterior of the unit for signs of wear, cracks, damage, or oil leakage. If any damage is present or there are signs of oil leakage, take the unit to your Yamaha dealer for service.

REAR SWING ARM

Refer to **Figure 17** for this procedure.

Removal/Installation

1. Remove the rear wheel as described under *Rear Wheel Removal/Installation*, this chapter.

2. Remove the final drive unit as described under *Final Drive Removal/Installation* in this chapter.

3. Slide back the rubber protective boot and remove the 4 bolts (A, **Figure 18**) securing the drive shaft to the middle gear housing.

4. Disengage the drive shaft and remove it through the rear.

5. Remove the right-hand lower shock absorber acorn nut.

6. Remove the caliper assembly from the swing arm. Tie it up to the frame with wire to relieve tension on the brake hose.

7. Remove the protective caps (B, **Figure 18**) and remove the locknut from the pivot bolt on both sides.

8. Remove both pivot bolts and the swing arm.

9. Install by reversing these removal steps, noting the following.

10. After the rear swing arm is installed, adjust side clearance as described under *Rear Swing Arm Adjustment* in this chapter.

11. Make sure that the swing arm moves up and down smoothly without tightness, binding or rough spots. If the movement is rough, the bearings should be replaced.

Inspection

1. Remove the rubber boot from the swing arm and inspect it for tears or deterioration; replace if necessary.

2. Remove the oil seals and bearings.

3. Thoroughly clean the bearings in solvent and dry with compressed air.

4. Turn each bearing by hand (**Figure 12**). Make sure bearings turn smoothly. Check the balls for evidence of wear or pitting. Replace if necessary. Always replace both bearings and inner and outer races at the same time.

5. If bearings have been replaced, the grease seals should be replaced also.

6. Pack the bearings with a lithium base, waterproof wheel bearing grease.

7. Install the bearings into the swing arm.

CAUTION
Tap the bearings squarely into place and tap on the outer race only. Do not tap on the inner race or the bearings might be damaged. Be sure that the bearings are completely seated.

Adjustment

1. Measure the distance between the frame and the swing arm on both right- and left-hand sides (**Figure 19**).

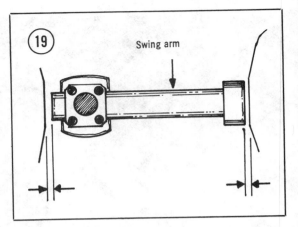

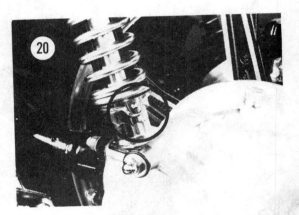

2. The difference between the two measurements should not be more than 0.062 in. (1.6mm).

3. If these measurements differ by more than that specified, adjustment should be made.

4. Remove the protective caps (B, **Figure 18**).

5. Loosen the pivot shaft locknuts on both sides.

6. Loosen the pivot shaft bolt on the side with the greatest dimension.

NOTE
Loosen only slightly, approximately 1/2 turn.

7. Tighten the opposite pivot shaft bolt slightly and measure the frame to swing arm distance as in Step 1.

8. If the dimension is still not within specifications (Step 2), repeat Step 6 and Step 7 until correct.

9. When correct, tighten the pivot shaft locknuts to 47 ft.-lb. (64 N•m).

NOTE: *Do not allow the pivot shaft bolts to rotate while tightening the locknuts.*

After tightening, recheck to make sure the dimensions are still correct.

REAR SHOCKS

The rear shocks are spring controlled and hydraulically dampened. Spring preload can be adjusted by rotating the cam ring at the base of the spring **(Figure 20)** — *clockwise to increase* preload and *counterclockwise to decrease it.*

NOTE: *Use the spanner wrench furnished in the XS750 tool kit for this adjustment.*

Both cams must be indexed on the same detent. The shocks are sealed and cannot be rebuilt. Service is limited to removal and replacement of the hydraulic unit.

Removal/Installation

Removal and installation of the rear shocks is easier if they are done separately. The remaining unit will support the rear of the bike and maintain the correct relationship between the top and bottom mounts.

1. Block up the engine or support it on the centerstand.

2. Adjust both shocks to their softest setting, *completely counterclockwise.*

3. Remove the upper and lower acorn nuts.

4. Pull the shock off.

5. Install by reversing removal steps. Torque the upper nut to 21 ft.-lb. (28 N•m) and the lower nut to 28 ft.-lb. (37 N•m).

9

NOTE: If you own a 1980 or later model, first check the Supplement at the back of the book for any new service information.

CHAPTER TEN

BRAKES

The XS750 has dual disc front brakes operated by the right-hand lever and a single disc rear brake operated by a foot lever. This chapter describes repair and replacement procedures for all brake components.

FRONT DISC BRAKES

The front disc brakes are actuated by hydraulic fluid and are controlled by a hand lever. As the brake pads wear, the brake fluid level drops in the reservoir and automatically adjusts for wear. However, brake lever free play must be maintained. Refer to *Front Brake Lever Adjustment* in Chapter Three.

When working on hydraulic brake systems, it is necessary that the work area and all tools be absolutely clean. Any tiny particles of foreign matter and grit in the caliper assembly or the master cylinder can damage the components. Also, sharp tools must not be used inside the caliper or on the piston. If there is any doubt about your ability to correctly and safely carry out major service on the brake components, take the job to a Yamaha dealer or brake specialist.

Master Cylinder Removal/Installation

1. Remove the rear view mirror.

CAUTION
Cover the fuel tank and instrument cluster with a heavy cloth or plastic tarp to protect them from accidental spilling of brake fluid. Wash any brake fluid off of any painted or plated surface immediately, as it will destroy the finish. Use soapy water and rinse completely.

2. Pull back the rubber boot and remove the union bolt (**Figure 1**) securing the brake hose to the master cylinder and remove it.

3. Remove the electrical leads from the brakelight switch (A, **Figure 2**).

4. Remove the bolt and nut (B, **Figure 2**) securing the brake lever and remove it.

5. Remove the 2 clamping bolts (**Figure 3**) securing the master cylinder to the handlebar, and remove it.

6. Install by reversing the removal steps.

7. Bleed the brake as described under *Bleeding the System* at the end of this chapter.

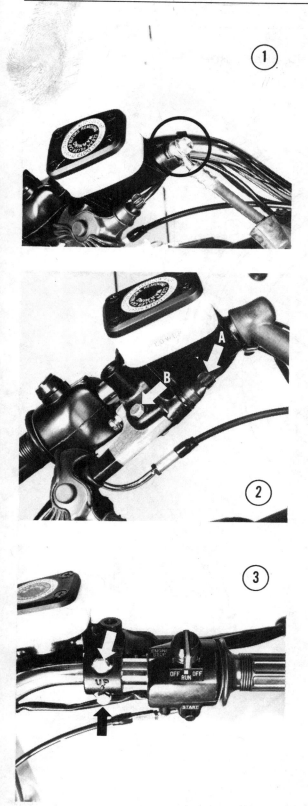

Master Cylinder Disassembly

Refer to **Figure 4** for the front and **Figure 5** for the rear master cylinder, for this procedure.

1. Remove the master cylinder as described under *Master Cylinder Removal/Installation* in this chapter.

2. Remove the top cap, diaphragm, and gasket; pour out the brake fluid and discard it — *never* reuse brake fluid.

3. Remove the boot and snap ring.

4. Remove the piston cap assembly.

Master Cylinder Inspection

1. Clean all parts in denatured alcohol or fresh brake fluid. Inspect the cylinder bore and piston contact surfaces for signs of wear and damage. If either part is less than perfect, replace it.

2. Check the end of the piston for wear caused by the hand lever or brake actuating rod and check the pivot bore in the front hand lever. Discard the caps.

3. Make sure the passages in the bottom of the brake fluid reservoir are clear. Check the reservoir cap and diaphragm for damage and deterioration and replace as necessary.

4. Inspect the condition of the threads in the bores for the brake line and the switch.

5. Check the front hand lever pivot lug for cracks.

6. Replace all internal seals every 2 years.

Master Cylinder Assembly

1. Soak the new caps in fresh brake fluid for at least 15 minutes to make them pliable.

2. Install the spring.

3. Install the primary and secondary caps into the cylinder.

4. Install the piston and washer and install the snap ring and boot.

5. Install the diaphragm, gasket, and top cap.

6. Install the front master cylinder on the handlebar and connect the brake hose and brakelight switch electrical leads.

7. Install the rear master cylinder to the frame and connect the brake hose. Tighten the brake hose union bolts to 18 ft.-lb. (24 N•m).

10

④ **FRONT MASTER CYLINDER AND BRAKE HOSE ASSEMBLY**

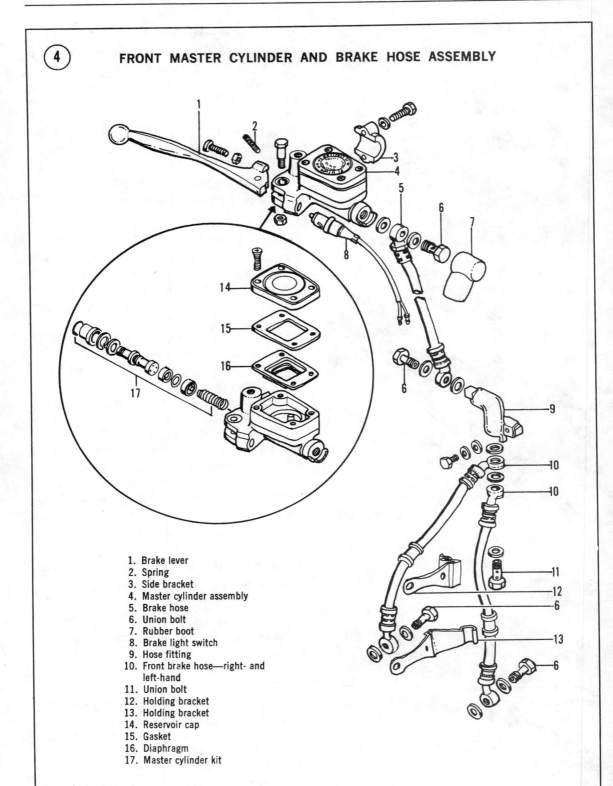

1. Brake lever
2. Spring
3. Side bracket
4. Master cylinder assembly
5. Brake hose
6. Union bolt
7. Rubber boot
8. Brake light switch
9. Hose fitting
10. Front brake hose—right- and left-hand
11. Union bolt
12. Holding bracket
13. Holding bracket
14. Reservoir cap
15. Gasket
16. Diaphragm
17. Master cylinder kit

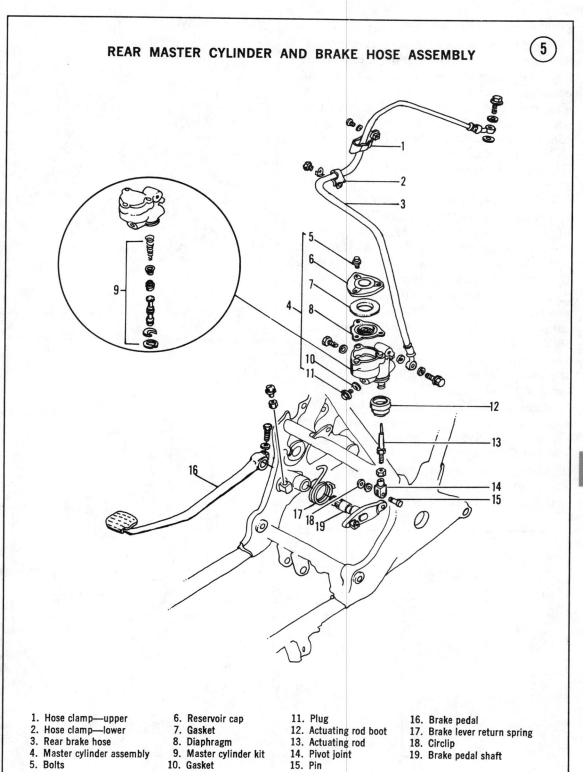

REAR MASTER CYLINDER AND BRAKE HOSE ASSEMBLY

⑤

1. Hose clamp—upper
2. Hose clamp—lower
3. Rear brake hose
4. Master cylinder assembly
5. Bolts
6. Reservoir cap
7. Gasket
8. Diaphragm
9. Master cylinder kit
10. Gasket
11. Plug
12. Actuating rod boot
13. Actuating rod
14. Pivot joint
15. Pin
16. Brake pedal
17. Brake lever return spring
18. Circlip
19. Brake pedal shaft

10

Front Brake Pad Replacement

There is no recommended mileage interval for changing the friction pads in the disc brake. Pad wear depends greatly on riding habits and conditions. The pads should be checked for wear every 2,500 miles (4,000km) and replaced when the wear indicator (**Figure 6**) reaches the edge of the brake disc. Always replace all four pads (two per disc) at the same time.

It is not necessary to remove the front wheel to replace the pads.

Refer to **Figure 7** for this procedure.

1. *On Models D, 2D, E and F:* Remove the upper mounting bolt (A, **Figure 8**) and the lower support bolt (B, **Figure 8**). Pull the caliper off the disc. Remove the screw (**Figure 9**) securing the pads in place.

2. *On Models SE and SF:* Remove the plastic protective cap (**Figure 10**) and remove the caliper mounting bolt assembly (**Figure 11**). Pull the caliper assembly off the disc. Pinch the spring retainer (A, **Figure 12**) together and slide the pad locating pin out (B, **Figure 12**) and remove the old pads.

3. Clean the pad recess and end of the piston with a soft brush. Do not use solvent, a wire brush, or any hard tool which would damage the cylinder or the piston.

4. Lightly coat the end of the piston and the backs of the new pads (not the friction material) with disc brake lubricant.

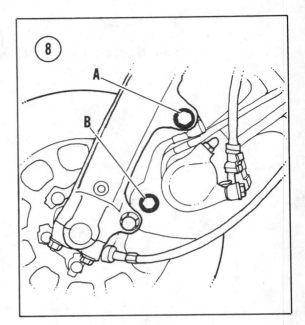

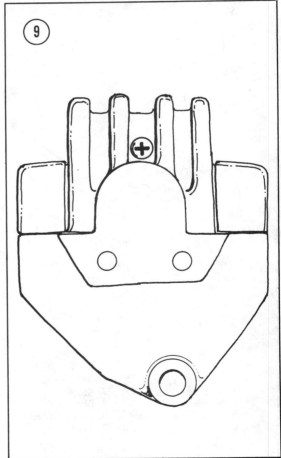

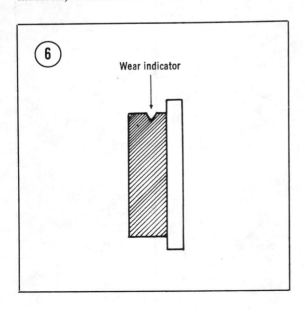

Wear indicator

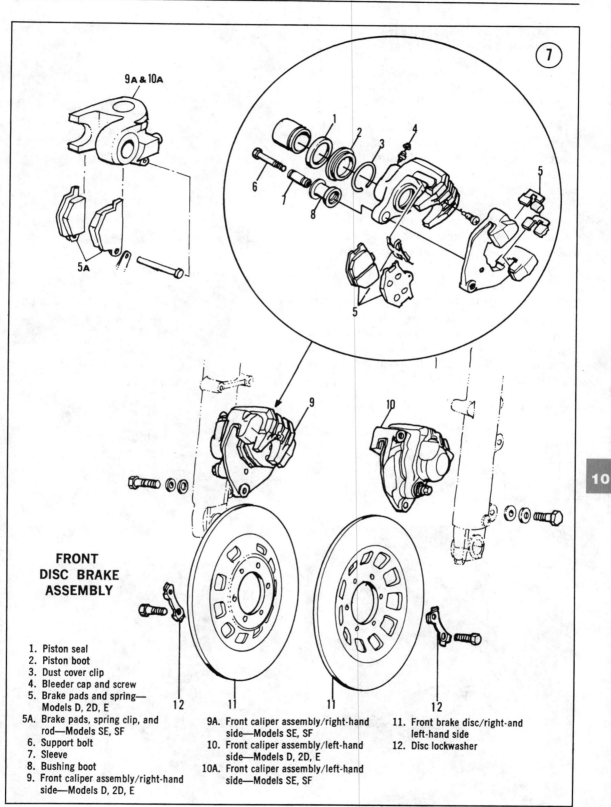

FRONT
DISC BRAKE
ASSEMBLY

1. Piston seal
2. Piston boot
3. Dust cover clip
4. Bleeder cap and screw
5. Brake pads and spring—
   Models D, 2D, E
5A. Brake pads, spring clip, and
   rod—Models SE, SF
6. Support bolt
7. Sleeve
8. Bushing boot
9. Front caliper assembly/right-hand
   side—Models D, 2D, E

9A. Front caliper assembly/right-hand
   side—Models SE, SF
10. Front caliper assembly/left-hand
   side—Models D, 2D, E
10A. Front caliper assembly/left-hand
   side—Models SE, SF

11. Front brake disc/right-and
   left-hand side
12. Disc lockwasher

NOTE: *Check with your dealer to make sure the friction compound of the new pads is compatible with the disc material. Remove any roughness from the backs of new pads with a fine cut file and blow clean with compressed air.*

5. Remove the cap from the master cylinder and slowly push the piston into the caliper while checking the reservoir to make sure the brake fluid does not overflow. Remove fluid necessary prior to overflowing. The piston should move freely. If it does not and there any evidence of it sticking in the cylinder, the caliper should be removed and serviced as described under *Caliper Rebuilding* in this chapter.

6. Push the caliper to the right and push the piston in to allow the new pads to be installed.

7. Install the new pads (**Figure 13**). *On Models D, 2D, E and F:* replace the 3 shims and the pad retaining screw. *On Models SE and SF:* install the caliper mounting bolt assembly in the order shown in **Figure 14**.

NOTE: *Do not forget to install the O-ring.*

CAUTION
On Models SE and SF: *Make sure the locating lug on front forks (**Figure 15**) is positioned into the caliper slot.*

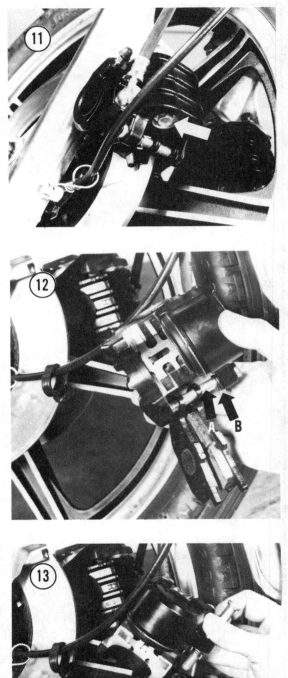

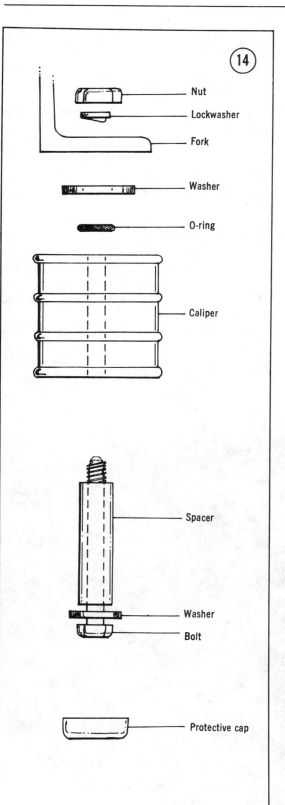

8. Carefully remove any rust or corrosion from the disc.

9. Block the motorcycle up so that the front wheel is off the ground. Spin the front wheel and activate the brake lever for as many times as it takes to refill the cylinder in the caliper and correctly locate the pads.

10. Refill the fluid in the reservoir if necessary and replace the top cap.

WARNING
Use brake fluid clearly marked DOT-3 only. Others may vaporize and cause brake failure. Always use the same brand name; do not intermix as many brands are not compatible.

WARNING
Do not ride the motorcycle until you are sure that the brake is operating correctly with full hydraulic advantage. If necessary, bleed the brakes as described under **Bleeding the System** *at the end of this chapter.*

11. Bed the pads in gradually for the first 50 miles by using only light pressure as much as possible. Immediate hard applications will glaze the new friction pads and greatly reduce the effectiveness of the brakes.

Front Caliper
Removal/Installation

It is not necessary to remove the front wheel to remove either or both caliper assemblies.

Refer to **Figure 7** for this procedure.

1. *On Models D, 2D, E and F:* Remove the upper and lower bolts (**Figure 8**). Pull the caliper assembly off the disc.

2. *On Models SE and SF:* Remove the plastic protective cap (**Figure 10**) and remove the caliper mounting bolt assembly (**Figure 11**). Slide the caliper assembly off the disc.

3. Remove the union bolt (**Figure 16**) securing the brake hose to the caliper and remove it. Drain the brake fluid from the hose and discard it; *never* reuse brake fluid.

4. Repeat Steps 1-3 for the other caliper.

5. Install by reversing these removal steps. *On Models E, SE, and SF:* make sure the locating lug on the front forks (**Figure 15**) is positioned correctly into the caliper slot. Carefully insert the caliper onto the disc. Avoid damage to the pads.

6. Torque the brake hose union bolts to 18 ft.-lb. (24 N•m).

7. *On Models D, 2D, E and F:* Torque the upper mounting bolt to 31 ft.-lb. (41 N•m) and the lower support bolt to 13 ft.-lb. (18 N•m).

8. *On Models SE and SF:* Torque the mounting assembly bolt to 18 ft.-lb. (24 N•m).

> NOTE: *Install caliper mounting bolt assembly in the order shown in* **Figure 14**.

9. Bleed the brakes as described under *Bleeding the System* at the end of this chapter.

WARNING
Do not ride motorcycle until you are sure that brakes are operating properly.

Caliper Rebuilding

If the caliper leaks, it should be rebuilt. If the piston sticks in the cylinder, indicating severe wear or galling, the entire unit should be replaced. Rebuilding a leaky caliper requires special tools and experience.

Caliper service should be entrusted to your Yamaha dealer or brake specialist. Considerable money can be saved by removing the caliper yourself and taking it in for repair.

The factory recommends that the internal seals of the calipers be replaced every two years.

Front Brake Hose Replacement

The factory recommends that all brake hoses be replaced every four years or when they show signs of cracking or damage.

Refer to **Figure 4** for this procedure.

> CAUTION
> *Cover the front wheel, fender, and fuel tank with a heavy cloth or plastic tarp to protect it from accidental spilling of brake fluid. Wash any brake fluid off of any painted or plated surface immediately, as it will destroy the finish. Use soapy water and rinse completely.*

1. Remove the union bolt (**Figure 17**) securing the brake hose to the caliper and remove it. Drain the brake fluid from the hose and discard it — *never* reuse brake fluid. Repeat for the other caliper.

2. Remove the union bolt (**Figure 18**) securing both hoses to the fitting. Release the hoses from the holding brackets and remove them.

3. Remove the union bolt (**Figure 19**) securing the upper hose to the fitting.

4. Remove the union bolt (**Figure 20**) securing the upper hose to the master cylinder and remove the hose.

5. Install new hoses, washers, and union bolts in the reverse order of removal. Be sure to install all washers in the correct position; refer to **Figure 4**. Torque all union bolts to 18 ft.-lb. (24 N•m).

6. Refill the master cylinder with brake fluid clearly marked DOT-3 only. Bleed the brakes as described under *Bleeding the System* at the end of this chapter.

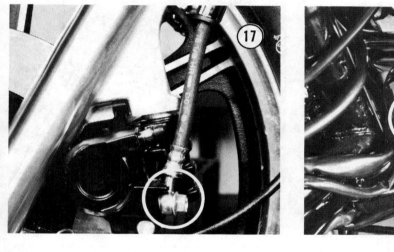

10

REAR DISC BRAKE

The rear disc brake is actuated by hydraulic brake fluid and is controlled by the foot operated brake lever. As the brake pads wear, the brake fluid drops in the reservoir and automatically adjusts for wear. However, brake lever free play must be maintained; refer to *Rear Brake Height and Free Play Adjustment* in Chapter Three.

Refer to the note regarding hydraulic brake work habits in *Front Disc Brakes* at the beginning of this chapter.

Rear Master Cylinder
Removal/Installation

> CAUTION
> *Cover the surrounding frame with a heavy cloth or plastic tarp to protect it from accidental spilling of brake fluid. Wash any brake fluid off of any painted or plated surface immediately, as it will destroy the finish. Use soapy water and rinse completely.*

Refer to **Figure 5** for this procedure.

1. Remove the union bolt (**Figure 21**) securing the brake hose to the master cylinder and remove the hose.

2. Remove the bolt and lockwasher (**Figure 22**) securing the master cylinder to the frame and remove it. Pull the master cylinder straight up and off the brake actuating rod.

3. Install by reversing these removal steps. Inspect the brake actuating rod boot on the bottom of master cylinder. Replace it if cracked or deteriorated.

4. Torque master cylinder to frame bolt to 13 ft.-lb. (18 N•m).

5. Torque the union bolts to 18 ft.-lb. (24 N•m).

6. Bleed the brake as described under *Bleeding the System* at the end of this chapter.

REAR MASTER CYLINDER

Disassembly/Inspection/Assembly

These procedures are identical for front and rear master cylinders. Refer to *Master Cylinder Disassembly/Inspection/Assembly* procedures under *Front Disc Brake*.

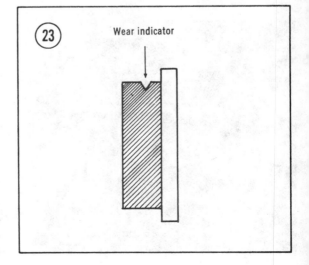

Wear indicator

Rear Brake Pad Replacement

There is no recommended mileage interval for changing the friction pads in the disc brake. Pad wear depends greatly on riding habits and conditions. The pads should be checked for wear every 2,500 miles (4,000km) and replaced when the wear indicator (**Figure 23**) reaches the edge of the brake disc. Always replace both pads at the same time.

It is not necessary to remove the rear wheel to replace the pads.

Refer to **Figure 24** for this procedure.

1. Place the bike on the centerstand.

2. Remove the cotter pin and rear axle nut (**Figure 25**).

3. Loosen the axle pinch bolt (A, **Figure 26**) and withdraw the axle from the right-hand side. Do not lose the axle spacer (B, **Figure 26**).

4. Remove the acorn nut and lockwasher (**Figure 27**) and pivot the caliper assembly up (**Figure 28**) and off the disc.

5. From the backside of the caliper assembly, remove the screw (**Figure 29**) securing the pads in place. Remove the pads and shims.

6. Clean the pad recess and end of the piston with a soft brush. Do not use solvent, a wire brush, or any hard tool which would damage the cylinder or the piston.

7. Lightly coat the end of the piston and the backs of the new pads (not the friction material) with disc brake lubricant.

10

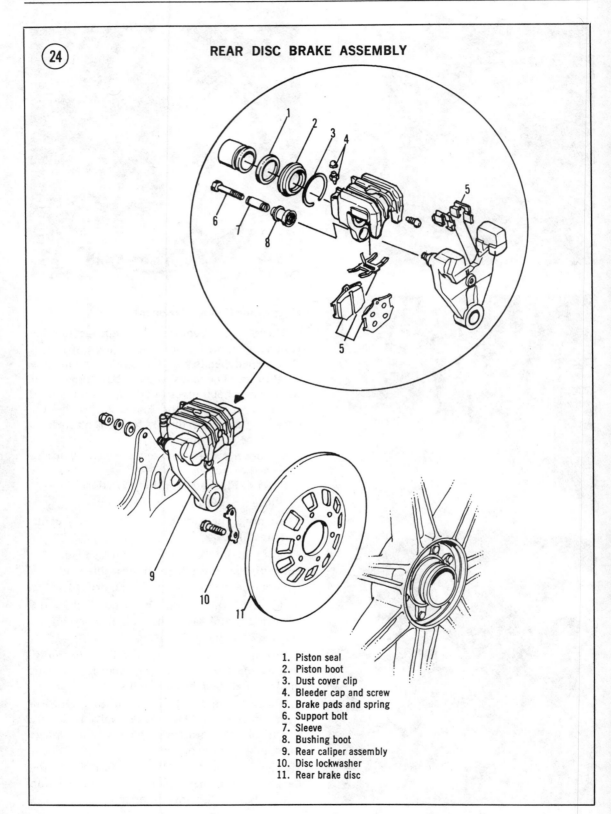

REAR DISC BRAKE ASSEMBLY

1. Piston seal
2. Piston boot
3. Dust cover clip
4. Bleeder cap and screw
5. Brake pads and spring
6. Support bolt
7. Sleeve
8. Bushing boot
9. Rear caliper assembly
10. Disc lockwasher
11. Rear brake disc

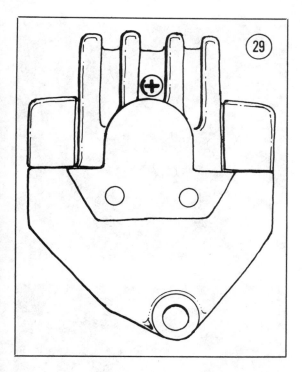

NOTE: *Check with your dealer to make sure the friction compound of the new pads is compatible with the disc material. Remove any roughness from backs of the new pads with a fine cut file and blow clean with compressed air.*

8. Remove the cap from the master cylinder and slowly push the piston into the caliper while checking the reservoir to make sure the brake fluid does not overflow. Remove fluid if necessary, prior to overflowing. The piston

should move freely. If it does not and there is any evidence of it sticking in the cylinder, the caliper should be removed and serviced as described under *Caliper Rebuilding* in this chapter.

9. Push the caliper to the right and push the piston in to allow the new pads to be installed.

10. Install the new pads and new shims.

11. Carefully remove any rust or corrosion from the disc.

12. Block the motorcycle up so that the rear wheel is off the ground. Spin the wheel and activate the brake pedal for as many times as it takes to refill the cylinder in the caliper and correctly locate the pads.

13. Refill the fluid in the reservoir if necessary and replace the top cap.

WARNING
Use brake fluid clearly marked DOT-3 only. Others may vaporize and cause brake failure. Always use the same brand name; do not intermix as many brands are not compatible.

WARNING
*Do not ride the motorcycle until you are sure that the brake is operating correctly with full hydraulic advantage. If necessary, bleed the brakes as described under **Bleeding the System** in this chapter.*

14. Bed the pads in gradually for the first 50 miles by using only light pressure as much as possible. Immediate hard application will glaze the new friction pads and greatly reduce the effectiveness of the brake.

15. Torque the rear axle pinch bolt to 5 ft.-lb. (6.8 N•m) and the axle bolt to 76 ft.-lb. (102 N•m).

Rear Caliper Removal/Installation

It is not necessary to remove the rear wheel to remove the caliper assembly.

Refer to **Figure 24** for this procedure.

1. Remove the union bolt **(Figure 30)** securing the brake hose to the caliper and remove the hose. Drain the brake fluid from the hose and discard it; *never* reuse brake fluid.

10

2. Perform Steps 1-4, *Rear Brake Pad Replacement* in this chapter.

3. Install by reversing these removal steps. Torque the rear axle pinch bolt to 5 ft.-lb. (6.8 N•m) and the axle bolt to 76 ft.-lb. (102 N•m).

4. Bleed the brake as described under *Bleeding the System* at the end of this chapter.

> **WARNING**
> *Do not ride the motorcycle until you are sure the brakes are operating properly.*

Caliper Rebuilding

If the caliper leaks, it should be rebuilt. If the piston sticks in the cylinder, indicating severe wear or galling, the entire unit should be replaced. Rebuilding a leaky caliper requires special tools and experience.

Caliper service should be entrusted to your Yamaha dealer or brake specialist. Considerable money can be saved by removing the caliper yourself and taking it in for repair.

The factory recommends that the internal caliper seals be replaced every two years.

Rear Brake Hose Replacement

The factory recommends that the brake hose be replaced every four years or when it shows signs of cracking or damage.

Refer to **Figure 5** for this procedure.

> **CAUTION**
> *Cover the surrounding frame area with a heavy cloth or plastic tarp to protect it from the accidental spilling of brake fluid. Wash any brake fluid off of any painted or plated surface immediately, as it will destroy the finish. Use soapy water and rinse completely.*

1. Remove the union bolt **(Figure 31)** securing the brake hose to the master cylinder. Drain the brake fluid from the hose and discard it — *never* reuse brake fluid.

2. Remove the union bolt **(Figure 30)** securing the brake hose to the caliper. Remove the hose from the holder brackets and remove the hose.

3. Install the new hose, washers, and union bolts in the reverse order of removal. Be sure to install all washers in the correct positions; refer to **Figure 5**.

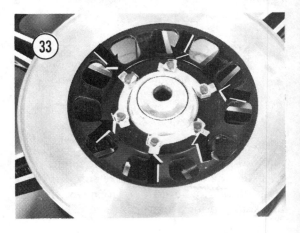

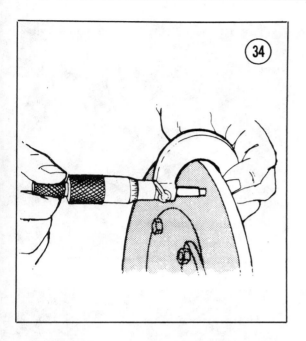

(34)

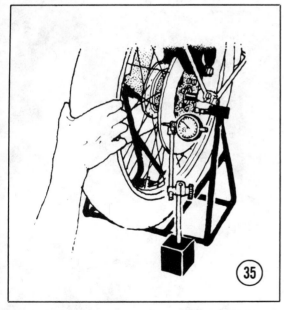

(35)

BRAKE DISC (FRONT AND REAR)

Removal/Installation

This procedure applies to both front and rear discs.

1. Remove the wheel as described under *Front* or *Rear Wheel Removal/Installation* in Chapters Eight or Nine respectively.

> NOTE: *Insert a piece of wood in the caliper(s) in place of the disc. This way, if the brake lever is inadvertently squeezed or depressed the piston will not be forced out of the cylinder. If this does happen, the caliper might have to be disassembled to reseat the piston, and the system will have to be bled. By using the wood, bleeding the brake is not necessary when installing the wheel.*

2. Straighten the locking tabs and remove the 6 bolts (**Figure 33**) securing the disc to the wheel.

3. Install by reversing these steps. Torque the bolts to 15 ft.-lb. (20 N•m). Always install new locking tabs and make sure to bend up one tab against a flat side of each bolt.

Inspection

10

It is not necessary to remove the disc from the wheel to inspect it. Small marks on the disc are not important, but deep radial scratches, deep enough to snag a fingernail, reduce braking effectiveness and increase pad wear. The disc should be replaced.

1. Measure the thickness at several points around the disc with vernier caliper or micrometer (**Figure 34**). The disc must be replaced if the thickness, at any point, is less than 0.26 in. (6.5mm).

2. Check the disc runout with a dial indicator. Raise the wheel being checked and set the arm of a dial indicator against the surface of the disc (**Figure 35**) and slowly rotate the wheel while watching the indicator. If the runout is greater than 0.006 in. (0.15mm), the disc must be replaced.

3. Clean the disc of any rust or corrosion with a non-petroleum based solvent.

4. Make sure the brake hose is positioned correctly in the holding bracket (**Figure 32**) so it will not come in contact with any moving parts (shock absorber, wheel, etc.). Tighten all union bolts to 18 ft.-lb. (24 N•m).

5. Refill the master cylinder with brake fluid clearly marked DOT-3. Bleed the brake as described under *Bleeding the System* at the end of this chapter.

BLEEDING THE SYSTEM

This procedure is not necessary unless the brakes feel spongy, there has been a leak in the system, a component has been replaced, or the brake fluid has been replaced.

This procedure pertains to both the front and rear brake systems. When bleeding the front system, do one caliper at a time.

1. Remove the dust cap from the brake bleed valve.

2. Connect a length of clear tubing to the bleed valve on the caliper. See **Figure 36** for the front and **Figure 37** for the rear. Place the other end of the tube into a clean container. Fill the container with enough fresh brake fluid to keep the end submerged. The tube should be long enough so that a loop can be made higher than the bleed valve to prevent air from being drawn into the caliper during bleeding.

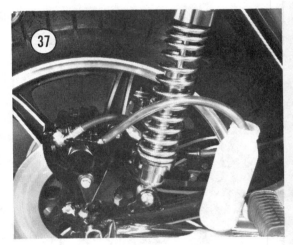

> CAUTION
> *Cover the fuel tank and instrument cluster or the rear frame area with a heavy cloth or plastic tarp to protect it from the accidental spilling of brake fluid. Wash any brake fluid off of any painted or plated surface immediately, as it will destroy the finish. Use soapy water and rinse completley.*

3. Clean the top of the master cylinder of all dirt and foreign matter. Remove the screws **(Figure 38)** securing the cap and remove the cap, diaphragm, and gasket. Fill the reservoir almost to the top lip, insert the diaphragm and gasket, and reinstall the cap loosely. Leave the cap in place during this procedure to prevent the entry of dirt.

> WARNING
> *Use brake fluid clearly marked DOT-3 only. Others may vaporize and cause brake failure. Always use the same brand name; do not intermix as many brands are not compatible.*

4. Slowly apply the brake lever or pedal several times. Pull the lever in or push the pedal down. Hold the lever or pedal in the ON position. Open the bleed valve about one-half turn. Allow the lever or pedal to travel to its limit. When this limit is reached, tighten the bleed screw. As the

fluid enters the system, the level will drop in the reservoir. Maintain the level at about ⅜ inch from the top of the reservoir to prevent air from being drawn into the system.

5. Continue to pump the lever or pedal and fill the reservoir until the fluid emerging from the hose is completely free of bubbles.

> NOTE: *Do not allow the reservoir to empty during the bleeding operation or more air will enter the system. If this occurs, the entire procedure must be repeated.*

6. Hold the lever or pedal down, tighten the bleed valve, remove the bleed tube, and install the bleed valve dust cap.

7. If necessary, add fluid to correct the level in the reservoir. It should be to the *upper* level line.

8. Install the reservoir cap tightly.

9. Test the feel of the brake lever and pedal. It should be firm and should offer the same resistance each time that it's operated. If it feels spongy, it is likely that there is still air in the system and it must be bled again. When all air has been bled from the system and the fluid level is correct in the reservoir, double check for leaks and tighten all the fittings and connections.

WARNING
Before riding the motorcycle, make certain that the brakes are operating correctly by operating the lever and pedal several times.

10

CHAPTER ELEVEN

FRAME AND REPAINTING

This chapter describes procedures for completely stripping the frame. In addition, recommendations are provided for repainting the stripped frame.

This chapter also includes procedures for the kickstand, centerstand, and footpegs.

KICKSTAND (SIDE STAND)

Removal/Installation

1. Place the bike on the centerstand.

2. Raise the kickstand and disconnect the return spring (A, **Figure 1**) from the frame with Vise Grips.

3. Remove the cotter pin and unbolt the kickstand from the frame (B, **Figure 1**).

4. Install by reversing these removal steps. Apply a light coat of multipurpose grease to the pivot surfaces of the frame tab and the kickstand yoke prior to installation.

CENTERSTAND

Removal/Installation

1. Block up the engine or support the bike on the kickstand.

2. Place the centerstand in the raised position and disconnect the return spring (A, **Figure 2**) from the frame loop with Vise Grips.

3. Loosen the self-locking nuts on the frame brackets (B, **Figure 2**). Remove the bolts and the centerstand.

4. Install by reversing these removal steps. Apply a light coat of multipurpose grease to all pivoting points prior to installation.

FOOTPEGS

Replacement

Remove the bolts securing the front and rear footpegs (**Figure 3**) to the frame. The rear bolt also secures the muffler in place.

When installing the footpegs, make sure the alignment tabs are correctly positioned.

FRAME

The frame does not require periodic maintenance. However, all welds should be examined immediately after any accident, even a slight one.

Component Removal/Installation

1. Disconnect the negative battery cable. Remove the fuel tank, seat, and battery.

2. Remove the engine as described in Chapter Four.

3. Remove the front wheel, steering, and suspension components as described in Chapter Eight.

4. Remove the rear wheel and suspension components. See Chapter Nine.

5. Remove the lighting and other electrical equipment. Remove the wiring harness. See Chapter Seven.

6. Remove the kickstand and centerstand as described in this chapter.

7. Remove the bearing races from the steering head tube as described in Chapter Eight.

8. Check the frame for bends, cracks, or other damage, especially around welded joints and areas which are rusted.

9. Assemble by reversing the removal steps.

Stripping and Painting

Remove all components from the frame. Thoroughly strip off all old paint. The best way is to have it sandblasted down to bare metal. If this is not possible, you can use a liquid paint remover like Strypeeze, or equivalent, and steel wool and a fine, hard wire brush.

CAUTION
The side panels, part of the rear fender, and the instrument housing, are plastic. If you wish to change the color of these parts, consult an automotive paint supplier for the proper procedure. Do not use any liquid paint remover on these components as it will damage the surface. The color is an integral part of component and cannot be removed.

When the frame is down to bare metal, have it inspected for hairline and internal cracks. Magnafluxing is the most common process.

Make sure that the primer is compatible with the type of paint you are going to use for the final coat. Spray one or two coats of primer as smoothly as possible. Let it dry thoroughly and use a fine grade of wet sandpaper (400-600 grit) to remove any flaws. Carefully wipe the surface clean and then spray the final coat. Use either lacquer or enamel and follow the manufacturer's instructions.

A shop specializing in painting will probably do the best job. However, you can do a surprisingly good job with a good grade of spray paint. Spend a few extra bucks and get a good grade of paint as it will make a difference in how well it looks and how long it will stand up. One trick in using spray paints is to first shake the can thoroughly — make sure the ball inside the can is loose; if not, return it and get a good one. Shake the can as long as is stated on the can. Then immerse the can *upright* in a pot or bucket of *warm water (not hot — not over 120°F).*

WARNING
Higher temperatures could cause the can to burst. **Do not** *place the can in direct contact with any flame or heat source.*

Leave the can in for several minutes. When thoroughly warmed, shake the can again and spray the frame. Several light mist coats are better than one heavy coat. Spray painting is best done in temperatures of 70°-80°F; any temperature above or below this will give you problems.

After the final coat has dried completely, at least 48 hours, any overspray or orange peel may be removed with *a light application* of rubbing compound and finished with polishing compound. Be careful not to rub too hard and go through the finish.

Finish off with a couple of good coats of wax prior to reassembling all the components.

An alternative to painting is powder coating. The process involves spraying electrically charged particles of pigment and resin on the object to be coated, which is negatively charged. The charged powder particles adhere to the electrically grounded object until heated and fused into a smooth coating in a curing oven. Powder coated surfaces are more resistant to chipping, scratching, fading and wearing than other finishes. A variety of colors and textures are available. Powder coating also has advantages over paint as no environmentally hazardous solvents are used.

SUPPLEMENT

1980 AND LATER SERVICE INFORMATION

The following supplement provides additional information for servicing these 1980 and later models:

a. 1980 XS850G, LG, SG.

b. 1981 XS850H, LH, SH.

Other service procedures remain the same as described in the basic book, Chapters One through Twelve.

The chapter headings in this supplement correspond to those in the main portion of this book. If a chapter is not referenced in this supplement, there are no changes affecting that chapter; follow the procedures described for the latest XS750 model in the basic book.

If your bike is covered by this supplement, carefully read the appropriate chapter in the basic book before beginning any work.

CHAPTER ONE

GENERAL INFORMATION

Refer to **Table 1** for general specifications for the XS850.

Table 1 GENERAL SPECIFICATIONS (XS850)

Engine type	Air-cooled, 4-stroke, DOHC, in-line triple
Bore and stroke	2.815 x 2.701 in. (71.5 x 68.8 mm)
Compression ratio	9.2:1
Carburetion	3 Hitachi, constant velocity, 32 mm
Ignition	Fully transistorized
Lubrication	Wet sump, filter, oil pump
Clutch	Wet, multi-plate
Transmission	5-speed, constant mesh
Transmission ratio	
1st	2.285
2nd	1.588
3rd	1.300
4th	1.095
5th	0.956
Starting system	Manual kick and electric
Wheelbase	
G, H	57.1 in. (1,450 mm)
SG, LG, SH, LH	58.7 in. (1,490 mm)
Steering head angle	
G, H	27°
SG, LG, SH, LH	29°
Trail	
G, H	5.16 in. (131 mm)
SG, LG, SH, LH	4.96 in. (126 mm)
Front suspension	Telescopic fork (air-assist)
Travel	6.9 in. (175 mm)
Rear suspension	Swing arm, adjustable shock absorbers
Travel	3.86 in. (98 mm)
Front tire	3.25H19-4PR (tubeless)
Rear tire	4.50H17-4PR (tubeless)
Ground clearance	
G, H	5.5 in. (140 mm)
SG, LG, SH, LH	5.9 in. (150 mm)

(continued)

12

Table 1 GENERAL SPECIFICATIONS (XS850) (continued)

Seat height	
G, H	32.1 in. (815 mm)
SG, LG, SH, LH	31.5 in. (800 mm)
Overall height	
G	46.9 in. (1,190 mm)
H	61.8 in. (1,570 mm)
SG, LG, SH, LH	49.8 in. (1,265 mm)
Overall width	
G, H	36.8 in. (935 mm)
SG, LG, SH, LH	36.4 in. (925 mm)
Overall length	
G, H	89.4 in. (2,270 mm)
SG, LG, SH, LH	86.6 in. (2,200 mm)
Fuel capacity	4.5 gal. (17 liters)
Oil quantity	
Oil change	2.96 qt. (2.8 liters)
Oil and filter change	3.28 qt. (3.1 liters)
Weight (dry)	
G	531 lb. (241 kg)
H	604 lb. (274 kg)
SG, LG, SH, LH	522 lb. (237 kg)

CHAPTER TWO

TROUBLESHOOTING

STARTER

For the XS850H and SH models, add the following steps to the *Starter* troubleshooting procedure:

4. *Starter only operates when the clutch lever is pulled in, even in NEUTRAL*—If the neutral light does not come on in NEUTRAL, but the engine starts when the clutch lever is pulled in, the neutral switch is defective or the connecting wire is open.

5. *Starter operates while transmission is in gear without pulling in the clutch lever*—The neutral switch or connecting wire is shorted to ground.

6. *Starter will not operate while transmission is in gear with the clutch lever pulled in*—The clutch lever switch or connecting wire is shorted to ground.

CHAPTER THREE

PERIODIC LUBRICATION, MAINTENANCE AND TUNE-UP

SERVICE INTERVALS

Refer to **Table 2** for service intervals for all 1980 and later models.

PERIODIC LUBRICATION

Front Fork Oil Specifications

New front fork oil capacity specifications are in **Table 3**.

Front Fork Oil Change

1. Remove the air valve cap and *bleed off all air pressure* from each fork by depressing the valve stem. See **Figure 1**.

> *WARNING*
> *Always bleed off all air pressure; failure to do so may cause personal injury when disassembling the fork.*

> *NOTE*
> *Release the air pressure gradually. If released too fast, fork oil may spurt out with the air. Protect your eyes and clothing accordingly.*

2. Place a drain pan under the drain screw and remove it. See **Figure 2**. Allow the oil to drain for at least 5 minutes. *Never reuse the oil.*

> *CAUTION*
> *Do not allow the fork oil to come in contact with any of the brake components.*

3. Pump the forks several times by pushing on the handlebars to make sure all oil is drained from the fork tube.
4. Inspect the gasket on the drain screw; replace it if necessary. Install the drain screw.
5. Repeat Steps 2-4 for the other fork.
6. Remove the bolts securing the handlebar clamps and remove the handlebar. Lay the handlebar over the instrument panel.
7. Depress the fork cap (**Figure 3**) and fork spring. Remove the spring wire circlip with a

12

small screwdriver. Remove the fork cap slowly as it is under spring pressure from the fork spring.

8. Remove the fork spring.

9. Refill the fork leg with the specified type and quantity fork oil. Refer to **Table 3**.

NOTE
In order to measure the correct amount of fluid, use a plastic baby bottle. These have measurements in cubic centimeters (cc) and fluid ounces (oz.) on the side.

10. After filling each fork tube, slowly pump the fork tubes several times to expel air from the upper and lower fork chambers and to distribute the oil.

11. Inspect the O-ring in the spring seat. Replace it if worn or damaged.

12. Install the fork spring.

13. Push the fork cap into the fork tube and hold it in place while you install the circlip (**Figure 3**).

14. Position the handlebar on the fork crown. Install the top handlebar clamps and install the bolts. Tighten the forward bolts first and then the rear bolts. Tighten all bolts to 13 ft.-lb. (18 N•m). After installation, sit on the bike and make sure the handlebar alignment is correct for your riding position.

15. Adjust the air pressure in both fork tubes as described in this supplement.

PERIODIC MAINTENANCE

Disc Brake Pad Wear
(XS850SG, LG, SH, LH)

To check brake pad wear on these models, look at the pad wear indicator tabs on the front of the caliper (**Figure 4**). If the red line on any pad aligns with the tab, replace all pads.

Clutch Cable Adjustment

Clutch cable free play is 3/32-1/8 in. (2-3 mm) on all 1980 and later models.

Air Cleaner

1. Remove the air cleaner cover wing nut (**Figure 5**) and slide the cover/filter assembly out of the air box. See **Figure 6**.

2. Pull the filter out of the cover (**Figure 6**).

3. Tap the filter lightly to remove most of the dust and dirt, then apply compressed air to the inside surface of the filter.

4. Inspect the filter; make sure it is in good condition. Replace it if necessary.

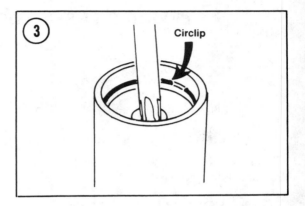

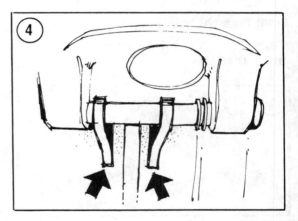

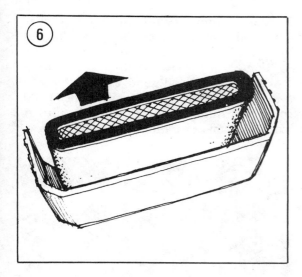

5. Reinstall the filter into the cover. Install the cover/filter assembly and secure it with the wing nut.

SUSPENSION ADJUSTMENT

Front Fork Air Pressure

The air pressure in the front forks must be adjusted for various load conditions (see **Table 4**). An easy way to accomplish this is with the S & W Mini-Pump (**Figure 7**) or equivalent.

1. Place the bike on the centerstand and raise the front wheel off the ground.
2. Attach the air pressure tool to the air fitting (**Figure 8**).
3. Inflate to the desired pressure.

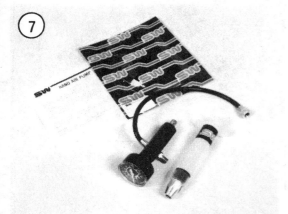

> *CAUTION*
> *Never exceed 36 psi (2.5 kg/cm²) or the oil seal will be damaged. The pressure difference between the two forks should be 1.4 psi (0.1 kg/cm²) or less.*

Rear Shock Absorber Adjustment

The rear shock absorbers must be adjusted to correspond to front fork adjustment and vehicle load (see **Table 4**).

12

1. Turn the upper damping adjuster (**Figure 9**) by hand or with a screwdriver to the desired setting.

> *NOTE*
> *Always turn the adjuster until it clicks into position. If it is set between any 2 click positions it will automatically be set at the maximum (No. 4) damping. Always set both shocks to the same position.*

2. The lower spring seat (**Figure 10**) must also be adjusted as shown in **Table 4**. Rotate the cam ring at the base of the spring—*clockwise to increase* preload and *counterclockwise to decrease* it.

> *NOTE*
> *Use a screwdriver to adjust the spring preload. Set both shocks to the same position.*

ENGINE TUNE-UP

Procedures for tuning the engine remain the same as for 1979 models except as noted under *Ignition Timing* in this supplement. See **Table 5** for tune-up specifications that have changed from those given in Chapter Three of the basic book.

Ignition Timing
(1981 Models)

The 1981 ignition system was modified for easier maintenance and requires inspection only when the pickup coil is disturbed.

Timing is set with a timing light by observing the alignment of the stationary pointer (1, **Figure 11**) in relation to the mark on the timing plate (2, **Figure 11**). The pointer should align with the upside-down "u" mark on the timing plate.

It is only necessary to check timing on the No. 1 cylinder; the other 2 cylinders will automatically be correct.

1. Place the bike on the centerstand.

2. Connect a portable tachometer following the manufacturer's instructions. The bike's tachometer is not accurate enough in the low rpm range for this adjustment.

3. Attach a timing light to the No. 1 cylinder (left-hand side) spark plug wire according to the manufacturer's instructions.

4. Remove the screws securing the ignition cover (**Figure 12**) and remove it.

5. Start the engine and allow it to idle (1,100 rpm). Continue to idle the engine until it reaches normal operating temperature.

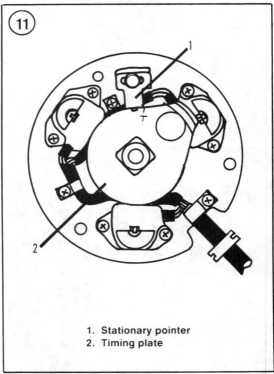

1. Stationary pointer
2. Timing plate

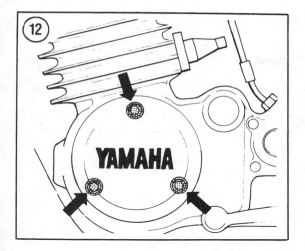

6. Aim the timing light at the timing plate.

7. The stationary pointer should align with the mark on the timing plate. If not, check the timing plate and pickup coil fasteners for tightness. If the ignition timing is not within specifications and the fasteners are tight, there is a problem with the ignition system; ignition timing is not adjustable. Refer to *Ignition System Troubleshooting* in Chapter Seven of the basic book and in the Chapter Seven section of this supplement.

8. If the ignition timing is within specifications, shut off the engine, reinstall the ignition cover and disconnect the portable tachometer and timing light.

Table 2 MAINTENANCE SCHEDULE*

Initial 600 miles (1,000 km) or 1 month
- Change engine oil and filter
- Check front and rear brake free play; adjust if required
- Check front brake pad and rear brake shoe thickness; replace if required
- Adjust clutch free play
- Lubricate all control cables
- Adjust cam chain tension

Initial 600 miles (1,000 km) or 1 month; then every 5,000 miles (8,000 km) or 12 months
- Check middle/final gear oil level

Initial 3,000 miles (5,000 km) or 6 months; then every 2,500 miles (4,000 km) or 6 months
- Check exhaust system mounting bolts and gasket
- Check engine idle speed; adjust if required
- Check carburetor synchronization and adjust if required
- Change engine oil and filter
- Check front and rear brake free play; adjust if required
- Check front and rear brake pad thickness; replace if required
- Adjust clutch free play
- Lubricate all control cables
- Lubricate clutch and brake lever pivot points
- Lubricate brake and shift lever pivot points
- Lubricate centerstand and side stand pivot points
- Check steering stem bearings for looseness; adjust if required
- Check front and rear wheel bearings for smooth rotation; replace if required
- Check battery fluid level and specific gravity

Initial 3,000 miles (5,000 km) or 7 months; then every 5,000 miles (8,000 km) or 12 months
- Check and adjust valve clearance
- Check crankcase ventilation hose for cracks or damage; replace if required
- Check fuel line and vacuum hoses for cracks or damage; replace if required
- Clean air filter. If filter is damaged or torn, replace it.

(continued)

12

Table 2 MAINTENANCE SCHEDULE* (continued)

Initial 8,000 miles (13,000 km) or 18 months; then every 7,500 miles (12,000 km) or 18 months	• Replace spark plugs
Every 10,000 miles (16,000 km) or 24 months	• Repack steering bearing grease • Repack swing arm bearings

* This Yamaha factory maintenance schedule should be used as a guide to general maintenance and lubrication intervals. Harder than normal use and exposure to mud, water, sand, high humidity, etc., will dictate more frequent attention to most maintenance items.

Table 3 FRONT FORK OIL CAPACITY

Model	Quantity (each fork)	Oil type
G, H	6.59 oz. (195 cc)	SAE 10 fork oil
SG, LG, SH, LH	9.30 oz. (195 cc)	SAE 10 fork oil

Table 4 RECOMMENDED SUSPENSION SETTING

		Rear Shock Absorber	
Load	Front Fork Air Pressure psi (kg/cm^2)	Lower Spring Seat	Damping Adjuster
Rider	5.7-14 (0.4-1.0)	A-E	1
Rider plus passenger[1]	5.7-14 (0.4-1.0)	A-E	2
Rider plus passenger[2]	14-21 (1.0-1.5)	C-E	3
Maximum vehicle load[3]	21 psi	E	4

1. Load weight of rider and passenger; no luggage.
2. Load weight of rider plus that of passenger and/or luggage.
3. See owner's manual for load limit for your particular model.

Table 5 TUNE-UP SPECIFICATIONS

Valve clearance (cold)	
Intake	0.0043-0.0059 in. (0.11-0.15 mm)
Exhaust	0.008-0.010 in. (0.20-0.25 mm)
Idle speed	1,100 rpm
Compression pressure	156 +/-14 psi
Cold at sea level	(11 +/-1.0 kg/cm^2)

CHAPTER FOUR

ENGINE

SPECIFICATIONS

In 1980, Yamaha increased displacement on the 3-cylinder engine from 45.59 cid (747 cc) to 50.4 cid (826 cc). This was done with a bore increase. Service procedures for the XS850 engine are identical to those for the XS750 engine described in Chapter Four of the basic book, unless otherwise noted in this supplement. Specifications for the XS850 engine are given in **Table 6** of this supplement. Revised engine torque specifications are listed in **Table 7**.

ENGINE

Removal/Installation

The XS850H is factory-equipped with a fairing. Remove it prior to removing the engine; see *Fairing Removal/Installation* in the Chapter Eleven section of this supplement.

KICKSTARTER

Procedures used to service the kickstarter are the same as for XS750 models, except that a spacer has been added between the idler gear circlip and shim washer. See 15, **Figure 13**.

12

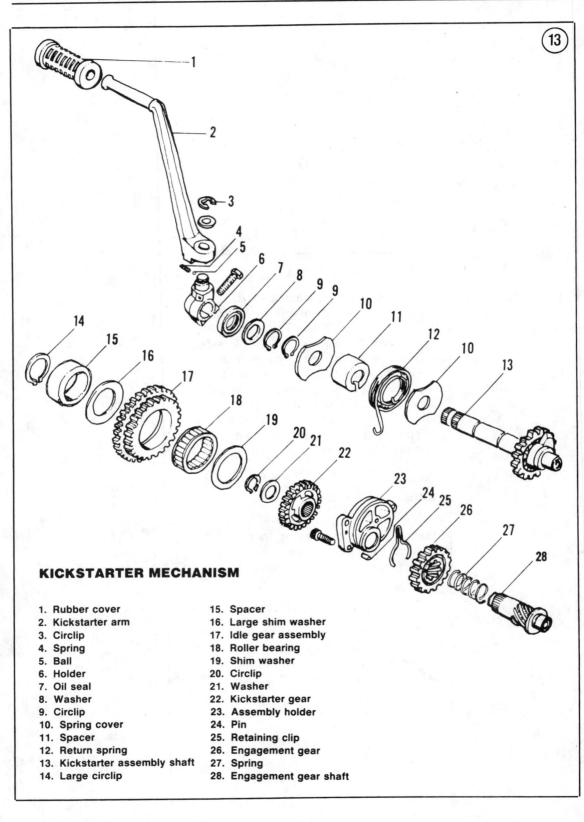

⑬

KICKSTARTER MECHANISM

1. Rubber cover
2. Kickstarter arm
3. Circlip
4. Spring
5. Ball
6. Holder
7. Oil seal
8. Washer
9. Circlip
10. Spring cover
11. Spacer
12. Return spring
13. Kickstarter assembly shaft
14. Large circlip

15. Spacer
16. Large shim washer
17. Idle gear assembly
18. Roller bearing
19. Shim washer
20. Circlip
21. Washer
22. Kickstarter gear
23. Assembly holder
24. Pin
25. Retaining clip
26. Engagement gear
27. Spring
28. Engagement gear shaft

Table 6 ENGINE SPECIFICATIONS

Item	Specifications	Wear Limit
General		
Number of cylinders	3	—
Bore x stroke	2.815 x 2.701 in. (71.5 x 68.6 mm)	—
Displacement	50.4 cu. in. (826 cc)	—
Compression ratio	9.2 to 1	—
Compression pressure		
Warm at sea level	156 +/- 14 psi (11 +/- 1 kg/cm^2)	—
Cylinders		
Bore	2.815-2.816 in. (71.50-71.52 mm)	2.8189 in. (71.60 mm)
Out-of-round	—	0.002 in. (0.05 mm)
Cylinder/piston clearance	0.0020-0.0022 in. (0.050-0.055 mm)	0.004 in. (0.1 mm)
Pistons		
Diameter	2.8130-2.8128 in. (71.450-71.455 mm)	—
Clearance in bore	0.0020-0.0022 in. (0.050-0.055 mm)	0.004 in. (0.1 mm)
Piston rings		
Number per piston		
Compression	2	—
Oil control	1	—
Ring end gap		
Top	0.008-0.016 in. (0.2-0.4 mm)	0.039 in. (1.0 mm)
Second	0.008-0.016 in. (0.2-0.4 mm)	0.039 in. (1.0 mm)
Oil control	0.0118-0.035 in. (0.3-0.9 mm)	0.059 in. (1.5 mm)
Ring side clearance		
Top	0.0016-0.0031 in. (0.04-0.08 mm)	0.0059 in. (0.15 mm)
Second	0.0012-0.0028 in. (0.03-0.07 mm)	0.0059 in. 0.15 mm)
Crankshaft		
Main bearing oil clearance	0.0024-0.0032 in. (0.060-0.082 mm)	—
Connecting rod oil clearance	0.0017-0.0025 in. (0.042-0.064 mm)	—
Main bearing journal runout	0.0012 in. (0.03 mm)	
Camshaft		
Cam lobe height		
Intake	1.449 +/-0.002 in. (36.805 +/-0.05 mm)	1.443 in. (36.65 mm)
Exhaust	1.429 +/-0.002 in. (36.305 +/-0.05 mm)	1.423 in. (36.15 mm)
Camshaft-to-cap clearance	0.0008-0.0021 in. (0.020-0.054 mm)	0.006 in. (0.16 mm)
Runout limit	—	0.004 in. (0.1 mm)
Valves		
Valve stem clearance		
Intake	0.0004-0.0016 in. (0.01-0.04 mm)	—
Exhaust	0.0010-0.0022 in. (0.025-0.055 mm)	—

(continued)

12

Table 6 ENGINE SPECIFICATIONS (continued)

Item	Specifications	Wear Limit
Valve guide inner diameter—intake and exhaust	0.276-0.277 in. (7.0-7.015 mm)	—
Valve seat width	0.0433 +/-0.004 in. (1.1 +/-0.1 mm)	—
Valve springs Free length (inner) Intake and exhaust	1.402 in. (35.6 mm)	1.322 in. (33.6 mm)
Free length (outer) Intake and exhaust	1.571 in. (39.9 mm)	1.491 in. (37.9 mm)
Allowable tilt from vertical Intake		0.063 in. (1.6 mm)
Exhaust		0.069 in. (1.75 mm)

Table 7 ENGINE TORQUE SPECIFICATIONS

Item	Ft.-lb.	N•m
Alternator rotor bolt	36	50
Engine mounting bolts 12 mm flange bolts and nuts	18	25

CHAPTER FIVE

CLUTCH AND TRANSMISSION

Minor modifications to the transmission and clutch assemblies were made in 1980 to accommodate the added power of the XS850 engine. Disassembly and assembly procedures are similar; note the following changes.

CLUTCH

One additional friction plate was added and clutch plates of 2 different thicknesses are now used. Observe the sequence which must be used during assembly (**Figure 14**). The thinner plates (3, **Figure 14**) are 0.063 in. (1.6 mm) thick and the thicker plates are 0.079 in. (2.0 mm) thick. Inspect and measure the plates as described in Chapter Five of the basic book. New clutch torque specifications are:

    a. Locknut—79 ft.-lb. (110 N•m).
    b. Screws—6.5 ft.-lb. (9 N•m).

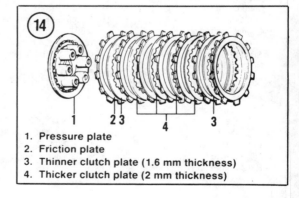

1. Pressure plate
2. Friction plate
3. Thinner clutch plate (1.6 mm thickness)
4. Thicker clutch plate (2 mm thickness)

TRANSMISSION

The transmission assembly for all XS850 models is shown in **Figure 15**. Procedures for servicing the transmission are the same as for models as described in Chapter Five of the basic book.

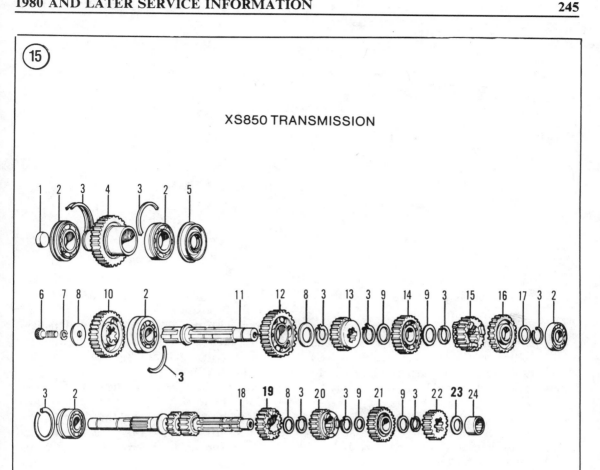

XS850 TRANSMISSION

1. Plug
2. Bearing
3. Circlip
4. Middle driven gear
5. Oil seal
6. Bolt
7. Lockwasher
8. Washer
9. Washer
10. Middle drive gear
11. Countershaft
12. Countershaft 1st gear
13. Countershaft 4th gear
14. Countershaft 3rd gear
15. Countershaft 5th gear
16. Countershaft 2nd gear
17. Shim
18. Main shaft
19. Main shaft 4th gear
20. Main shaft 3rd gear
21. Main shaft 5th gear
22. Main shaft 2nd gear
23. Shim
24. Bearing

12

CHAPTER SIX

FUEL AND EXHAUST SYSTEMS

CARBURETORS

Service

The XS850 carburetor is similar to the one used on 1979 XS750 models. **Table 8** lists specifications for XS850 carburetors. Refer to **Figure 16** for disassembly and reassembly.

> *NOTE*
> *The idle mixture is pre-set at the factory with the use of special equipment. It must not be reset.*

Fuel Level Measurement (1981 Models)

The bike must be exactly level for this measurement to be accurate. Place pieces of wood or shims under each side of the centerstand or place a suitable size jack under the engine and position the bike so that the carburetor assembly is level from side to side.

Use a piece of clear vinyl tubing with an inside diameter of 0.24 in. (6 mm). The tubing should be long enough to reach from one side of the carburetor assembly to the other.

> *WARNING*
> *Before starting any procedure involving gasoline have a class B fire extinguisher rated for gasoline or chemical fires within reach. Do not smoke, allow anyone to smoke or work where there are any open flames. The work area must be well-ventilated.*

1. Turn the fuel shutoff valve to the ON or RESERVE position.
2. Start with the No. 1 carburetor (left-hand side). Place a small container under the carburetor to catch any fuel that may drip from the float bowl.
3. Connect the tube to the float bowl nozzle.
4. Hold the loose end of the tube up above the float bowl and loosen the drain screw. Fuel will flow into the tube. Be sure to hold the loose end up or fuel will flow out of the tube.
5. Start the engine and let it run for 2-3 minutes. This is necessary to make sure the fuel level is at the normal operating level in the float bowl.
6. Hold the loose end of the tube up against the No. 1 carburetor body (**Figure 17**). Check

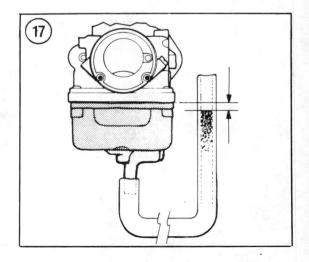

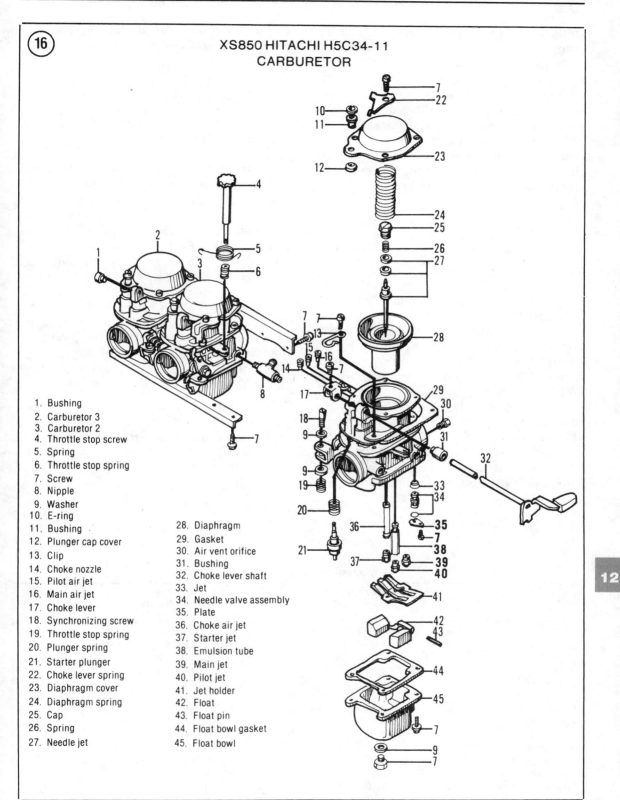

(16)

**XS850 HITACHI H5C34-11
CARBURETOR**

1. Bushing
2. Carburetor 3
3. Carburetor 2
4. Throttle stop screw
5. Spring
6. Throttle stop spring
7. Screw
8. Nipple
9. Washer
10. E-ring
11. Bushing
12. Plunger cap cover
13. Clip
14. Choke nozzle
15. Pilot air jet
16. Main air jet
17. Choke lever
18. Synchronizing screw
19. Throttle stop spring
20. Plunger spring
21. Starter plunger
22. Choke lever spring
23. Diaphragm cover
24. Diaphragm spring
25. Cap
26. Spring
27. Needle jet

28. Diaphragm
29. Gasket
30. Air vent orifice
31. Bushing
32. Choke lever shaft
33. Jet
34. Needle valve assembly
35. Plate
36. Choke air jet
37. Starter jet
38. Emulsion tube
39. Main jet
40. Pilot jet
41. Jet holder
42. Float
43. Float pin
44. Float bowl gasket
45. Float bowl

12

the fuel level in the tube and mark it with a grease pencil or a piece of masking tape.

7. Insert a golf tee into the open end of the tube so fuel will not drain out when moving the tube from side to side.

8. Move the tube to the other side of the bike and remove the golf tee. Repeat Step 6, holding the tube up against the No. 3 (right-hand) carburetor body. The dimension should be the same; if not, the bike and carburetor assembly are not level.

NOTE
Always insert the golf tee in the tube whenever moving the tube with gasoline in it.

9. Readjust the shims under the centerstand or adjust the jack until exactly level—*this is necessary to obtain correct measurements.* Repeat Steps 6-8 until the bike is level.

10. After the carburetor assembly is level hold the loose end of the tube up against the No. 1 carburetor body. Check the fuel level in the tube. It should be 0.04 ±0.04 in. (1 ±1 mm) below the top surface of the float bowl (**Figure 17**).

11. Tighten the drain screw and hold both ends of the tube at the same height so fuel will not drain out. Remove the tube from the carburetor float bowl nozzle. Immediately wipe up any spilled fuel on the engine.

WARNING
Do not let any fuel spill on the exhaust system as it is hot.

12. Repeat Steps 2-6, 10 and 11 for the No. 2 and 3 carburetors. Record the measurements of all 3 carburetors.

13. If the fuel level is incorrect on any of the carburetors, remove the carburetor assembly and adjust the float as described under *Float Adjustment* in Chapter Six of the main book. Do not use the float level specification in that procedure; it is for earlier models.

14. Adjust the float tang on affected carburetor(s). If the fuel level on one or more of the carburetors is correct, use that as a guide for correct float height.

15. Bend the float tang upward very slightly to lower the fuel level; bend the float tang downward to raise the fuel level.

16. Install the carburetor assembly and repeat this procedure until all fuel levels are correct.

CAUTION
The 3 carburetors must be adjusted to exactly the same position to maintain the same fuel-air mixture to all 3 cylinders.

Table 8 CARBURETOR SPECIFICATIONS

Item	Models G, SG, LG	Models H, SH, LH
Type	Hitachi	Hitachi
Model	3J3-00	3J2-00
Main jet	142	142
Pilot jet	40	40
Starter jet	40	40
Jet needle	Y-01	Y-01
Float height	0.492 in. (12.5 mm)	—
Fuel level	—	1/32 in. (1 mm)
Pilot screw	Preset	Preset
Main air jet	50	50
Pilot air jet	155	155
Float valve seat	2.0	2.0
Engine idle speed	1,100 rpm	1,100 rpm

CHAPTER SEVEN

ELECTRICAL SYSTEM

Procedures used to check the transistorized ignition system are the same as for 1979 and earlier models, except that pickup coil testing specifications have changed.

1. Unplug the 8-prong pickup coil connector from the ignitor unit.
2. Using an ohmmeter set on the R×100 scale, measure the resistance at the following wires:
   a. Yellow to black.
   b. Gray to black.
   c. Orange to black.
3. In all cases, the resistance should be 700 ohms ±20%. If the test results were incorrect in any one check, the pickup coil must be replaced.

PICKUP COIL ASSEMBLY (1980 MODELS)

Removal

1. Place the bike on the centerstand.
2. Remove the screws securing the ignition cover (**Figure 12**) and remove it.
3. Loosen the Allen bolt securing the governor in position. Remove the Allen bolt and the special nut.
4. Remove the neutral switch wire. Remove the pickup coil wires from the clamps on the crankcase.

NOTE
When the timing plate was installed at the factory, special bolts were used. They have a head that shears off when the correct torque is achieved, thus leaving no bolt head for removal.

5. Flatten the special bolt heads on the timing plate with a flat punch (A, **Figure 18**), then punch a starting hole in the center of each bolt.

CAUTION
Make sure the punch mark is centered, otherwise the drilled hole will be offset and will damage the threads in the crankcase.

6. With a 1/8 in. (3 mm) drill bit, drill a hole approximately 1/4-1/2 in. deep in each bolt (B, **Figure 18**).
7. Tap a screw extractor into the hole with a hammer (C, **Figure 18**) and unscrew the bolt (D, **Figure 18**). Repeat for the other bolt.
8. Remove the pickup coil and governor assemblies from the crankcase.

Installation/Adjustment

This procedure must be performed when you are installing a new pickup coil/governor assembly. The ignition timing must be calibrated.

1. Install the governor assembly on the end of the crankshaft. Make sure to align the slot in the back of the governor plate with the pin in the end of the crankshaft.
2. Install the pickup coil assembly. Install the bolts snugly; do not tighten.

NOTE
Yamaha uses special Torx bolts and washers which require a special driver. The bolt heads snap off when tightened. You may prefer to install another type

12

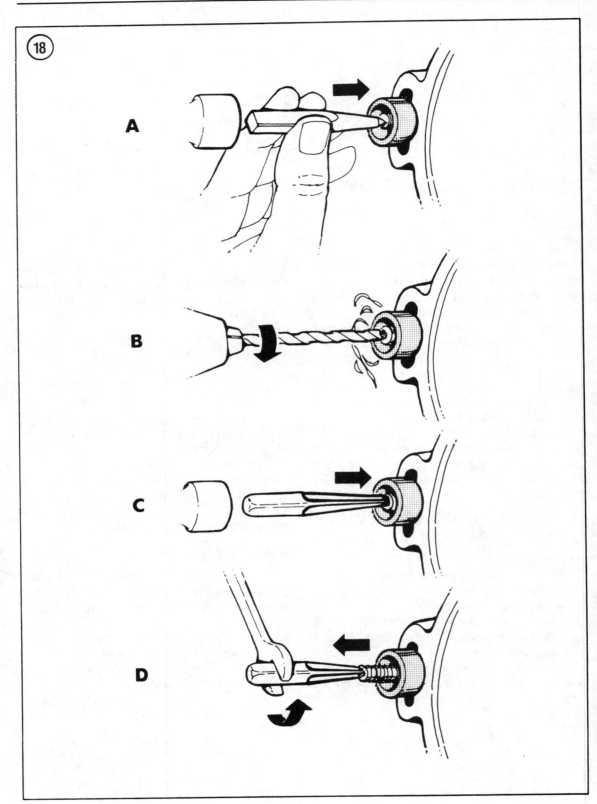

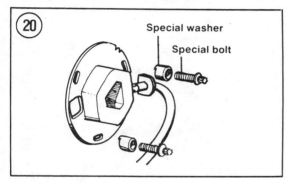

Special washer

Special bolt

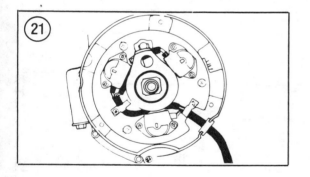

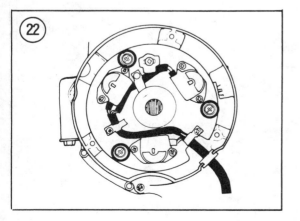

of bolt to ease disassembly later if necessary.

3. Install the crankshaft turning nut and the Allen bolt. Tighten the Allen bolt to 17 ft.-lb. (23 N•m).

4. Remove the left cylinder spark plug. Install a dial indicator as shown in **Figure 19** with the pointer touching the top of the piston. Using the crankshaft turning nut, rotate the engine *counterclockwise* until the left piston is exactly at TDC (top dead center).

5. With the dial indicator showing the No. 1 cylinder piston at TDC, check that the "T" mark on the governor is aligned with the stationary pointer. If the alignment is incorrect, loosen the screw securing the stationary pointer and align it with the governor "T" mark. Tighten the screw securely.

6. Remove the dial indicator and install the left cylinder spark plug. Reconnect the spark plug cap.

7. Using a stroboscopic timing light, check the ignition timing as described in Chapter Three of main book. If the "1F" mark on the governor does not align with the stationary pointer, loosen the pickup coil as required to align the "1F" governor mark with the stationary pointer.

8. When the engine is properly timed, tighten each Torx bolt using a Torx socket (**Figure 20**) until its head breaks off.

PICKUP COIL (1981 MODELS)

Pickup coil mounting on 1981 models has changed from 1980 to aid in removal. In addition, the governor assembly has been replaced with a rotor.

Removal/Installation

1. Place the bike on its centerstand.

2. Remove the screws securing the ignition cover (**Figure 12**) and remove it.

3. Remove the Allen bolt (**Figure 21**) holding the rotor in place.

4. Remove the screws securing the pickup coil (**Figure 22**) and remove the pickup coil assembly.

12

5. Installation is the reverse of these steps, noting the following.

6. When installing the rotor, make sure the slot in the end of the rotor aligns with the pin in the end of the crankshaft. See **Figure 23**.

7. Tighten the Allen bolt to 21 ft.-lb. (30 N•m).

8. Check the ignition timing as described in the Chapter Three section of this supplement. The ignition timing is not adjustable. If incorrect, refer to *Ignition System Troubleshooting* in this supplement and in Chapter Seven of the basic book.

9. Install the ignition cover.

STARTER SYSTEM
(1981 MODELS)

The starting system consists of the starter motor, starter solenoid, starter button and (on all 1981 models) a cut-off relay. The starter system is shown in **Figure 24**.

When the starter button is pressed, it engages the solenoid that closes the circuit. The solenoid will only close when the cut-off relay is closed. The cut-off relay is closed when the sidestand is up and either the clutch is pulled in or the transmission is in NEUTRAL. Once these conditions are met, electricity flows from the battery to the starter motor.

LIGHTING SYSTEM

The reserve lighting system circuit diagram for all XS850 models is shown in **Figure 25**. The self-cancelling flasher system is shown in **Figure 26**. All procedures used to service these systems are the same as described in Chapter Seven of the basic book.

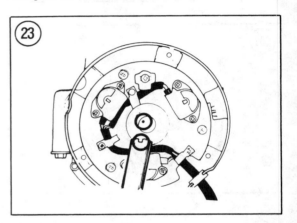

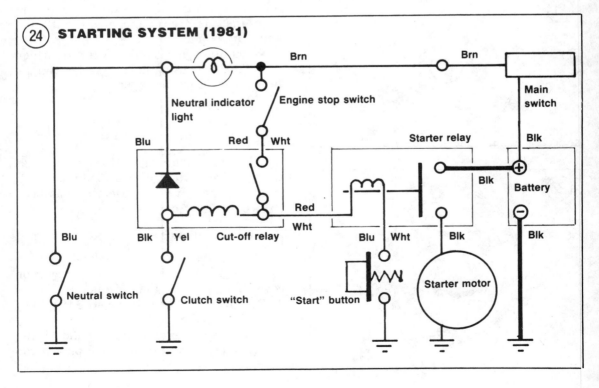

STARTING SYSTEM (1981)

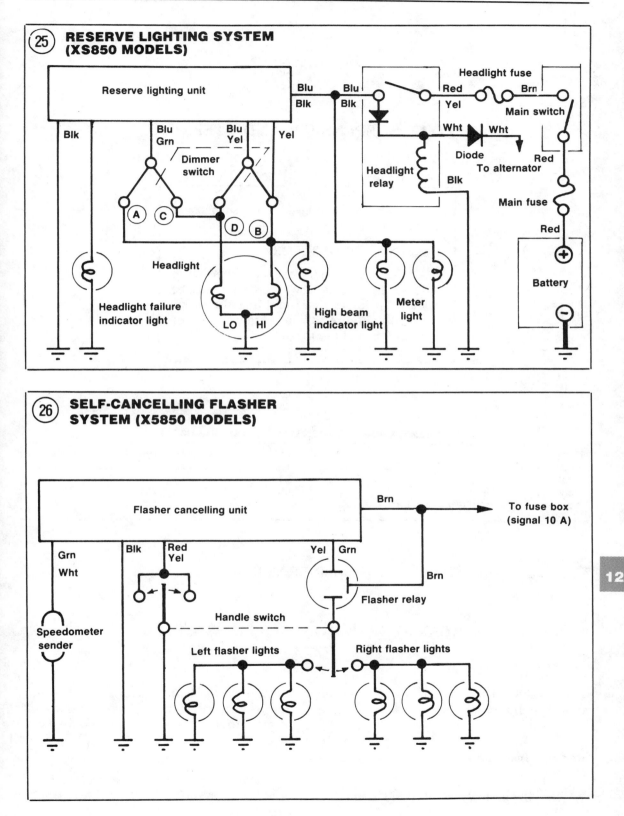

RESERVE LIGHTING SYSTEM (XS850 MODELS)

Reserve lighting unit

Blk

Blu Grn

Blu Yel

Yel

Dimmer switch

A C D B

Headlight

Headlight failure indicator light

LO HI

High beam indicator light

Meter light

Blu / Blk Blu / Blk

Headlight fuse

Red Brn
Yel
Main switch

Wht Wht Diode To alternator

Headlight relay Blk

Red

Main fuse

Red

Battery

SELF-CANCELLING FLASHER SYSTEM (X5850 MODELS)

Flasher cancelling unit

Brn To fuse box (signal 10 A)

Grn Wht

Blk

Red Yel

Yel Grn

Brn

Flasher relay

Handle switch

Speedometer sender

Left flasher lights

Right flasher lights

12

CHAPTER EIGHT

FRONT SUSPENSION AND STEERING

See **Table 9** for revised front suspension torque specifications.

FRONT FORKS

All XS850 models are equipped with air-assist front forks. The air pressure must be released prior to disassembling the forks. Refer to **Figure 27** or **Figure 28** for disassembly and assembly.

Table 9 FRONT SUSPENSION TORQUE VALUES

Item	ft.-lb.	N•m
Front axle nut	77.4	107
Front axle holding nuts (G, H)	14.5	20
Front axle pinch bolt (SG, LG, SH, LH)	14.5	20

CHAPTER NINE

REAR SUSPENSION AND FINAL DRIVE

See **Table 10** for revised rear suspension torque specifications.

REAR WHEEL

**Removal/Installation
(1980 Models)**

1. Place the motorcycle on its sidestand.

2. Remove the bottom left-hand side shock absorber mounting nut and pull the shock off of its mounting stud on the final drive housing.

NOTE
Remove the factory wire hook tool from the motorcycle's tool kit; it will be used

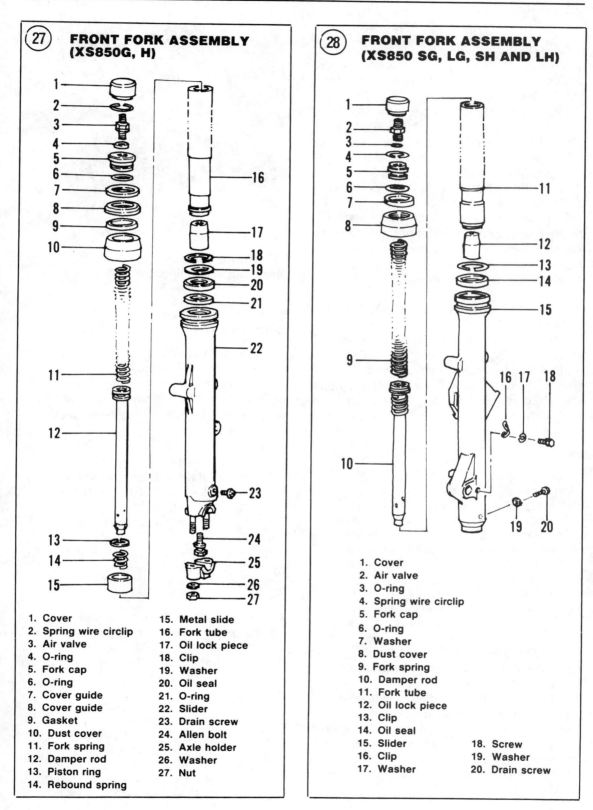

27 **FRONT FORK ASSEMBLY (XS850G, H)**

1. Cover
2. Spring wire circlip
3. Air valve
4. O-ring
5. Fork cap
6. O-ring
7. Cover guide
8. Cover guide
9. Gasket
10. Dust cover
11. Fork spring
12. Damper rod
13. Piston ring
14. Rebound spring
15. Metal slide
16. Fork tube
17. Oil lock piece
18. Clip
19. Washer
20. Oil seal
21. O-ring
22. Slider
23. Drain screw
24. Allen bolt
25. Axle holder
26. Washer
27. Nut

28 **FRONT FORK ASSEMBLY (XS850 SG, LG, SH AND LH)**

1. Cover
2. Air valve
3. O-ring
4. Spring wire circlip
5. Fork cap
6. O-ring
7. Washer
8. Dust cover
9. Fork spring
10. Damper rod
11. Fork tube
12. Oil lock piece
13. Clip
14. Oil seal
15. Slider
16. Clip
17. Washer
18. Screw
19. Washer
20. Drain screw

12

*in the next step. If the tool is missing,
use a bent coat hanger or similar wire.*

2. Attach one end of the hook tool to the frame mount beside the upper right-hand shock absorber mount bolt.

3. With an assistant sitting on the seat, further compress the right-hand shock absorber by pulling up on the swing arm until the bottom end of the hook tool can be attached to the swing arm.

4. Place the motorcycle on its centerstand.

5. Remove the seat. Then remove the bolts (**Figure 29**) securing the rear fender assembly to the frame. Reinstall the bolts and allow the fender to rest on top of them to prevent it from slipping down.

6. Remove the rear axle cotter pin and axle nut.

7. Loosen the rear axle pinch bolt from the right-hand side of the swing arm.

8. Remove the rear axle from the right-hand side.

9. Pull the rear brake torque stopper plate out from its position on the swing arm. Then pull the brake caliper assembly up and rest it on the swing arm.

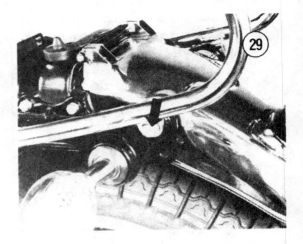

13. Torque the axle nut to 108 ft.-lb. (150 N•m) and the axle pinch bolt to 4 ft.-lb. (5 N•m).

Removal/Installation
(1981 Models)

The shorter mufflers used on 1981 model simplify rear wheel removal.

1. Place the motorcycle on the centerstand.

2. Remove the saddlebags (if so equipped) as described in the Chapter Eleven section of this supplement.

3. Remove the seat. Then remove the bolts (**Figure 29**) securing the rear fender assembly to the frame. Reinstall the bolts and allow the fender to rest on top of them to prevent it from slipping down.

4. Remove the rear axle cotter pin and axle nut.

5. Loosen the rear axle pinch bolt from the right-hand side of the swing arm.

6. Remove the rear axle from the right-hand side.

7. Pull the rear brake torque stopper plate out from its position on the swing arm. Then pull the brake caliper assembly up and hang it on the helmet holder using the wire tool from the tool kit.

NOTE
Insert a piece of wood in the caliper in place of the disc. This way, if the brake pedal is inadvertently depressed, the piston will not be forced out of the cylinder. If this does happen the caliper might have to be disassembled to reseat the piston and the brake system will have to be bled. By using the wood, bleeding the brake should not be necessary when installing the wheel.

10. Slide the wheel to the right to disengage it from the hub drive splines and remove the wheel.

11. Install by reversing these removal steps. Apply molybdenum disulfide grease to the final drive flange splines on the wheel and the ring gear. Lightly grease the seals on each side of the wheel.

12. Make sure that the wheel hub splines engage with the final drive.

NOTE
Insert a piece of wood in the caliper in place of the disc. This way, if the brake lever is inadvertently depressed, the piston will not be forced out of the cylinder. If this does happen the caliper

might have to be disassembled to reseat the piston and the brake system will have to be bled. By using the wood, bleeding the brake should not be necessary when installing the wheel.

8. Slide the wheel to the right to disengage it from the hub drive splines and remove the wheel.

9. Install by reversing these removal steps. Apply molybdenum disulfide grease to the final drive flange splines on the wheel and the ring gear. Lightly grease the seals on each side of the wheel.

10. Make sure that the wheel hub splines engage with the final drive.

11. Torque the axle nut to 108 ft.-lb. (150 N•m) and the axle pinch bolt to 4 ft.-lb. (5 N•m).

Table 10 REAR SUSPENSION TORQUE VALUES

Item	Foot-pounds	Newton Meters
Rear axle nut	108	150
Rear axle pinch bolt	4.5	6

CHAPTER TEN

BRAKES

See **Table 11** for revised brake torque specifications.

FRONT DISC BRAKES

The front disc assembly on XS850SG, LG, SH and LH models has changed slightly. Refer to **Figure 30** for disassembly and assembly procedures.

Front Disc Pad Replacement (XS850SG, LG, SH and LH Models)

There is no recommended mileage interval for changing the friction pads in the disc brake. Pad wear depends greatly on riding habits and conditions. The pads should be checked for wear every 2,500 miles (4,000 km) and replaced when the wear indicator (**Figure 4**) reaches the red line on the pad.

Always replace all four pads (two per disc) at the same time.

It is not necessary to remove the front wheel to replace the pads.

1. Use pliers and pinch the retaining pin coil spring. Then pull the pin out of the pad and housing assembly. See **Figure 31**.

2. Remove the brake pads and the pad spring and caliper retainer.

3. Clean the pad recess and the end of the caliper piston with a soft brush. Do not use a solvent, a wire brush or any hard tool which would damage the cylinder or the piston.

4. Lightly coat the end of the piston and the backs of the new pads (not the friction material) with fresh disc brake lubricant.

5. Install the brake pads along with the pad spring and caliper retainer. Position the coil spring (**Figure 31**). Hold the spring open with a pair of pliers and install the retaining pin. Release the coil spring.

12

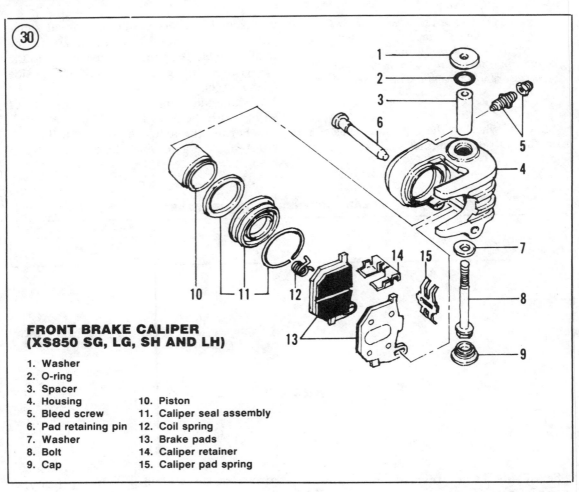

(30)

**FRONT BRAKE CALIPER
(XS850 SG, LG, SH AND LH)**

1. Washer
2. O-ring
3. Spacer
4. Housing
5. Bleed screw
6. Pad retaining pin
7. Washer
8. Bolt
9. Cap
10. Piston
11. Caliper seal assembly
12. Coil spring
13. Brake pads
14. Caliper retainer
15. Caliper pad spring

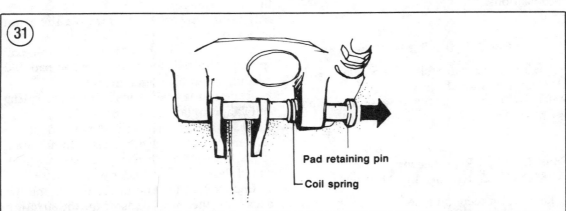

(31)

Pad retaining pin

Coil spring

Table 11 BRAKE TORQUE SPECIFICATIONS

Item	Ft.-lb.	N•m
Front caliper assembly mounting bolt	19	26
Rear master cylinder to frame	16	23

CHAPTER ELEVEN

FRAME AND REPAINTING

TOURING COMPONENTS

Some XS850 models are equipped with a fairing and saddlebags. These items will have to be removed to gain access to some components.

FAIRING

Removal

1. Place the bike on the centerstand.
2. Disconnect the negative battery lead.
3. Disconnect the wiring harness from the left-hand side of the fairing.
4. Remove the bolts securing the lower left- and right-hand fairing sections and remove them.

> *NOTE*
> *The next step requires the aid of an assistant. The fairing is not that heavy, but is bulky and could be damaged if you try to remove it by yourself.*

5. Remove the fairing mounting bolts and remove the fairing.

Installation

1. Have a helper hold the fairing in position while you install the fairing mounting bolts. Install the bolts but do not tighten fully at this time.
2. Install the lower fairing sections in place and align with the fairing. Tighten all screws securely. Do not overtighten the screws as the keeper nuts will pull out of the fairing.

3. Plug in the wiring harness; make sure the connection is tight.
4. Reconnect the battery negative cable.

Windshield Replacement

1. Remove all fasteners, both clips and the old windshield.
2. Remove all traces of the old foam tape from the fairing where the windshield was attached. The surface must be clean to achieve a watertight seam for the new windshield.
3. On the new windshield, puncture the foam tape at each attachment bolt hole. Use one of the nylon attachment bolts for this purpose. Do not use a metal bolt as it may fracture the hole, causing a crack in the windshield.
4. Position the 2 clips on the windshield about 4 5/8 in. (118 mm) above the upper hole on each side of the windshield.
5. Place the windshield on the fairing and slightly bend the windshield inward so that the clip studs will align with the holes in the fairing.
6. Insert the studs of the 2 clips through the top fairing mounting holes. Install a black bushing and a 6 mm keeper nut on each stud.
7. From the outside (or front of the fairing) install a nylon bolt through the windshield and fairing. Slide a small nylon washer onto the bolt from the inside and install the nut. Tighten the nut only finger-tight. Repeat for all remaining bolts.
8. Tighten the bolts in the torque sequence shown in **Figure 32**.

12

9. Install a rubber protective tip over the exposed clip studs.

NOTE
Always remove the windshield from the fairing when moving the bike on a trailer or open bed truck. Never use the fairing as a tie-down point when securing the bike to the trailer or truck.

Windshield Cleaning

Be very careful when cleaning the windshield as it can easily be scratched or damaged. Do not use a cleaner with an abrasive, a combination cleaner and wash or any solvent that contains ethyl or methyl alcohol. Never use gasoline or cleaning solvent. These products will either scratch or totally destroy the surface of the windshield.

To remove oil, grease or road tar, use isopropyl alcohol or naptha. Then wash the windshield with a solution of mild soap and water. Dry gently with a soft cloth or chamois—do not press hard.

NOTE
When removing grungy road tar make sure there are no small stones or sand imbedded in it. Carefully remove any abrasive particles prior to rubbing with a cleaner. This will help minimize scratching.

Many commercial windshield cleaners are available (such as Yamaha Windscreen Cleaner). If using a cleaner other than the one from Yamaha, make sure it is safe for use on the plastic and test it on a small area first.

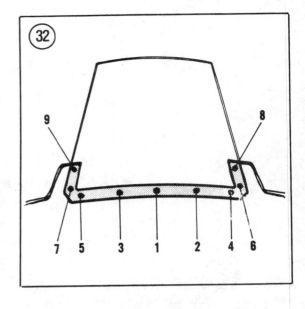

SADDLEBAG

Removal/Installation

1. Place the motorcycle on the centerstand.
2. Remove the seat and rear luggage rack.
3. Disconnect the left and right hand turn signal wire connectors.
4. Remove the guard rail pinch bolts at the frame rails.
5. Remove the saddlebag mount bolt at the frame guard bracket.
6. Remove the rear saddlebag mount bolts at the rear of the frame.
7. Remove the side plates from the shock absorber studs. Then remove the saddlebags from the motorcycle.
8. Install by reversing these removal steps.

INDEX

13

13

WIRING
DIAGRAMS

XS750D & 2D

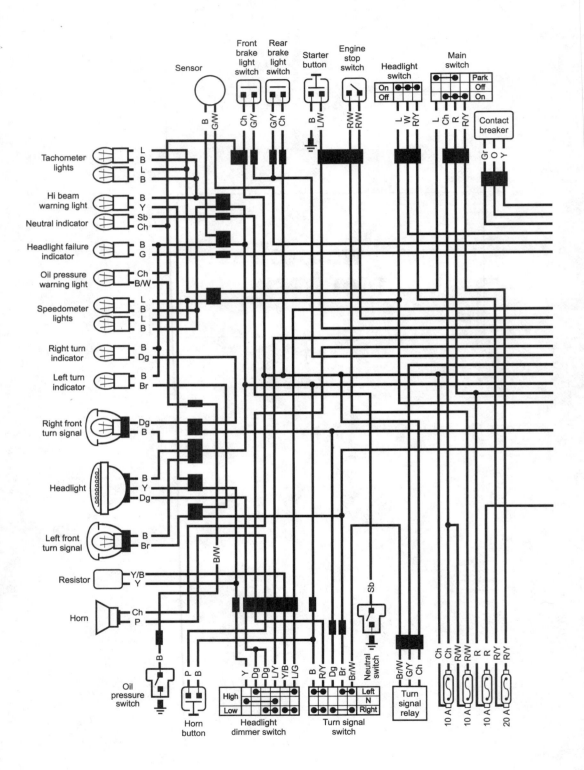

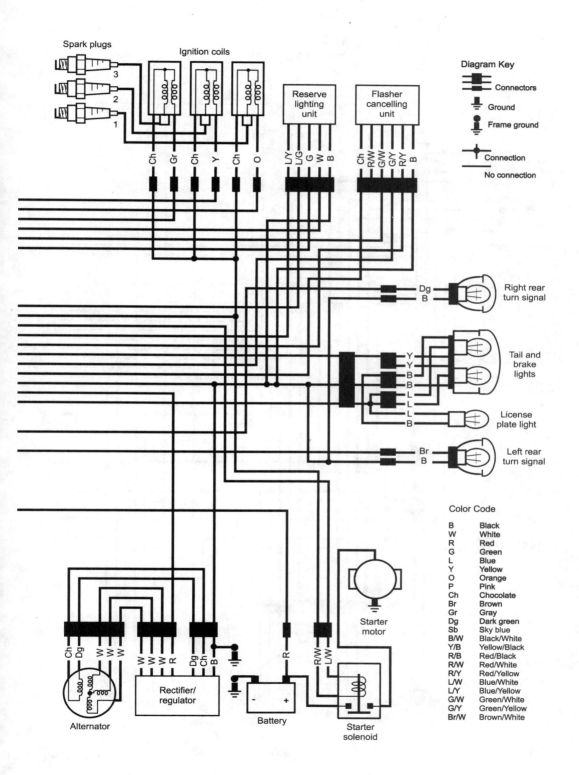

XS750E, SE, F & SF

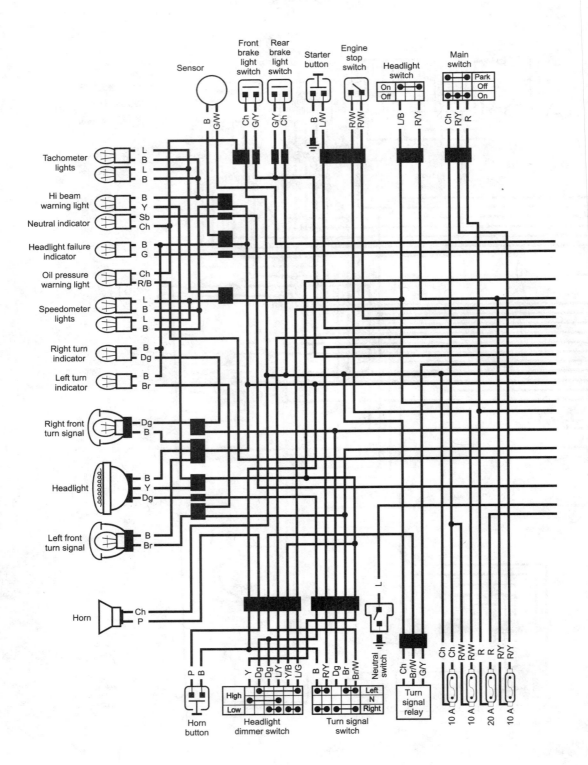

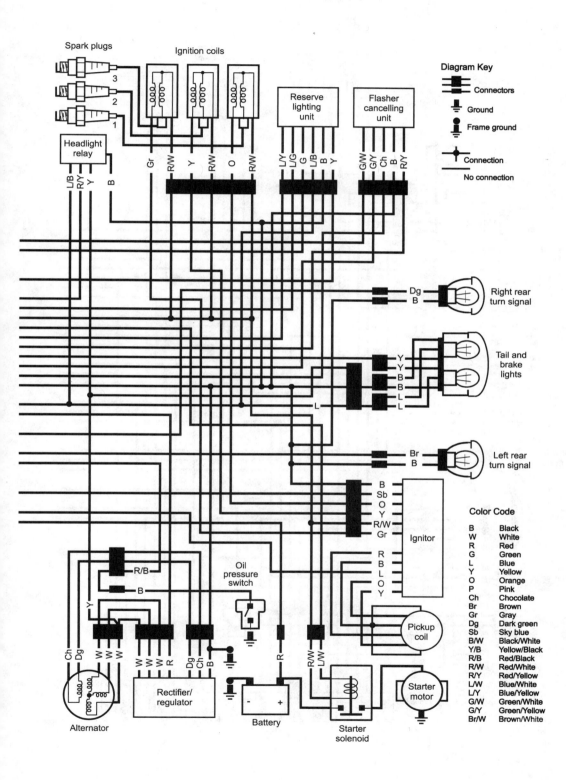

XS850G, LG & SG

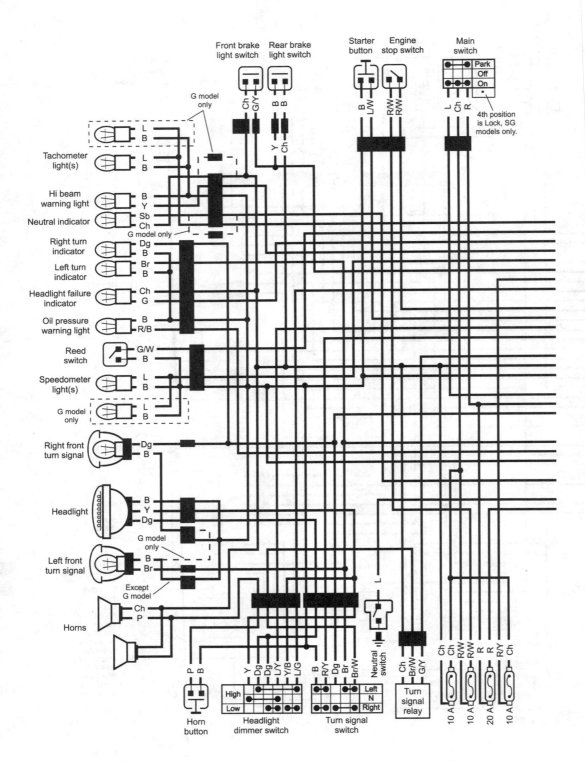

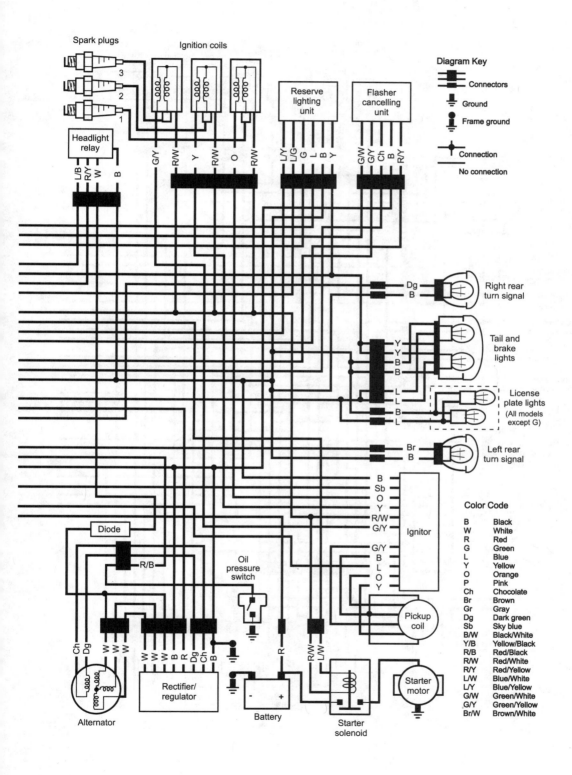

XS850H, LH & SH

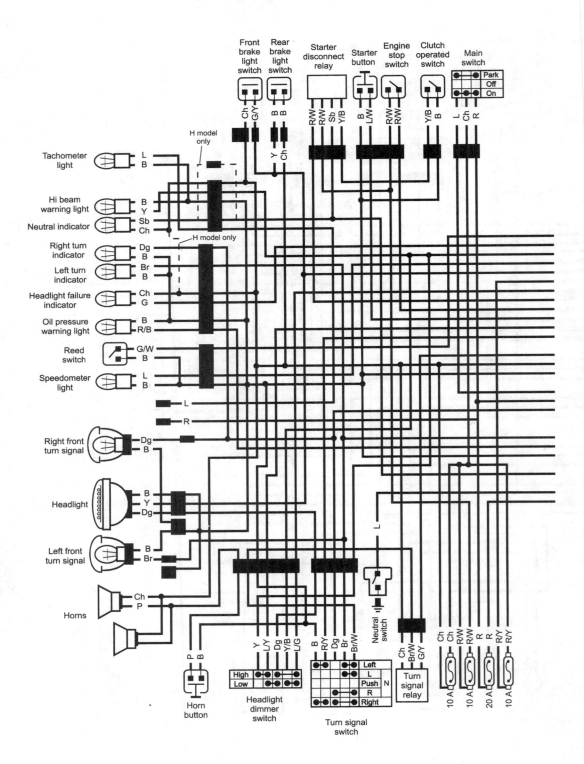

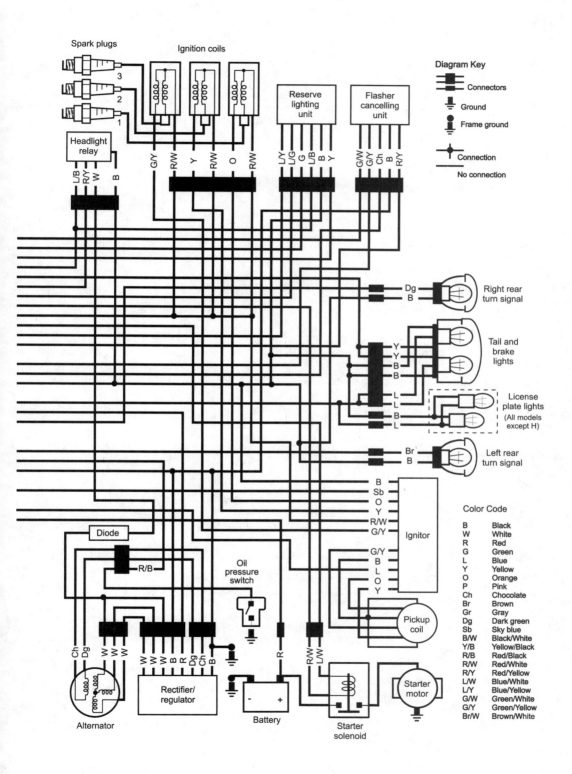

Spark plugs

Ignition coils

3
2
1

Headlight relay

Reserve lighting unit

Flasher cancelling unit

Diagram Key

Connectors

Ground

Frame ground

Connection

No connection

Right rear turn signal

Tail and brake lights

License plate lights
(All models except H)

Left rear turn signal

Ignitor

Diode

Oil pressure switch

Pickup coil

Starter motor

Alternator

Rectifier/ regulator

Battery

Starter solenoid

Color Code

B	Black
W	White
R	Red
G	Green
L	Blue
Y	Yellow
O	Orange
P	Pink
Ch	Chocolate
Br	Brown
Gr	Gray
Dg	Dark green
Sb	Sky blue
B/W	Black/White
Y/B	Yellow/Black
R/B	Red/Black
R/W	Red/White
R/Y	Red/Yellow
L/W	Blue/White
L/Y	Blue/Yellow
G/W	Green/White
G/Y	Green/Yellow
Br/W	Brown/White

13

NOTES

NOTES

MAINTENANCE LOG

Date	Miles	Type of Service

BMW

M308	500 & 600 CC Twins, 55-69
M309	F650, 1994-2000
M500-3	BMW K-Series, 85-97
M501	K1200RS, GT & LT, 98-05
M502-3	BMW R50/5-R100 GSPD, 70-96
M503-2	R850, R1100, R1150 and R1200C, 93-04

HARLEY-DAVIDSON

M419	Sportsters, 59-85
M428	Sportster Evolution, 86-90
M429-4	Sportster Evolution, 91-03
M427	Sportster, 04-05
M418	Panheads, 48-65
M420	Shovelheads, 66-84
M421-3	FLS/FXS Evolution, 84-99
M423-2	FLS/FXS Twin Cam, 00-05
M422-3	FLH/FLT/FXR Evolution, 84-99
M430-4	FLH/FLT Twin Cam, 99-05
M424-2	FXD Evolution, 91-98
M425-3	FXD Twin Cam, 99-05

HONDA

ATVs

M316	Odyssey FL250, 77-84
M311	ATC, TRX & Fourtrax 70-125, 70-87
M433	Fourtrax 90 ATV, 93-00
M326	ATC185 & 200, 80-86
M347	ATC200X & Fourtrax 200SX, 86-88
M455	ATC250 & Fourtrax 200/250, 84-87
M342	ATC250R, 81-84
M348	TRX250R/Fourtrax 250R & ATC250R, 85-89
M456-3	TRX250X 87-92; TRX300EX 93-04
M446-2	TRX250 Recon & ES, 97-04
M346-3	TRX300/Fourtrax 300 & TRX300FW/Fourtrax 4x4, 88-00
M200	TRX350 Rancher, 00-03
M459-3	TRX400 Foreman 95-03
M454-3	TRX400EX 99-05
M205	TRX450 Foreman, 98-04
M210	TRX500 Rubicon, 98-04

Singles

M310-13	50-110cc OHC Singles, 65-99
M319-2	XR50R, CRF50F, XR70R & CRF70F, 97-05
M315	100-350cc OHC, 69-82
M317	Elsinore, 125-250cc, 73-80
M442	CR60-125R Pro-Link, 81-88
M431-2	CR80R, 89-95, CR125R, 89-91
M435	CR80, 96-02
M457-2	CR125R & CR250R, 92-97
M464	CR125R, 1998-2002
M443	CR250R-500R Pro-Link, 81-87
M432-3	CR250R, 88-91 & CR500R, 88-01
M437	CR250R, 97-01
M352	CRF250, CRF250X & CRF450R, CRF450X, 02-05
M312-13	XL/XR75-100, 75-03
M318-4	XL/XR/TLR 125-200, 79-03
M328-4	XL/XR250, 78-00; XL/XR350R 83-85; XR200R, 84-85; XR250L, 91-96
M320-2	XR400R, 96-04
M339-7	XL/XR 500-650, 79-03

Twins

M321	125-200cc, 65-78
M322	250-350cc, 64-74
M323	250-360cc Twins, 74-77
M324-5	Twinstar, Rebel 250 & Nighthawk 250, 78-03
M334	400-450cc, 78-87
M333	450 & 500cc, 65-76
M335	CX & GL500/650 Twins, 78-83
M344	VT500, 83-88
M313	VT700 & 750, 83-87
M314-2	VT750 Shadow (chain drive), 98-05
M440	VT1100C Shadow, 85-96
M460-3	VT1100C Series, 95-04

Fours

M332	CB350-550cc, SOHC, 71-78
M345	CB550 & 650, 83-85
M336	CB650, 79-82
M341	CB750 SOHC, 69-78
M337	CB750 DOHC, 79-82
M436	CB750 Nighthawk, 91-93 & 95-99
M325	CB900, 1000 & 1100, 80-83
M439	Hurricane 600, 87-90
M441-2	CBR600F2 & F3, 91-98
M445	CBR600F4, 99-03
M434-2	CBR900RR Fireblade, 93-99
M329	500cc V-Fours, 84-86
M438	Honda VFR800, 98-00
M349	700-1000 Interceptor, 83-85
M458-2	VFR700F-750F, 86-97
M327	700-1100cc V-Fours, 82-88
M340	GL1000 & 1100, 75-83
M504	GL1200, 84-87
M508	ST1100/PAN European, 90-02

Sixes

M505	GL1500 Gold Wing, 88-92
M506-2	GL1500 Gold Wing, 93-00
M507	GL1800 Gold Wing, 01-04
M462-2	GL1500C Valkyrie, 97-03

KAWASAKI

ATVs

M465-2	KLF220 & KLF250 Bayou, 88-03
M466-4	KLF300 Bayou, 86-04
M467	KLF400 Bayou, 93-99
M470	KEF300 Lakota, 95-99
M385	KSF250 Mojave, 87-00

Singles

M350-9	Rotary Valve 80-350cc, 66-01
M444-2	KX60, 83-02; KX80 83-90
M448	KX80/85/100, 89-03
M351	KDX200, 83-88
M447-3	KX125 & KX250, 82-91 KX500, 83-04
M472-2	KX125, 92-00
M473-2	KX250, 92-00
M474	KLR650, 87-03

Twins

M355	KZ400, KZ/Z440, EN450 & EN500, 74-95
M360-3	EX500, GPZ500S, Ninja R, 87-02
M356-4	Vulcan 700 & 750, 85-04
M354-2	Vulcan 800 & Vulcan 800 Classic, 95-04
M357-2	Vulcan 1500, 87-99
M471-2	Vulcan Classic 1500, 96-04

Fours

M449	KZ500/550 & ZX550, 79-85
M450	KZ, Z & ZX750, 80-85
M358	KZ650, 77-83
M359-3	900-1000cc Fours, 73-81
M451-3	1000 & 1100cc Fours, 81-02
M452-3	ZX500 & 600 Ninja, 85-97
M453-3	Ninja ZX900-1100 84-01
M468-2	Ninja ZX-6, 90-04
M469	ZX7 Ninja, 91-98
M453-3	Ninja ZX900, ZX1000 & ZX1100, 84-01
M409	Concours, 86-04

POLARIS

ATVs

M496	Polaris ATV, 85-95
M362	Polaris Magnum ATV, 96-98
M363	Scrambler 500, 4X4 97-00
M365-2	Sportsman/Xplorer, 96-03

SUZUKI

ATVs

M381	ALT/LT 125 & 185, 83-87
M475	LT230 & LT250, 85-90
M380-2	LT250R Quad Racer, 85-92
M343	LTF500F Quadrunner, 98-00
M483-2	Suzuki King Quad/Quad Runner 250, 87-98

Singles

M371	RM50-400 Twin Shock, 75-81
M369	125-400cc 64-81
M379	RM125-500 Single Shock, 81-88
M476	DR250-350, 90-94
M384-3	LS650 Savage, 86-04
M386	RM80-250, 89-95
M400	RM125, 96-00
M401	RM250, 96-02

Twins

M372	GS400-450 Twins, 77-87
M481-4	VS700-800 Intruder, 85-04
M482-2	VS1400 Intruder, 87-01
M484-3	GS500E Twins, 89-02
M361	SV650, 1999-2002

Triple

M368	380-750cc, 72-77

Fours

M373	GS550, 77-86
M364	GS650, 81-83
M370	GS750 Fours, 77-82
M376	GS850-1100 Shaft Drive, 79-84
M378	GS1100 Chain Drive, 80-81
M383-3	Katana 600, 88-96 GSX-R750-1100, 86-87
M331	GSX-R600, 97-00
M478-2	GSX-R750, 88-92 GSX750F Katana, 89-96
M485	GSX-R750, 96-99
M377	GSX-R1000, 01-04
M338	GSF600 Bandit, 95-00
M353	GSF1200 Bandit, 96-03

YAMAHA

ATVs

M499	YFM80 Badger, 85-01
M394	YTM/YFM200 & 225, 83-86
M488-5	Blaster, 88-05
M489-2	Timberwolf, 89-00
M487-5	Warrior, 87-04
M486-5	Banshee, 87-04
M490-3	Moto-4 & Big Bear, 87-04
M493	YFM400FW Kodiak, 93-98
M280-2	Raptor 660R, 01-05

Singles

M492-2	PW50 & PW80, BW80 Big Wheel 80, 81-02
M410	80-175 Piston Port, 68-76
M415	250-400cc Piston Port, 68-76
M412	DT & MX 100-400, 77-83
M414	IT125-490, 76-86
M393	YZ50-80 Monoshock, 78-90
M413	YZ100-490 Monoshock, 76-84
M390	YZ125-250, 85-87 & YZ490, 85-90
M391	YZ125-250, 88-93 WR250Z, 91-93
M497-2	YZ125, 94-01
M498	YZ250, 94-98 and WR250Z, 94-97
M406	YZ250F & WR250F, 01-03
M491-2	YZ400F, YZ426F, WR400F WR426F, 98-02
M417	XT125-250, 80-84
M480-3	XT/TT 350, 85-00
M405	XT500 & TT500, 76-81
M416	XT/TT 600, 83-89

Twins

M403	650cc, 70-82
M395-10	XV535-1100 Virago, 81-03
M495-4	V-Star 650, 98-05
M281-2	V-Star 1100, 99-05
M282	Road Star, 99-05

Triple

M404	XS750 & 850, 77-81

Fours

M387	XJ550, XJ600 & FJ600, 81-92
M494	XJ600 Seca II, 92-98
M388	YX600 Radian & FZ600, 86-90
M396	FZR600, 89-93
M392	FZ700-750 & Fazer, 85-87
M411	XS1100 Fours, 78-81
M397	FJ1100 & 1200, 84-93
M375	V-Max, 85-03
M374	Royal Star, 96-03
M461	YZF-R6, 99-04
M398	YZF-R1, 98-03
M399	FZ1, 01-04

VINTAGE MOTORCYCLES

Clymer® Collection Series

M330	Vintage British Street Bikes, BSA, 500-650cc Unit Twins; Norton, 750 & 850cc Commandos; Triumph, 500-750cc Twins
M300	Vintage Dirt Bikes, V. 1 Bultaco, 125-370cc Singles; Montesa, 123-360cc Singles; Ossa, 125-250cc Singles
M301	Vintage Dirt Bikes, V. 2 CZ, 125-400cc Singles; Husqvarna, 125-450cc Singles; Maico, 250-501cc Singles; Hodaka, 90-125cc Singles
M305	Vintage Japanese Street Bikes Honda, 250 & 305cc Twins; Kawasaki, 250-750cc Triples; Kawasaki, 900 & 1000cc Fours